The Entrepreneurial Bureaucracy:
Biographies of Two Federal Programs in Education

CONTEMPORARY STUDIES IN SOCIOLOGY, VOL. 1

Editor: John Clark, *Department of Sociology, University of Minnesota*
Series Editors: Robert Althauser, *Department of Sociology, Indiana University,*
John D. Kasarda, *Department of Sociology, University of North
Carolina,* Clark McPhall, *Department of Sociology, University of
Illinois*

CONTEMPORARY STUDIES IN SOCIOLOGY
Theoretical and Empirical Monographs

Editor-in-Chief: John Clark
Department of Sociology, University of Minnesota
Series Editors: Robert Althauser, *Department of Sociology, Indiana University,* John D. Kasarda, *Department of Sociology, University of North Carolina* and Clark McPhail, *Department of Sociology, University of Illinois*

To My Mother, Beulah Corwin

The Entrepreneurial Bureaucracy:

Biographies of Two Federal Programs in Education

by RONALD G. CORWIN
Department of Sociology
The Ohio State University

 JAI PRESS Inc.

Greenwich, Connecticut   *London, England*

Library of Congress Cataloging in Publication Data

Corwin, Ronald G.
  The entrepreneurial bureaucracy.

  (Contemporary studies in sociology ; v. 1)
  Bibliography: p.
  Includes index.
  1. Federal aid to education—United States—
Administration. I. Title. II. Series.
LB2825.C639 1983   379.1'21'0973   82-81210
ISBN 0-89232-314-0

Copyright © 1983 JAI PRESS INC.
36 Sherwood Place
Greenwich, Connecticut 06830

JAI PRESS INC.
3 Henrietta Place
London WC2E 8LU
England

ISBN NUMBER 0-89232-314-0
Library of Congress Catalog Card Number: 82-81210
Manufactured in the United States of America

CONTENTS

PART IV. REFLECTIONS

List of Figures

List of Tables

Foreword

Since the National Institute of Education (NIE) in Washington, D.C. was created in 1972, it has awarded millions of dollars annually in grants and contracts to universities, private firms, and state and local governments. These funds have been used to support a wide range of research, development and demonstration programs, and projects relating to education. This book consists of studies of two of the more ambitious of these programs, namely (1) the Research and Development Utilization Program (RDU) funded at $10 million, which operated between 1976 and 1979, and (2) the Rural Experimental Schools Program (ES), which was funded at $6.4 million during the years 1970 to 1978.

These programs had many features in common. Both were initiated by a federal agency. Both had a fixed life span. Both entailed direct working relationships between federal officials and educators at the state, intermediate, and local school district levels. Both provided large sums of money to a select number of schools or school districts for the purpose of helping practitioners make certain changes in their practices and procedures which they had identified as necessary for their own improvement. And both included a smaller, but nonetheless substantial, research component for the purpose of learning from the experience.

Underlying these similarities, however, were some critical differences that evolved from the unique origin and history of each program. These distinctive features have fortuitously served to illuminate different properties of their parent organization, the National Institute of Education. In particular, RDU was solely the product of NIE, designed and administered to meet this fledgling agency's emerging priorities and needs. RDU has thus provided a rare opportunity to observe up close how a program came into being in the precarious social climate of this new agency. Therefore, in the case of RDU I have chosen to focus on the dynamics behind program *design* and to give only secondary attention to the way the program was managed.

ES had a slightly different history. It was instituted by the U.S. Office of Education (OE) shortly before NIE was created and later transferred to NIE as one of numerous ongoing programs that NIE reluctantly "inherited" from OE. What has proved to be most sociologically revealing about ES is the way the program was *managed.* Therefore, in the case of ES, I have chosen to focus on the various roles and management styles exhibited by NIE program officers as they administered the program. While the designs of both programs impacted their operations, I am less interested in comparing the two cases than in capitalizing on the distinctive ways that each program can contribute to an understanding of some critical features of the policy process in this federal agency. Taken together, the two programs include a broad range of the activities that marked the early stages of NIE. A close examination can serve to expose aspects of the social milieu that prevailed there during its first decade. Of course, as only two of innumerable programs that could have been chosen for study, RDU and ES can obviously provide only a partial and selective picture of this complex agency. No two programs can be said to be representative. But when considered as pieces of the larger mosaic, RDU and ES do provide a valid portrayal of at least some critically important features that characterized NIE during its formative years.

Some of the events associated with these two programs can help illuminate a number of intellectual issues which are of general interest to social scientists, policymakers, and the practitioners associated with federal programs. Some of the issues to be addressed here include:

- The key identifying features of an emergent type of organization, the entrepreneurial bureaucracy.
- How discretionary programs come into existence (in contrast to many other studies of federal programs which have focused on existing, legislated programs).

- How program designs are shaped and altered by the organizational context of their sponsoring organizations—the structural constraints, the incentives, and the internal politics of such organizations.
- How the fate and impact of a program are determined by the processes used to design it.
- Various ways in which program designs can become accommodated to the realities under which programs must operate.
- How relationships between federal agencies and local communities are influenced by the competing roles that program officers are expected to perform.
- How a program officer's choice of role priorities is, in turn, fixed by features of his/her social context.
- The benefits and costs that accrue when federal agencies attempt to provide technical assistance to local communities.

Details from the two programs, RDU and ES, pertaining to these and related issues will be described in the following pages.

Part I

The Setting

Chapter I

The Life and Times of an Entrepreneurial Bureaucracy

The National Institute of Education (NIE) is a relatively new federal agency which has had a stormy career. Established by the Nixon administration and funded in 1972, NIE, with a vague, often controversial mission and harboring grandiose ambitions, has sometimes seemed naively smug to an incredulous Congress. Pushed and pulled by its constituencies and bothered by opposing factions within the Congress, it remains, a decade later, a favorite target. As part of the new Department of Education, one of the agencies the Reagan administration has singled out for termination, its fate is uncertain. As this publication goes to press, it remains to be seen whether NIE will be dismantled, consolidated with another agency, or reorganized in some other way. The persistent vulnerability of this agency is an important and inescapable part of the story behind ES and RDU.

AN ARCHITECTURE OF CONTRADICTIONS

NIE had an inauspicious beginning. It was the product of a multitude of consultants and much advanced planning in its parent agency and within the federal structure (Levien, 1971). Tacked onto a larger bill, the authorization moved through Congress without arousing much interest. From the beginning, NIE has been torn over whether its primary mission is policy analysis, fundamental research, or delivery services. While confusion over such matters is probably not uncommon in Washington, in this

3

case much of it can be attributed to the traumas associated with the transfer to NIE of the educational research mission which had previously been the responsibility of a subordinate unit within the huge U.S. Office of Education (OE). Two consequences followed from that move which were to hamper the new agency. First, educational research became more visible and hence more exposed to congressional scrutiny. The fact that the director of NIE reported to the assistant secretary of Education and submitted budget requests directly to Congress shattered the covering from congressional pressure that had previously protected educational research at OE, where its budget had been obscured by other activities and had been merged with higher levels of the hierarchy. While research had been subject to pressures from external constituencies at OE, it was less visible to Congress. Second, with the transfer from OE, research now lost contact with OE's powerful constituents.

But even if its creators had anticipated these problems, NIE would have remained a bewildering array of anomalies. For one thing, by the 1960s Congress had become wary of costly R & D in every field and was demanding proof of results for the millions of dollars it appropriated for research each year. Some members of Congress and some NIE planners were convinced that past R & D efforts in education had been abysmal failures. And yet, despite this lack of foundation on which to build, the appropriations committees expected the virgin agency to yield tangible improvements in schooling within a few years. Raizen (1979:260–61) observes that:

> The Institute came into existence at a paradoxical time for its mission. The social programs of the '60s had brought disenchantment with education as a means for equalizing life chances regardless of ethnic origin or socioeconomic status. At the same time, there was disenchantment with the power of research, and particularly the findings of social science research, to alleviate societal ills. To some degree, these perceptions came together in an emphasis on dissemination: The case against research was not proven, since much of what we knew was not applied in classrooms, and schools would work better if available knowledge (derived from both research and experience) were put to use to improve education as an art, science, and profession.

Even if it had been possible for a new agency to meet these demands, Congress ingeniously embroidered another set of contradictions that charted a course to certain trouble. It was clear from the congressional hearings that NIE's sponsors in Congress intended for it to be completely independent from OE. In the words of Congressman Brademas: "NIE must be able to spit in the eye of the Office of Education" (Sproull et al., 1978; see also Dershimer, 1976:129). Many observers believed this course was preferable to dependence on OE. At the same time, however, deals were made that resulted in the transfer of $110 million worth of OE programs to NIE at the direction of the commissioner of Education. Included among them was the Experimental Schools Program. The antagonistic relationship between OE and NIE would later haunt that program. Of the $162 million requested in the 1974 NIE budget, $137 million was needed to support OE transfer programs.[1] Still other programs were transferred from the controversial Office of Economic Opportunity (OEO). The net effect of these transfers put NIE in a "no win" position with respect to Congress. Conservatives were suspicious because of the ties with OEO, and the heavy dose of research in social programs made liberals impatient.

If this were not enough to defeat the legislative intent, a clash between the government employees' union and NIE managers would have done the job. Under threat of legal action from the government employees' union, NIE was compelled to hire 80 OE employees, most of them through a lottery system. The NIE management then tried to fill the more than 200 remaining personnel slots with outsiders—typically, young men and women in their early thirties who generally, and often by intent, lacked substantial government experience. Sproull et al. (1978:119) wrote: "In the words of one of the members of the inner circle, (we are) immodest, young, foolishly willing to deal with a broad range of issues beyond our competence."

The predictable schism between the OE transfers and the mobile outsiders produced an enduring stratification hierarchy in the agency which hampered its efforts to take new directions. It is perhaps true that some of the transferred personnel lacked the kind of skills that might have been secured from the outside, but the smug sense of superiority occasionally manifest among the outsiders who were in charge of the agency did not help to produce the internal support that would be necessary for their refreshing ideas to be implemented.

In engineering the competitive relationship between OE and NIE, Congress put the Institute in an untenable position. OE was charged with responsibility for most service programs, which left research as NIE's primary domain. But it would take a long time for newly initiated research projects to prove themselves useful to practitioners, and in the meantime, how was NIE supposed to demonstrate its utility to practitioners when prohibited from providing the direct services that might be of immediate use to them? Given the amount of time required to demonstrate the utility of research, dissemination was the logical basis on which to build a new constituency of people in the field.

The Institute also had to contend with the tensions involved in fostering creativity within the staff and the requirements of responsible management, as well as with the assumption that R & D can be managed from a federal level by scholar bureaucrats (Sproull et al., 1978). But many of these outside scholars, who frequently came expecting to do their own intramural research (which never fully materialized), brought with them laissez-faire approaches characteristic of the major universities. Consequently, NIE has seldom been able to design coherent R & D plans. While it is not being claimed that this characterization of the Institute as a whole applies in every respect to all of the units, plans for dissemination were clearly impacted by this factor. On this point Raizen (1979:282–83) writes, "NIE never developed institute-wide dissemination policy despite many attempts to do so." NIE has operated as a diffuse, free market, entrepreneurial enterprise where each major program is contrived to operate independently. For example, twelve separate sets of activities were identified in the 1975 budget request, all of which were to be funded at relatively low levels (Sproull et al., 1978:99).

This decentralized decision-making structure was the product of several circumstances. First, some of the programs transferred from OE brought with them their own managers and their own small, unofficial constituencies. Second, during the first years, several management slots went unfilled, which allowed individual programs to assert their autonomy in the fluid and expanding environment that existed at that time. Third, the administrative style of the first NIE director firmly implanted a competitive atmosphere within NIE. It was his practice to provide limited amounts of money to be awarded to the program manager who submitted the winning plan chosen from among a formal competition. Finally, the managers from universities and research institutes brought with them the conviction that it was possible to create programs and comprehensive plans through extensive debate and analysis (Sproull et al., 1978:183), which only produced indecisiveness: in one sixteen-month period, program plans went through fourteen separate drafts. On this point, Sproull et al., (1978:183) note:

> In an organization with aggressive managers and support staff, inconclusive decision processes can be generated by competition for recognition and promotion. This would occur if competition was based not on program achievement but on the exigencies of process-oriented skills. If the competitors perceive the game as one in which the ability to debate skillfully is paramount, and if there are two or more competitors of roughly equal ability, we would expect lengthy processes.

The authors go on to say that one reason that some NIE managers have done well within the agency is at least partially due to their interpersonal skills (presumably in addition to, or in lieu of, their knowledge skills). This early history left its mark even though the Institute was already changing by the time RDU took form.

Perhaps the diffuse decision-making structure did foster creativity *within* the agency, but the agency remained poorly adapted for responding to external crises. And by 1974, as the belief that NIE was failing spread among the public, crisis had become familiar to the Institute. The National Education Association, for example, had launched a public attack on NIE programs, charging that they were too esoteric and irrelevant to be useful to teachers. Several congressmen expressed concern that NIE's programs did not seem to be helping people in any direct or demonstrative way (Sproull et al., 1978:102). Finally, in April and May of 1974, the House and Senate disapproved NIE's request for supplemental funds, and over the summer of that year, the $134.5 million budget requested for fiscal year 1975 was slashed almost in half. Critics blame the cut on poor planning and ineffective advocacy.

With NIE's budgets and the Institute's very survival in the balance, NIE managers were pressed to take action. In retrospect, it is not clear what the NIE managers *did plan* to do. However, what they *did do* is clear enough: they reorganized. In fact, in a short

Figure I.1. NIE Organization Chart for 1974

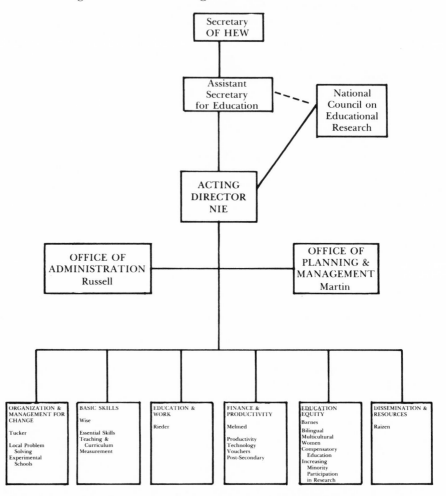

two and one-half year period (by November 1974), the agency had been "reorganized" five times. (See Figure I.1., NIE Organization Chart for November, 1974.) That this shuffling around would not help much was probably predictable, mainly because the changes were driven by competition and this competition was not resolved by setting up new organization charts. There were cases in which separate units were created to pacify small cliques who protested their place within the organization chart. One such instance occurred in connection with the dissemination program that was taking shape during this troubled time.

In place of centralized managerial control and supervision, NIE management chose to offer autonomy as an incentive for those staff members who ventured to take iniative. As a natural outgrowth of the decentralization and the rampant interpersonal competition throughout the agency, the agency's programs often have been, and continue to be, extensions of the individuals who created and managed them. Most of these people are of course sincerely committed to improving education and are convinced of the inherent worth of the ideas they advocate. Moreover, the programs are often based on sound rationale and information. Nevertheless, the stress on personal initiative seems to promote a "revisionist" mentality that quickly grows disdainful of everything that one's competitors are doing. Moreover, scholar/bureaucrats are in a unique position with respect to their colleagues in research firms and universities. It can be tempting to hold out money to researchers who embrace their ideas almost as a condition for obtaining federal dollars. The very destiny of entire programs can get mixed up with the rise and fall of the individuals who are closely associated with them. We can call this type of managerial system an "entrepreneurial bureaucracy."

I will deal more fully with the notion of entrepreneurial bureaucracy (EB) in the concluding pages of this volume, but for now it will be sufficient to define it as a large hierarchical organization in which subordinate employees are encouraged to assume the risks associated with initiating new activities and approaches. As an emergent type of organization, EBs are not prevalent. However, NIE is not the only example. Some other new agencies in Washington seem to function like EBs, as do some research firms and some other established organizations when they are threatened with survival. Indeed, the EB may be viewed as a generic response to a confluence of conditions: dependence on research and new technologies; newness and being the product of a recent historical era; and threats to survival when an organization is situated in a precarious environment (see Chapter XIII: Summary).

EBs are bureaucracies in the sense that they are administrative systems managed by experts within legal guidelines. They consist of elaborate divisions of labor, well-defined hierarchies of authority, codified rules, separation of official duties from personal considerations, an equitably administered system of rewards and promotions based on explicit criteria, and similar characteristics. However, EBs represent an emergent, hybrid type of organization which is distinctive in at least three respects. First, the incentive system encourages subordinate employees to use their initiative to start up new activities and develop new approaches to problems. Such organizations are not merely decentralized. What is critical is that employees are explicitly *rewarded* for assuming the managerial initiatives and the risks associated with launching new programs and fostering new roles and relationships.

Secondly, careers in EBs are not confined to job transfers and promotions within a particular bureaucratic system (e.g. government or higher education), and longevity in the system is not a critical basis for advancement. Instead, they rely heavily on specialists recruited from outside the system on temporary appointments. These specialists do not have longevity in the system and do not plan to confine their careers to it. Entrepreneurical bureaucracies are thus characterized by high rates of turnover.

Third, entrepreneurial bureaucracies place very high priority on specialized knowledge (expertise). Persons with specialized training in an academic field are accorded authority and esteem on that basis alone. While knowledge is respected in many modern organizations, in EBs expertise displaces seniority (or experience) and often official rank as well, as the primary basis of authority. Specialized expertise is the primary source of status, and it is not necessarily closely associated with either rank or with experience (except that expertise can take precedence over experience for certain promotions).

In addition to these basic features, EBs also have other properties, such as a fluid division of labor (with concomitant disputes over domain and boundaries), the utility of political and interpersonal skills, wide spheres of autonomy, and allegiances to external consistencies. Some of these qualities will become evident in the course of the following narrative. But they can be more profitably discussed after ES and RDU have been described.

SUMMARY

The fate of each program, ES and RDU, was shaped by the precarious posture of NIE during its early days. A Congress already disdainful toward social research set expectations beyond the capacity of such an agency. More specifically, this agency was intended to be independent from, and in some sense, better than the OE research programs. But it was saddled with OE programs and personnel. It was supposed to foster creative, untested, long-range approaches to complex problems. But it was nonetheless held accountable for producing immediate results. Circumstances and managerial philosophies had produced a decentralized, loosely coordinated organization. But the managers were charged with responsibility for setting clear priorities and initiating coordinated attacks on problems. With this history in mind we can now turn to consider how the Research and Development Utilization Program was shaped by this environment.

NOTE

1. Moreover, some of the most active OE research programs, including those in the areas of vocational education and the handicapped, remained at OE.

Part II

The Politics of Program Design

Chapter II

RDU as a Discretionary Program

In December 1975 the National Institute of Education (NIE) issued a request soliciting proposals for three-year projects to help solve educational problems. Proposers were required to show that they could provide assistance to schools that wished to make use of available educational research and development materials. Three and one-half years later, seven projects, which constituted the $10 million "Research and Development Utilization Program" (RDU), had earned a reputation as successful, and were being prepared to phase out according to plan. Between these two events a story unfolded of clashes between personal initiative and political necessity, of strong personalities, and of machinations not uncommon to complex organizations such as federal bureaucracies. What follows is a biography of this federal program from its inception to its demise.

After briefly outlining the major parameters of the program, I describe my data collection methods and then outline some of my assumptions and perspectives used to interpret the data.

RDU IN PROFILE

The RDU program was initiated by the National Institute of Education in the summer of 1976 as a three-year $10 million action research program with a twofold purpose (Dissemination and Resources Group, 1976):

(1) to help select education agencies alleviate identified problems by acquainting school and community personnel with revelant products
and R & D; and
(2) to increase knowledge on how local improvement processes could,
through deliberate linkage mechanisms, be made more effective by
increased use of research and exemplary practice.

Seven different projects were supported in different places and
with different types of sponsors. The projects shared several characteristics. First, each included a number of stages through which
schools were expected to go in the process of problem solving and
knowledge utilization. These stages included problem identification, examination of alternative solutions, and selection, implementation, and incorporation of selected solutions. Second, each
was to deal directly with local schools or school districts and set up
specific linking agents that would both serve those schools and
emphasize local problem identification and decision making. Finally, each was to make use of an identified source of knowledge
pertinent to the problem at hand. Since NIE itself had identified
"basic skills" and career education as major educational problems,
it supported a great deal of work in these areas. The R & D
utilization projects were encouraged to use the resulting knowledge resources, though they were not limited either to them or to
the two problem areas.

The intent was to give every school in the program external
assistance with a staged sequence of decisions,[1] and in particular,
to give each assistance with:

- identification of curriculum needs or problems in areas of
reading, math, career education, or teaching skills (these
needs assessments were conducted by the local school staff);
- selection of specific R & D products from a pool of materials
specified in advance by each project which promised to alleviate the problems identified; and
- evaluation and follow-up of the entire process and its results.

RDU operated through seven project offices: four housed in
single state education agencies (SEAs), one operated by a consortium of SEAs, another by a consortium of regional and local educational service agencies, and another by the National Education
Association (see Louis et al., 1979). Each project initially received

awards from NIE in June 1976, with continuation funds made available in 1977, 1978, and 1979. The total amount of support provided by NIE for this program (exclusive of a research component) was roughly $1 million per project spread over approximately three and one-half year years. Each of the seven projects was itself complex, consisting of several components and working with different kinds of organizations. Structurally each project consisted of:

1. An office of project director, usually situated in the host organization. All project directors were concerned with the administration of the project, including project design, planning, budgeting, monitoring, supervision, and evaluation.

2. Technical assistance affiliates, usually separate, nonprofit organizations based in a university, an educational lab or a service district in the school system and usually operating on a subcontract to the project director. These affiliates provided services such as the development and maintenance of the pool of information and products and the provision of training and technical assistance.

3. Two or more "linking agents" employed by intermediate service agencies, who were usually full-time employees of their own host organizations and who worked either part-time or full-time on RDU activities depending upon the number of schools served. The work loads of these linkers varied considerably. In one project each linker worked with one school; in several other projects each linker was responsible for seven or more schools.

4. School personnel consisting of ad hoc teams composed of full-time administrators, teachers, and other practitioners in the school system. These personnel often formed what was called a "local action team" which administered the RDU process at each local school site.

The projects also encompassed a range of governmental boundaries. In four projects the participating schools were located within single states; three other projects worked with schools located in several different states. Overall, the schools participating in RDU were distributed across ten states. By design, the knowledge pools differed in size and in the frequency with which they were updated. Five of the projects emphasized basic skills, one emphasized teacher skills and one other emphasized career education.

SOURCES OF INFORMATION FOR THE STUDY

The events reported here have been reconstructed from retrospective interviews with key actors who were involved with various stages of the program and from documents graciously made available by NIE staff members. On the premise that no one individual or group of individuals would be able to comprehend all facets of a program of this scope—one that encompassed so many years and became altered over time—I selected knowledgeable informants from various *sectors* of the program, including:

> *time sectors*—people associated with various stages of the program, including its conception, its operation, and decisions about its future;
>
> *organizational role sectors*—the original architects of the program, the persons responsible for the action research component, the project monitors, and program directors; and
>
> *institutional sectors*—staff members and administrators in different parts of the NIE hierarchy.

Information from these disparate sources was pieced together in a manner analogous to legal research or investigative reporting. The accuracy test for this type of analysis is whether it conveys a plausible picture based upon convergent reports from knowledgeable informants. An analogy can be made with the way an attorney presents a case before a grand jury. The purpose here, however, is not to find fault but to illuminate and make sense out of a complex situation that would otherwise remain incomprehensible.

I began by conducting a round of informal conversations with four persons who had been closely associated with the program throughout its history. I also read available program documents. I then designed an extensive informal interview guide that consisted of open-ended questions with extensive probes. This guide was organized around five focal questions:

- How has the federal policy been formulated, interpreted and implemented during the course of this program?
- How has the program been managed?
- How do local project directors and their staffs view NIE policies and the procedures that govern the local projects?
- Where does the program fit within the federal bureaucracy, both administratively and substantively?
- How do federal managers view action research programs such as RDU?

Specific questions were posed about the personal and professional backgrounds and constituencies of those who operated the program; about communication patterns, turnover, and replacement of key policy makers, program directors and program officers; about pressures from different constituencies, bureaucratic procedures, rules, and resource limitations; about the visibility of the program within NIE and its priority within the Institute; and about how program managers intended to use the findings.

I then interviewed fourteen persons who had been closely associated with the program at NIE. Three of these interviews were conducted by telephone; the remainder were conducted in person. The interviews ranged in length from 30 minutes to several hours.

Finally, I sent a preliminary draft of the present report to several key informants for their comments. Since it was a preliminary draft, I took the liberty of expressing in an extremely provocative form some conjectures that had been offered by informants and some of my own tentative interpretations in order to elicit opposing views. The reactions were candid, occasionally defensive, and (in one case) abusive. Nevertheless, the procedure proved effective. Indeed, I think that it was more useful than a second round of formal interviews might have been, because it provided informants with the context of my questions, and gave them a chance to elaborate on and correct interpretations and information.

It has not always been easy to reconstruct this story. Informants sometimes gave conflicting accounts of the same events, and even when they agreed on the facts they sometimes offered different interpretations of their meaning. I have tried to report some of these differences at critical junctures, but the reader is cautioned to keep the fluidity of the data base in mind at all times.

It is worth considering why certain informants and I have occasionally interpreted an event differently. Some of the obvious reasons have already been mentioned: the fact that the program design was in a constant state of flux, memory lapses, the various roles played by different informants in the program, and the fact that informants were involved at different phases. Also, I have chosen to focus on certain sociological dimensions within an evolutionary framework, and this is not necessarily the framework that most people use.

This last consideration (i.e., the matter of sociological perspective) merits further comment. I refer not merely to the theoretical structure that was used, for while I admit to being partial to evolutionary and conflict perspectives, the appropriateness of the framework I used was suggested by the events as described by the informants themselves. I think that what is critical about my perspective is that I have interpreted the program from the standpoint of an outsider, rather than a participant. As a consequence, it is possible that I have not conveyed sufficient appreciation for what each actor in the program did accomplish. Perhaps my optimism about RDU has been too strongly tempered by the inconsistencies and other problems I saw, or by the concepts I have used. These are real risks.

However I want to stress that this report is not intended to be a *diary* of events as seen through the eyes of a participant (or participants). How could it be? My task has been to accommodate the various versions of events that were reported by different participants. Of necessity I have had to consolidate, simplify and abstract information pertaining to complex situations. The effect has been to temper the extreme views of both the critics and the apologists for the program. It has not always been possible for me to present everyone's view with equal vigor; I have applied my own judgment about the validity of alternative versions and I do not claim to have captured the total truth. This is my version of a very complex story.

In choosing to focus on RDU as only one of a myriad of activities going on at NIE at this time, I have also run the risk of distorting the *importance* of the program as it might have been seen by the actors involved. Although at one time one of the

Institute's largest programs, RDU was never of pressing interest within NIE. Even within the dissemination unit where it was lodged, it occupied a relatively small amount of the associate director's time. For her, RDU might have consisted of little more than a few conversations each week. The events described here were embedded in a larger set of activities at NIE, which it is not my intention to describe in a concrete way.

PERSPECTIVES USED

An *evolutionary* perspective has been employed to interpret much of what transpired during the program. Accordingly, the focus is on program life-cycle processes—how RDU was conceived and designed, how it developed, and its eventual entropy. As a result of my interviews, I concluded that in addition to calculated adjustments and revisions, RDU evolved in two different but overlapping ways: (1) accumulation of unplanned policy actions, which I call *institutional drift;* and (2) *group conflict,* resulting from the incessant struggles among groups seeking to protect and aggrandize their philosophies, values, and self-interests. These two evolutionary forces produced contradictions that were reconciled in a variety of ways, including in some cases the emergence of mutant concepts and practices. Much of the conflict was generated by the different traditions and dissemination strategies that had been included in the RDU design itself.

The program design was not derived from a clear or pure model. It started as little more than a good intention, a gleam in someone's eye. Consequently, even people closely associated with the program did not always agree upon facts surrounding certain events or their meaning. While the program was perhaps clear to various people at different times, it was conceived in *different* ways as it materialized, matured, and then wound down. The conceptions held at one phase imposed the constraints and the options that shaped the program in its next phase. My thesis is that the events that transpired early in the history of the program left a visible impact on the way it operated, and in fact these events ultimately determined its final destiny.

RDU is only one among many short-lived federal programs that come and go each year. It is nonetheless important to study such programs, and in particular to understand how they are *designed.*

Much of the social policy research in recent years has been concerned with program *implementation*. This is so because some promising projects have produced disappointing results.

Various explanations for these disappointing results emphasize the following (see McGowan, 1976; Williams, 1976):

- resistance or other obstacles encountered in the local settings;
- management control problems associated with large-scale projects;
- "specification" failures resulting from lack of concrete detail about what is to be done, how it is to be done, and whether the outcomes are sufficiently measurable; and
- vague, diffuse, and internally inconsistent designs.

These explanations are not distinctly different, of course, but they do represent different emphases that are traceable to alternative assumptions about the nature of implementation. The first two explanations do not directly challenge the design of the program. Presumably, problems can be corrected by changing the settings or by finding more compatible ones, and by applying more rational control techniques. The third explanation acknowledges that certain aspects of design can be at fault, but not the basic ideas which are, presumably, essentially clear and sound and merely require elaboration. Only the last explanation suggests that implementation problems are often created by the design itself. McGowan's (1976) study of NIE's Experimental Education Project (EEP) is a case in point. She concluded that the central problem was the uncertainty produced by the project's vague and unclear goals. Neither systematic planning nor evaluation proved to be of much help. The program "stumbled into existence" and was developed in a loose and intuitive way. In short, one reason that programs are not effectively implemented is because they are not clearly designed. And yet it seems that in comparison to the other explanations this simple truth has not been a prevailing theme in the research on implementation.

In calling attention to design, I have in mind not only the logic of program design, on which many authors have commented, but also the social history of design or, in other words, the progression of visions and concrete ideas that compete for survival and prominence during a program's formative period. With some notable exceptions (Bailey and Moser, 1968; Banfield, 1976), too little attention has been paid to how federal programs come into being in first place. And yet the sources of design inconsistencies are contained in a program's biographical history. In particular, the events surrounding a program's birth will often continue to affect its later course of development.

Federal programs are designed within administrative constraints as well as within political and economic ones, and all these affect the designer's ability to plan. Even coherent, clearly planned programs can evolve in unanticipated directions because they are shaped by administrative, political, and economic constraints. These programs are often the products of compromises, are implemented by persons who did not design them, and are then adapted to existing circumstances. Indeed, some features of the program design can themselves impose the very obstacles to implementation that the design was supposed to overcome.

The magnitude and force of these constraints depend upon the agency. Programs become entangled in the bureaucratic politics peculiar to different agencies. However, virtually no attention has been given to how organizational characteristics of different *types* of federal bureaucracies shape programs. RDU was a product of a troubled new federal agency with features resembling what I have called "entrepreneurial bureaucracy." The social climate prevailing at NIE at the time formed a context for RDU, and this program, in turn, tells us something about this type of bureaucracy.

In addition to the light it can shed on how programs are designed and then function in entrepreneurial bureaucracies, RDU is important for another reason. The bulk of social science research conducted on federal programs in recent years has been concerned with congressionally *mandated* programs created in response to legislation (see the references in this book). The host of *discretionary* programs such as RDU, that are conceived and initiated each year by employees of federal agencies, have not received enough attention. Even in some exceptional instances in which discretionary programs have been studied (cf. McGowan, 1976), little attention has been paid to understanding how agencies make decisions to use their discretionary funds.

There are some important differences between discretionary and mandated programs. First, discretionary programs are less likely to have influential sponsors in Congress who can protect them (Pressman, 1975). Second, design ambiguities in discretionary programs cannot be blamed on legislative imprecision. For example, the contradictions that crept into the Model Cities program design during the legislative process were due to congressional politics (Banfield, 1976). But discretionary programs are conceived in the offices of federal agencies, where they are presumably freer from congressional politics and, perhaps as a consequence, more subject to the forces of bureaucratic politics.

Third, and most important, discretionary programs are indicative of the autonomy and influence available to some federal agencies, and in particular to employees at middle levels of the federal hierarchy. While any agency has leeway to interpret and operationalize congressional mandates, many have even wider latitude to formulate programs on their own—programs that are not normally subject to congressional review.

As an investigation into the forces that shaped one discretionary program, this study does not claim that the events reported will be repeated or are generalizable, although I suspect that RDU does fit certain patterns. Nor is it my purpose to evaluate or pass judgment on the program. Rather, I hope to portray some of the human drama that drives federal agencies so that we can better appreciate how some discretionary programs evolve, and so that we can understand some of the reasons for their success or difficulties.

SUMMARY

RDU was initiated by NIE in the summer of 1976 as a three-year $10 million action research program intended to assist education agencies with identifying R & D products relevant to their needs and with trying out new ways of linking R & D knowledge with the practitioners who could use it. This program provides a propitious opportunity to examine the birth of a discretionary program. Some federal agencies have a great deal of latitude in establishing programs on their own, but little has been written about how they use their discretion. Accordingly, the focus will be on how the program was designed on the premise that the early history of the program impacted how it operated later on. As Michelson has said, "some programs are *conceived* to fail. Others, though they could succeed, are *designed* to fail. Few, I think are conceived and designed well, but managed badly; and even fewer are conceived, designed, and managed well, but foiled by irresponsible workers beyond managements' control" (Michelson, 1976:196).

Such a study also can illuminate an intriguing type of agency, the entrepreneurial bureaucracy (EB), as it was nurtured during the early stages of the National Institute of Education. One of the outstanding features of the EB is that subordinates act as the driving force behind new program thrusts. Through its managerial incentives, NIE cultivated such initiative until it became a major distinguishing characteristic of the agency.

Information was obtained through in-depth interviews with the key people who were associated with the program in different capacities at various times, as well as from NIE files. I have used a sociological framework to piece together information from different sources and perspectives. This is my version of a complex story.

NOTE

1. However, in practice the RDU staff treated the decisions as an iterative, interactive process. Alternative sequences were both permitted and expected.

Chapter III

Maneuvering

Most of the consultants who planned NIE had recommended that the dissemination activities, then housed in the National Center for Educational Communication (NCEC), should remain intact at OE. However, the chairman of the House Select Subcommittee on Education was convinced that unless NCEC was under the control of NIE, the Institute's products would never get into circulation. He prevailed, and in OE's dissemination programs were transferred to the Institute (see Sproull et al., 1978). The Institute was thereby equipped with an array of dissemination capabilities, from the most sophisticated machine information retrieval system to the use of field agents. OE was to continue supporting dissemination activities related to its own programs.

DISSEMINATION AS A VEHICLE FOR SERVICE

The largest component of the NCEC program was the Educational Research Information Center Program (ERIC), a network of sixteen decentralized information clearing houses and four centralized processing and management centers. Initiated by OE in the mid-1960s in response to criticisms that practitioners were uninformed about OE-sponsored research, ERIC provides access to a data base containing over 300,000 documents and journal articles. At nominal cost, users can obtain paper or microfiche copies of ERIC noncopyrighted holdings. Some experts say that it is the best mechanized information retrieval system in the world.

At the time of its transfer, NCEC was also sponsoring a pilot study in three states experimenting with the use of "linking" agents, or educational field agents with responsibilities loosely modeled after agricultural extension agents. This program was not developed by NIE, although it did provide some of the guidelines for the agency's State Capacity Building Grant Program.

The NIE managers were not entirely pleased with this "gift" of dissemination programs. In fact, during the first two years they were reluctant to promote dissemination at all. Sproull et al. (1978:132) reported that:

> after the transfer, the director of the dissemination group found himself and his group shut off from top management. The NIE directors took the view that dissemination was an issue to be studied. They believed that this program, which was based on the assumption that dissemination was primarily an issue of information transfer, needed reassessment, and that the dissemination director needed to be redirected.

Unwilling to bend, he resigned.

The truth is that a more important thrust for dissemination was coming from outside the agency. The Congress had decided that dissemination should be housed at NIE. And by 1974, the Chief State School Officers' Organization also had begun to press Congress for dissemination programs—largely channeled through State Departments of Education.[1] Some of the members of this organization reportedly were not pleased that the State Pilot Dissemination Project had been dropped. But within the agency, NIE management had concluded from a review that the NCEC programs were not highly regarded. Practitioners were critical of ERIC because they did not know what was in the system or how to gain access to it, and they also found it jargon-laden and of doubtful relevance. Furthermore, the new leadership had been recruited to NIE with the promise that they would do research. They were expecting a "honeymoon period" before they would have to demonstrate that NIE's programs were improving school practice (Sproull et al., 1978). The dissemination program seemed to them to be too service-oriented and out of place in a research shop. It was perceived as another encumbrance from OE.

The transfer of R & D knowledge is a complex undertaking. It must filter through a web of different academic disciplines, educational organizations, federal and state government agencies, and private firms. Add to this the massive number of school districts, schools, and the decentralized nature of American education, and dissemination must have seemed to be an overwhelming task to a management faced with all of the problems associated with starting a new agency.

Eventually the NIE management was forced to reassess its position. Appropriations committees in Congress were making it clear that there would be no honeymoon. In fact, there would be no more money unless NIE could demonstrate that it was improving educational practice. But prohibited from offering immediate service and entirely dependent on the long-term effects of spasmodic and intermittent research programs, how could the Institute demonstrate that it was doing that? The answer was obvious. The NCEC dissemination programs were, after all, service programs! Dissemination activities were the means by which NIE could provide the direct service to local education agencies (LEAs) that Congress had not authorized in any other way. Management now saw dissemination as the most immediate way for NIE to show that the products it had supported and developed were useful. Indeed, they had now come to believe that the future of the Institute hinged on an effective dissemination program.

It would not be enough, however, to merely continue the OE activities. NIE needed to show that it had something of its own. Expenditures for dissemination increased 72 percent between fiscal years 1973 and 1974. A new associate director for the Office of Dissemination was appointed in late spring of 1974. She had earlier worked on a task force with the Institute while on loan from NSF, where she was special assistant to the associate director for Education and in charge of curriculum for elementary programs. She had subsequently joined the Rand Corporation where she was responsible for designing policy evaluations for large-scale social intervention programs.

In retrospect, it seems fair to say that the R & D Utilization program was part of a larger thrust within this troubled agency to use dissemination for strategic purposes in response to congressional pressures on the Institute at the time. The establishment of seven new RDU projects was one of several political moves that were being made to show Congress and the public that NIE was taking serious steps on its own to improve the utility of research.

This proved to be the only feasible way for NIE to offer direct service to the states and the LEAs in its effort to build constituencies of practitioners.

A STRATEGIC RECRUITMENT

This chain of events prompted the deputy director of NIE to set out in 1974 to find someone able to devise new mechanisms for communicating knowledge about R & D to practitioners. He subscribed to the director's view that ERIC's computerized retrieval information system was not adequate. The management team was looking for some "new blood" for the Institute who could come up with something in addition to ERIC.

While attending some meetings at an educational laboratory, he met a creative, mercurial scholar named Larry Hutchins. Hutchins had recently written a paper describing effective strategies for disseminating R & D products. During the meetings, Hutchins expressed concern about the narrow concept of "information transfer" that seemed implicit in the ERIC system. These comments struck a responsive chord in the deputy director. Subsequently, the two engaged in several conversations that culminated in a three-year term appointment for Hutchins at NIE.

Larry Hutchins was known and respected among his colleagues for his assertiveness and his entrepreneurial skills. He was a fitting choice for the agency. He was, in a sense, hired with an "open portfolio" and with no specific assignment. Some people say that the NIE management had no firm ideas about what was needed. True, there was some talk about revising a catalogue of NIE-sponsored R & D products and renewing an initiative to develop consumer information "packages" that could be easily understood by practitioners. But the management of NIE had made it clear to Hutchins that they were looking to him for new directions, and encouraged him to use the opportunities at the Institute to develop his own ideas.

Hutchins's job would not be easy. When he arrived in the spring of 1974, he found a new associate director taking over a newly reorganized dissemination program, and a staff divided among itself and still nursing wounds from the most recent round of personnel reassignments. Hutchins's supervisor had no voice in his appointment,[2] but the two found some points of agreement. She also felt that the ERIC program was not capable of meeting all of the Institute's needs. She wanted to see a proactive, outreach initiative that would bring NIE into a more sustained relationship with practitioners. Both persons were encouraged by a recently released Rand Corporation report that stressed the need for "linking mechanisms" to bring outside innovations into schools. And so, with this backing, Hutchins settled in and began to chart a course.

Some of Hutchins's original notions would eventually be modified, but in essence he was planning an aggressive consumer information program that would be designed and administered nationwide by NIE—a program that would work through organizations already in existence at regional, state, intermediate, and local levels. His objective was to inform teachers, administrators and other practitioners about R & D-based materials available from NIE and elsewhere, which they might have overlooked or whose advantages and disadvantages they might not fully appreciate. Hutchins undoubtedly shared with other leaders in educational dissemination, a concern about the variable quality of the products being disseminated. But what seems to be the most critical assumption among many dissemination specialists is that *in general* teaching practices will benefit more from the use of research-based materials than from continuing to rely upon tradition, testimonials, and other unsystematic approaches. But there is an important proviso: practitioners must receive technical assistance concerning how to use materials and instruction concerning their potential disadvantages as well as their advantages.

Although Hutchins planned to design the program with plenty of advice from practitioners in the field, this would be an NIE initiative, a "top-down," proactive effort from Washington. Some of Hutchins's critics were also under the mistaken impression that he intended to advocate certain materials in a "product pushing" posture. This image undoubtedly complicated his life at NIE, but it was not Hutchins's intent to push any particular product. He originally thought that it would be possible for NIE to identify a large pool of reasonably good materials and publish clearly written information booklets to enable practitioners to make more informed choices on their own. While he had originally visualized one product pool for the nation, his objective was not to restrict the choices available to practitioners, but rather to expand their awareness by including as many products as possible.

Hutchins was keenly aware of the need for a closer working relationship between practitioners and curriculum experts in universities, state education agencies, R & D centers and the like. Therefore, he wanted to explore new forms of "linkage" among such agencies. While he probably had nothing definite in mind at this point, his view of linkage seems to have gone beyond the use of staff specialists from state education agencies who work with schools in the role of "extension agents." "Linkage" included workshops, joint appointments, working committees, and other institutional arrangements for cutting across stubborn organizational boundaries.

Hutchins's thoughts had been influenced by an exploding volume of dissemination literature. Perhaps the intellectual direction this field was taking is best illustrated in the linkage model described by Havelock et al. (1973), which attempted to fuse the best-documented features of several available models to improve the exchange between R & D and the practice system. According to Raizen (1979):

> Both the user system and the resource or R & D system are viewed as problem-solving, but with meaningful connections to each other. The user and the resource systems are engaged in a reciprocal and collaborative relationship that encourages a process of mutual adaptation. Linkage between the two, based on face-to-face contact, is the most important element in effective dissemination and use of knowledge. Successful practice improvement comes about through adequate diagnosis of need and through careful organization of resources to assure their relevance to the user. Unless those charged with carrying out the proposed improvements are involved early in the process of problem identification and consideration of alternative strategies for amelioration, effective implementation and maintenance of any innovation are unlikely.

NIE saw the importance of this model to its dissemination program in the following way:

> Because of the linkage perspective's synthesis of all the important factors that appear to affect knowledge use in education, it has great promise for generating effective programs. Therefore, NIE's dissemination efforts are devoting substantial resources to understanding and improving linkage

mechanisms between R & D and user communities in education (Dissemination and Resources Group, 1976).

The concepts running through Hutchins's mind at this point were still vague. The actual plan was to be given shape and substance by subsequent events, not the least of which included the harsh internal politics of the Institute. While he had been given an "open portfolio," he did not yet have a budget. Nor was he assigned to manage the staff of a functioning unit. Either he would have to work within the existing program structure, or find his own money and staff. On the surface, the first option had some merit. As we shall see, the RDU program that eventually materialized was in some respects compatible with several existing NIE dissemination programs, and it could have made a real contribution to these ongoing efforts. However, organizations have their own logic. What program manager wants to relinquish part of a budget and reassign staff members to a newcomer from outside for the purpose of revising (even if to augment) an already established program? Thus, existing dissemination programs that might have housed Hutchins's efforts were either inappropriate or inhospitable or both. To understand the barriers he now faced, some background information will help.

NIE DISSEMINATION PROGRAMS

A federal agency can establish one of three types of legal relationships with state and local units of government: it can support local initiative through field-initiated *grants;* it can offer a specific *service;* or it can *contract* for participation in federally directed experimental programs. The essence of a grant is that the initiative and plan come from the client. Also, by precedent, grants exercise fewer restrictions over how clients may use the funds than do contracts. The project grant has been described as a conditional gift wherein the grantee is largely free to conduct himself as he or she sees fit and without liability for damages for failure to perform. The government does not control the manner of performance (The Federal Domestic Assistance Catalog, 1976: VII, cited in CPI, 1977).

The service delivery mode usually requires the agency to make a long-term commitment to operate the service, but the agency can then decide which services to offer.

According to the "Project Officer's Guide to Contracting" (1974:i–ii), the contract mechanism is used where the purposes of government require the services of the non-federal sector. The government is required to monitor the contractor's activities in order to assure proper performance. (See CPI, 1977:55). Contracts for experimental programs are the most directive form of intervention, and they therefore can place an agency in a delicate bind between cooperating with and exercising supervision over other levels of government. Federal contracts can put appointed federal employees in positions of authority over elected officials at state and local levels.

NIE's Dissemination and Resource Group (DRG) operated activities that used all three strategies. The State Capacity Building Grants Program has provided three- to five-year grants to forty-three states for the purpose of helping them accomplish their objective to develop and coordinate comprehensive programs for the delivery of educational knowledge to LEAs. Each project is required to provide leadership and a pool of products (some for assistance to schools, etc.), but within broad, federal guidelines, the intent was to decentralize dissemination activities. The funds are used to develop information bases, provide technical assistance to LEAs, support the work of linking agents, and aid in leadership and management training. ERIC, on the other hand, is a service delivery program which has made information available to anyone who requested it. RDU represents the third mode of operation—an experimental program, designed and directed by NIE, which contracted with participants to cooperate in the experiment.

No Room at ERIC

It might seem that a program like RDU, with its consumer information thrust, was suited to the ERIC operation. On that assumption Hutchins said that he went "hat in hand" to an assistant director of a unit that included ERIC, in the hope of working out his ideas through that program. This never happened. It is not now easy to piece together the myriad of motives involved then, but some philosophical, political and pragmatic considerations do seem reasonably clear.[3]

The two men held different philosophical outlooks about the appropriateness of federally directed programs. Although they both eventually modified their positions, the director of ERIC, a thoughtful and humane person, believed that the federal government should confine itself to a "bottom-up" facilitative, supportive role with respect to disseminating R & D. ERIC was there to help whomever asked for its service. By contrast, he perceived that Hutchins planned to start with a "top-down," product-pushing outreach type of activity. Furthermore, as director of ERIC, he did not look forward to having to enforce contractual agreements with the states; the State Capacity Building Grants Program, which he was also directing, was being criticized by some outsiders for not being strict enough about enforcing requirements that pertained to state education agencies. His whole posture, then, had been in direct conflict with the NIE management's desire to take more initiative in promoting R & D products.

Some informants also believe that the ERIC director was concerned that ERIC might be placed in an untenable position by being held accountable for more than could reasonably be accomplished by a federal program (such as improving students' test scores). According to one informant, he advocated responsible "stewardship," which was his way of saying that a program can achieve no more than it has the resources to accomplish. Given the available evaluation technology, he felt that it would be impossible to ever prove that ERIC had favorably affected schools or students; any program that tried to use ERIC to impact schools, he firmly believed, could taint ERIC with an undeserved sense of failure.

Perhaps management could have forced a closer working relationship between the two men, but the associate director was convinced that there were simply too many obstacles impeding the wholesale modifications in the ERIC system that would have been required for it to eventually deliver R & D "products." ERIC had been designed to store and retrieve research information. It was not yet capable of disseminating these products themselves. Most ERIC clearinghouse directors were housed in universities with small staffs and did not have the skills or the manpower to actively disseminate products without jeopardizing the quality of what they were already doing so well.

Perhaps Another Program

ERIC was not the only option. There was the State Capacity Building Grants Program (SCBGP). With hindsight it seems that the procedures to be tried out in RDU probably would have been useful additions to what many state education agencies (SEAs) were trying to accomplish. As one informant noted, there was nothing about RDU that could not have been developed within the parameters of the SCBGP.

However, SCBGP was a *grant* program that was developed cooperatively with the states. SEAs had wide discretion over project designs and over how federal money would be used. It was therefore not a feasible vehicle for the kind of centrally planned program that Hutchins was contemplating.

The Problem Solving Program

Another activity at the Institute that Hutchins had to take into account was the School Capacity for Problem Solving Project. The project director had been appointed to head a task force to review and evaluate dissemination activities at NIE. The document that was produced by the task force (*Building Capacity for Renewal and Reform*, 1973) laid the foundation for a new unit to be directed by its principal author. Some tense controversy arose between him and others as to whether this new unit should be formed within the dissemination group or independent of it. In the end the unit was given relatively independent status within the Institute.

The Problem Solving Project had already initiated a tack that eventually would become an aspect of RDU, namely providing technical assistance to help schools identify and solve problems. But there the similarities ended. The Problem Solving Project was based on the assumption that practitioners would find or create their own resources. By contrast, RDU emphasized the practitioners' dependence on external assistance and on resources drawn from specific product pools. By virtue of his own interests and the circumstances that had brought him to NIE, Hutchins was under a mandate to disseminate R & D products. But the staff of the Problem Solving Project would not be saddled with such a narrow pool of possible "solutions." Moreover, the elaborate top-down system they saw in the RDU design was foreign to their philosophy, which presumed at its core that each local school faces peculiar problems that cannot be remedied with standardized products. The staff were relying on local initiative, not R & D. It seemed to them that Hutchins was working on solutions to problems before it was clear what the real problems were. Moreover, while the Problem Solving Project staff thought of their mission as research, the RDU program was to contain a heavy *service* component, in addition to the research component.

But beneath these surface differences, it must be recognized that in this era of competing "fiefdoms" at NIE, the Problem Solving Project was also defending its "turf." Not that RDU was a serious threat. The Problem Solving Project had already been funded and had achieved its own independent status within NIE. Rather, RDU seemed unnecessary. In the words of one observer, the Problem Solving Project's staff considered themselves more "pure," and they were reluctant "to give a competitor an idea." Given the strained relationship between the programs, and the complexity and evolving nature of the design, the project remained aloof from RDU.

OE's National Diffusion Network (NDN)

There was another logically attractive option, although it was never actively pursued. OE was operating a dissemination program called the National Diffusion Network (NDN) that used a personal assistance strategy similar to the approach RDU eventually took. In fact, the similarities between the "state facilitators" in NDN and the "linkers" in RDU were so striking that after RDU was funded a congressional committee raised questions about possible overlapping duplication. In one sense, RDU proved, in effect, to be a test of some of the ideas from the NDN design. However, the two programs were put into place on different assumptions. In particular, RDU provided more money per site, which increased the potential impact of the change agents. NDN was a product-pushing effort, while the objective of RDU was to provide consumer information about a wide range of products without necessarily endorsing any of them. Some observers also doubt whether NIE products would have met the standards used to screen products for the NDN pool.[4] However, NDN did not advocate a problem-solving approach to the extent of the one that eventually materialized in the RDU projects. In any case, it would not do for NIE to be identified with the very agencies whose shadow it was so desperately trying to escape.

FRAGMENTATION: THE PRICE OF SUCCESS

Hemmed in by a maze of alternative programs that were performing some parallel functions and that were competing for the same constituencies and resources, there seemed no choice but to initiate still another program, using still another approach. Rather than designing RDU to be symbiotic with and a supplement to existing programs, Hutchins opted for a distinctive alternative that would not exactly duplicate them but that would compete with them. Indeed, he hoped that RDU would jolt the Institute's other dissemination programs into adopting a consumer information perspective. Rather than cooperate closely with what he was beginning to see as rival programs, he sought to minimize any connection with them. RDU was tailored accordingly. The State Capacity Building Grants Program was relatively open-ended; RDU would be a contract arrangement under which the government would specify certain conditions required for action research. NDN was limited to the dissemination of *locally* invented products developed under Title III grants; RDU would include a different pool of R & D products and processes. The Problem Solving Project shunned R & D products; RDU would rely heavily on providing consumer information about specific R & D-based materials and ideas. Thus, the new program had established a niche in the Institute.

Hutchins has said that a major purpose of RDU was to prod ERIC and other dissemination programs at NIE to modify their operations, to place more stress on consumer information, to utilize more field agents, and to become more sensitive to the need to work with other agencies. And he is convinced that RDU has had some of these effects. Other informants dismiss such claims as fantasy. But whatever the effect of RDU, one thing is certain: all of the maneuvering that was required to get the program off the drawing board had a price. Ultimately the program was isolated by its own competiveness, which in turn contributed to the already fragmented federal dissemination effort. One can also wonder whether the squabbles diluted NIE's potential impact on the field, and (as some observers believe) whether they undermined the legitimacy and, perhaps ultimately, the utility of the findings that were drawn from the experience.

The naive outsider will wonder whether these autonomous programs were merely replicating services in a self-serving effort to survive. Insiders maintain that the proliferation of programs is unimportant, because there are enough problems and enough things to do to justify different approaches even if it means some duplication. What is important, though, is that *the way RDU was created clearly isolated it from any institutionalized, ongoing collaboration with those other federal programs that might have been able to use the results of the effort.* There was not even a formal connection between the people who managed RDU and the R & D Exchange Network (RDx), which was also established by Hutchins during his term at NIE.[5]

SUMMARY

The chief architect of what evolved as RDU was recruited with "open portfolio." But without a budget or staff, he was faced with the option of either finding a home within an existing program or initiating an entirely new endeavor. He soon decided against the first option, partly because he considered some of the other programs too protective and inhospitable. In addition, certain programs were not entirely compatible with the top-down, aggressive consumer information approach he was contemplating, with its focus on products and its ambitious vision of a new coalition among relevant but stubbornly autonomous R & D organizations. As others have been observed, a new agency and program must cope with crowded program space filled with similar programs competing for legitimacy and influence. "It has to negotiate issues of duplication and overlap, incompatibilities in eligibility requirements and territorial boundaries of service" (Weiss, 1979:15).

One critic questioned the "intervention" strategy behind RDU, which seemed to him based on the smug assumption that people at the federal level know more than people at the state level about how to design a dissemination program. Instead, he advocated cost sharing programs designed by states and supported jointly by the federal government and the states. While the federal government would then lose control, he maintained that there would at least be more chance that whatever was developed would continue.

But most of the staff members in the seven projects in RDU had more favorable comments. One project manager saw RDU as the first theory-driven program in education which had been planned on the basis of a model drawn from the literature. He admired Hutchins' willingness to put his ideas on the line for others to review and modify. In contrast to some of the NIE staff, he thought that the vagueness in the original RFP had contributed to the success of the projects, because it gave contractors the leeway they needed to design projects that conformed to local needs and conditions. Some people believed that RDU represented a step forward from what most dissemination programs had been doing, based largely on the notion that dissemination is a communication process.

The fact that RDU materialized as an independent program rather than as a constituent component of existing programs can be explained by a combination of formidable political realities in the Institute as well as the substantive characteristics of the existing programs. The true balance between logic and politics is perhaps debatable, but what is certain is that RDU was shaped by the prevailing institutional forces governing NIE at the time. The maneuvering had produced a new program, but it had also isolated RDU from other parts of the system where the findings from the program might have been put to use. Some knowledgeable observers vigorously maintain that formal arrangements are not necessary for a demonstration program to impact practice, and that is probably so. *But it is indeed ironic that a program established on the premise that more effective, formalized linkages are needed between the R & D community and practitioners itself was not formally linked into relevant ongoing programs in Washington.* The program had been sucked into a policy vacuum (Louis and Corwin, 1980). RDU was too remote from other dissemination programs at NIE as well as from the long-term service delivery programs at OE for its findings to be *readily* incorporated by them. The Institute was forced to rely upon informal word of mouth, dissemination forums, and publications to communicate the findings from the

RDU experience. Perhaps, as advocates for the program also maintain, some of the findings will be used by some state education agencies. But the fact remains that here too, no formally *institutionalized* mechanisms were ever established to ensure that that would happen on a national scale. In this respect, RDU may have hurt itself by claiming to be so distinctive. The conditions under which the program was designed triggered many of the problems that were to develop later. But features of the design also guided some of the responses to those problems.

NOTES

1. This group's pressure was instrumental in the subsequent development of the State Capacity Building Grants Program and in the National Dissemination Leadership Project.

2. Officially, Senta Raizen was not appointed until June 29, 1974, many weeks after Hutchins arrived. However, she had actually commenced her duties on a consultant basis in the early spring.

3. The former director of ERIC is now deceased, which makes this part of the report especially subject to conjecture.

4. In a July 18, 1975 memo from Senta Raizen to NIE Director Harold Hodgkinson, she wrote, "Our recent solicitation of product information revealed that almost 700 NIE products are developed or near completion but less than 100 present evidence of effectiveness in the Dissemination Status Report."

5. Cooperation was of course hampered by the fact that RDx did not take form until RDU was well under way. However, in addition, the NIE managers responsible for RDx coveted unspent RDU funds.

Chapter IV

The Politics of Getting Started

The decision to create a new program was only a beginning. There was still no money, and indeed it would be a struggle to find it. The next few months would be punctuated with a sequence of obstacles and issues spawned by bureaucratic politics. In the meantime, Hutchins and his staff braced themselves for the awesome tasks required to craft a program and get it underway.

THE "CONCEPT PAPER"

During his first few months at NIE, Hutchins and his staff traveled extensively through twenty-one states, visiting several hundred educators associated with state and local education agencies. These talks helped to sharpen and modify some of his original notions. Soon Hutchins and his staff were working on a position paper that outlined some tentative proposals for a formal program. This paper was sent to over 1,000 people, including SEAs, practitioners, and some well-known scholars in the field of dissemination.

Roots of the Paper

Intellectually, the paper reflected an eclectic body of research and theory. One can detect different themes from various well-known pieces of literature (see for example, Havelock, 1973; NIE, 1973; Berman and McLaughlin, 1977). While he had read most of this literature and knew many of its authors, Hutchins maintains that he was not swayed by any particular piece of literature. He was especially dubious about relying too heavily on the use of change agents, or "linkers." It seemed to him far too visionary and expensive an approach to work for the complex problems involved in the dissemination of educational R & D.

The Rationale

In his Foreword, Hutchins described the concept paper as a rationale and description for a dissemination program that was soon to be developed by the School Practice and Service Division of NIE. Calling the program "a venture into uncharted areas in an attempt to build additional linkages between research and development and the educational system," the paper warned that the proposed program would be substantially smaller than its conceptual scope. And, while conceding that the targeted approach being advocated could be viewed as an "intrusion upon local autonomy," the paper promised that RDU would operate in a manner compatible with local control.

The paper began with a reference to the fact that Congress had specifically authorized dissemination as a major activity of the Institute, and it stressed that the Senate intended a broad interpretation of dissemination which, in addition to spreading information about R & D innovations, included *helping* schools adopt and implement them. The proposed program would be based on the premise that adequate and useful R & D outcomes were available, but were not being used because practitioners were uninformed about them, and did not have the assistance needed to adapt them to their own needs. While research *findings* were readily available through ERIC, it had been difficult to make many R & D *products* available because publishers were not interested in limited-market items such as models, or teacher and administrator guides, and because ERIC did not include them.

Six program objectives were identified in the concept paper. Three of these related to the development of a knowledge base: information gathering; searching, screening and evaluating alternatives; and securing the innovation. These functions define what is required to select (adopt) a product and comprise the "consumer information" component of the program. The other three objectives pertained to helping to implement a program after it was selected. These objectives form the "R & D utilization component:" promoting linkage between developers and users, providing technical assistance to adopters, and installing R & D outcomes. The consumer information component was to be coordinated centrally with "input and help from the field," while the R & D utilization component would be predominately coordinated by state and local agencies "with advice and counsel from NIE." The idea was to start with a locally defined problem and marshall a national pool of R & D products and services to aid practitioners in assessing their needs. The options they selected would then be modified and the new programs would be implemented with the aid of state, intermediate, and regional agencies, as well as R & D organizations.

Hutchins had gone to NIE with the conviction that practitioners were primarily in need of *information* to help them select appropriate R & D products. But after talking extensively with specialists in the field, he became more fully appreciative of the practitioners' need for *assistance* in using the products they had chosen. His initial thinking about establishing a viable consumer information program quickly expanded into a two-pronged approach that encompassed adoption and implementation strategies.

Two strategies would be employed: (1) providing potential users with alternatives; and (2) using a "linkage strategy" based on the work of existing dissemination programs and agencies (rather than creating new ones). Two levels of coordination were to be included: (1) intra-state network activities (in the twenty-five states with regional intermediate service agencies for local service functions); and (2) interstate network activities that would focus on a large number of schools with relatively homogeneous problems without regard to state boundaries.

According to the concept paper, the projects would evolve through stages requiring from three to five years before any given topical problem had been "comprehensively addressed" in any given state or region.[1] During the first year, the program would be confined to two, or tentatively three, topical areas: reading, education and work, and an additional topic to be named later. These two topics were picked because they had been designated as NIE priorities and because "in our judgment, NIE's existing R & D involvement has yielded the largest number of tested, available outcomes in these areas." The authors also expected that two or three problem areas would be addressed in each subsequent year, and would be selected on the basis of user needs. The term "outcomes" was used advisedly to include many types of knowledge and research. But as a result, different parties never fully agreed on a precise meaning.

Finally, a major evaluation or assessment component was proposed to collect information needed "to inform program management decisions, and ultimately, policy makers who will determine the amount of public funding used to support the utilization of R & D in education." But it was cautioned that "this evaluation goal will not be easily met" because of the complexity of the governance structure, the potentials for conflict over the data, and the difficulties of finding direct measures for some of the objectives.

WRITING THE REQUEST FOR PROPOSALS

The concept paper was the first hint to the field that an RDU program was in the offering. It prodded potential bidders to begin thinking about their proposals many months before the formal request for proposals (RFP) was issued in November 1975. One project manager recalled a night in the fall of 1975, when several people sat at a table in a restaurant, writing notes on a napkin in anticipation of the RFP. They were well along in their thinking by the time they saw the RFP.

Preparing the RFP had proved to be a formidable undertaking. Indeed, it went through approximately thirty tortuous revisions. Part of the problem was that Hutchins had delegated some of the writing to staff members who were perhaps not entirely clear about what he had in mind. Moreover, the staff had conscientiously tried to include comments solicited from readers who had received the concept paper. In addition, however, some major conceptual issues emerged that split the staff.

One issue concerned how much emphasis to give to the two objectives outlined in the concept paper, that is, publicizing consumer information (CI) and providing technical assistance for implementation (TA). Both CI and TA were deemed important. As a practical issue, however, the question was raised about how many resources should be devoted to developing a consumer information program vs. how many resources should be devoted to hiring "linking agents" who would provide expensive technical assistance directly to chosen target schools. Raizen has written,

"Individually tailored assistance to 80,000 school buildings fits neither the resources nor the role of the federal government in education" (1979:264). In this sense, there was a threat that "the tail would wag the dog," that the technical assistance component would eclipse the consumer information thrust which had precipitated the program. At the same time, the rival Problem Solving Project staff was convinced that too much emphasis would be placed on pushing R & D products instead of on helping schools. Wanting the resources to go directly to schools, on the premise that local practitioners must learn to help themselves, the Problem Solving staff also objected to plans to channel the money through state or other intermediate service agencies.

In seeking to meld the strengths of CI and TA dissemination approaches and philosophies into the RDU design, the designers had also perpetuated the tensions between these two approaches. While both dimensions are logically important, in practice they compete for resources, and the actual balance remained to be worked out in the course of the program.

A closely related question being debated was whether the primary purpose of the TA component of the project was to help schools install specific R & D products or whether there was a larger objective—namely, to use the occasions when schools were deciding on R & D products as opportunities to strengthen local problem-solving *capacities*. Hutchins had come to NIE with the conviction that if practitioners were better informed about the products available, this would go a long way toward helping them solve their problems. However, some persons in the Institute were convinced that encouraging schools to use standard R & D products was secondary to helping them develop a long-term capacity to solve all sorts of problems on their *own*, including many problems for which standard R & D products might not be relevant. The issue was whether it was possible to build that long-term capacity through a project like RDU. Hutchins was convinced that it was not. Nonetheless, these two objectives were to continue to compete for priority throughout the course of the program.

Finally, some of the NIE staff were uneasy about the failure of the RFP to specify and operationalize more explicitly what was to be done and who was to do it. Awarding contracts is of course an inherently judgmental process, and the way awards were made in RDU was not necessarily exceptional. However, the contracts office was particularly nervous about the "looseness" in the RDU request for proposals, and some of the more experienced staff members at NIE complained that the wide range of activities permissible within the RFP made it difficult to establish concrete criteria for selecting the winners. One staff member asked, "How do programs like this get into existence when the initial idea is little more than an 'ink blot' to which everyone applies his own meaning?"

Part of this controversy stemmed from alternative views of how a program should be designed—as an operational plan or as a flexible guide (Williams, 1976). There is no question about the sincerity of the RDU staff. Indeed, they had conscientiously tried to give proposers the latitude they felt was required to tailor activities to the priority needs of different service areas. But the looseness might also have had some unintended effects. It probably aided and abetted some overlap already extant among the alternative programs, and as Seiber observes about federal RFPs in general, "vagueness permits federal managers to select proposals that are compatible with their private expectations on how the evaluation (program) should be conducted and allows leeway later on in defining more sharply the rules of the game" (Seiber, 1982).

CHOOSING THE WINNERS

Before the RFP was written, Hutchins took steps to encourage some good people to apply for projects, first by directing the concept paper to them, and second by talking with a large number of people during his visits in the field. He hoped to encourage people whom he knew were already committed to trying new directions.

Forty-one eligible proposals were received, thirteen of them from state education agencies (SEAs), nine from institutions of higher education, and four from R & D labs and centers. Only four proposals were received from school districts. The heavy response from the SEAs was predictable. They were strategically located in the communication chain between the federal agencies and the local education agencies. They had a history of working with dissemination. Many of them had already been awarded federal State Capacity Building Grants. Moreover, it would have been difficult for local education agencies to form the broad-based consortia that would cut across authority lines as called for in the RFP.

The issues that were debated during earlier stages of the procurement reappeared when trying to operationalize criteria for selecting the winning projects. One informant recalls that RDU staff spent a great deal of time raising questions among themselves about what the RFP actually called for. The reference to "R & D outcomes," for example, could be applied to a wide range of materials and ideas—anything from validated products to research findings, and even to customary practices. As a result, however, different people applied their own specific meanings. The RFP had called for projects that would provide variations in accordance with a matrix of approaches, but some cells of the matrix proved to be cost-ineffective, which necessitated some adaptation.

Approximately $10 million was eventually authorized for RDU: $8.3 million for the program and $1.7 million for the research. Budgets for seven projects ranged in size from $1.4 million to $835,000 for the three-year period. It was originally expected that there would be enough money to fund from five to seven projects. When it became apparent that six of the first-rank projects had consumed most of the money, a reduction in budget was negotiated with at least one project and, as Hutchins recalls, he bargained with the Institute for enough additional money to fund a seventh project by trading a reduction in the length of the program (from four to three years) for more money during the first three years.

Two members of the NIE panel responsible for reviewing the proposals protested that the RDU staff had exercised too much control over the procurement process. NIE guidelines for large procurements provided for an Internal Review Committee (IRC) comprised of NIE staff from throughout the Institute to oversee writing the technical scope of work, the review of proposals, and the recommendations for awards. The RDU staff had weeded out about 20 of the 41 proposals on grounds that they were ineligible or unresponsive. The remaining 21 proposals were assigned to members of a review panel comprised of eminent social scientists and practitioners outside of NIE as well as NIE staff members. It is customary when a large work load is involved (21 proposals of

100 to 300 pages each) to assign each member of the panel a subset of the proposals. The RDU program staff then took over, with the NIE-wide IRC exercising only a peripheral role from that point on. In effect, no one outside the program staff had a comprehensive or comparative grasp of the entire set of proposals. As Hutchins recalls, there were scheduling problems and some members of the panel simply failed to attend the crucial meeting at which the final decisions were made. While there were some quibbles about why a certain project was chosen over others, the primary issue seemed to be a struggle for control within the Institute rather than complaints about the merits of the projects chosen. It was nonetheless a turbulent birth for this program.[2]

STAFFING UP

As one of the largest programs in NIE at the time, RDU would seem to require substantial staff support. However, the program had suffered from the misfortune of being initiated during a government hiring "freeze." Consequently, Hutchins was unable to hire persons from outside the agency. He had to rely on existing staff, many of whom were assigned to the project on the basis of their availability.[3] It seems fair to say that if management had the option, many of the Institute staff who were reassigned to work on RDU probably would not have been hired specifically for this type of work; and probably many of them would have preferred assignments that were more compatible with their own training and experience.

As the program began, Hutchins removed himself from managerial details and turned his attention to writing consumer information materials. The job of running the program fell to an associate who had transferred to the Institute from OE in 1972. He joined the dissemination unit in February 1975 in a shift from a career education program. With a background in public administration, he was not well versed in the literature on dissemination, but he had gained some practical experience with the topic during his eight years of service on a county school board. He was well aware that the consumer information packages that were presumably being prepared for the RDU dissemination effort would not be available; the delivery system had been put into place before this information base was ready. He and Hutchins were forced to rely on the available R & D products themselves.

The projects were not funded until June 1976, and it then took some time before they were actually under way. In some states, authorization to spend money became stalled in the red tape of state bureaucracies, and it was still necessary to hire project directors and to select sites. Several of the projects did not get under way until midway through the first year, and they were not really at their full peak of operation until the following year.

THE RESEARCH CONTACT MUDDLE

RDU was sold to NIE management as "action research." In other words, it was to be a program created for the express purpose of learning something from it. Research was, therefore, an integral component of the program's design. Indeed, the research is what justified the program as part of NIE's mission. The plan was to choose a third-party research contractor when the program RFP was issued. That did not happen. While each project had started to collect some data in the fall of 1977, the major research component was repeatedly delayed. Not until the spring of 1978, almost two years after the seven projects became operational, did a study team from an external evaluation contractor make its first informal visits to the project sites. The first formal data collection from schools was not to occur until September 1978. This episode is a prime example of the politics of research—namely, the clash that frequently occurs between methodologies, bureaucracy, and political forces.

The chain of events responsible for the extended delay began innocently enough with a roadblock that was inadvertently created by the civil service freeze on hiring mentioned earlier. Hutchins was devoting much of his time to involving staff from the projects in the task of designing the research, and he was also preoccupied with the consumer information program. Unable to hire a full-time research specialist to develop the research RFP, Hutchins turned to a deputy who was forced to sandwich this task between his other responsibilities.

At about this time a new position had been created in the Dissemination Group. It would be the responsibility of this Evaluation Coordinator to work on all research and evaluations performed by the Dissemination Group. Mary Ann Millsap was recruited for this position in mid-May 1975, when the RFP for the research was first being considered. There was some confusion about her role. According to her supervisor, the Associate Director for dissemination, Millsap was a technical resource person available to program people if they wished to solicit her help. But Millsap was convinced that the position carried with it some responsibility for assuring quality control. In any case, Millsap soon found herself in competition with Hutchins for control over the research design. She felt hedged in by the lack of authority that she would have needed to fulfill any real or imagined quality control responsibilities. Hutchins controlled the budget and much of the information required to design the research. He began to view Millsap as an adversary and an "intruder" who was trying to grasp control over an internal part of the RDU program. Their stalemate once again deadlocked progress on the research.

After some disputes between Hutchins and Millsap, Millsap was removed from the project by her supervisor who felt that not to have backed Hutchins would have doomed the project in an early, vulnerable stage. A third-party evaluation now seemed less important than mobilizing some kind of evaluation that would be useful to Hutchins and his staff. Few subordinates command the experience and professional stature that Millsap would have needed to win an all-out confrontation with the director of a fledgling project.

The RFP languished for months until the late spring of 1976 when an outside consultant was hired to work out a research strategy. However, Hutchins was not satisfied with his proposal; it called for more quantitative data than Hutchins believed was possible to obtain. The consultant, finding that he was being asked to take on more responsibility than he had anticipated, soon resigned.

More months passed. In the fall of 1976, with the program well under way, Hutchins turned in desperation to a colleague who was performing related work at an NIE-sponsored R & D center. Hutchins contracted with the colleague's organization to collect some preliminary information as a stop-gap measure.[4] Then in the spring of 1977, when he was nearly out of time and resources, Hutchins again asked Millsap to work with a member of his staff on the RFP. She agreed, and Hutchins went along with the RFP design.

The political deadlock between Hutchins and Millsap had roots in an ideological controversy that exists in the social sciences concerning the relative merits of different approaches. Hutchins and some of his consultants were advocating case studies of the 120 individual school sites in the program, because they believed that ethnographies were the only way to capture the rich uniqueness of each individual project. Hutchins was insisting that the information must be helpful to people at the individual sites, and that it would be possible to extract from the cases the variables of common interest, even though this would have to be done at some later time. However, Millsap was dubious. She had been grounded in experimental and survey methods and was also knowledgeable about qualitative methods. How could one understand a *program* by concentrating on the unique properties of specific projects that were operating under a myriad of conditions at individual schools? Whereas Hutchins had hoped to triangulate the data that was drawn from different sources, Millsap had little hope that comparable data would emerge when it was drawn from so many different situations. It also seemed to her burdensome and inefficient to try to undertake so many case studies. She opted for a sample. Cases would yield large quantities of information perhaps, but most of this information would not address program-level issues.

There were some practical issues buried in these lofty arguments. One was whether the primary objective was to obtain a broad understanding of the processes taking place or whether it was to evaluate certain outcomes. The latter would be threatening to the persons who staffed the projects, while the former might encourage these people to "buy in" and cooperate with the study.

Another question raised was whom the research should serve and who should have access to the data. Some of the NIE staff felt that all information should be given directly to the people in the local projects to use for their own purposes. Others felt that all data should be controlled exclusively by the contractor and used solely for the purpose of portraying the program as a whole.

Finally, overlaying on these issues was the renewed disagreement about how much stress should be put on the consumer information approach. Hutchins was especially interested in whether participating in the project made people more aware of certain types of materials; other people were more interested in learning about how to make the implementation process work (e.g., how the linkers functioned).

The Predicament with OMB

Just when it seemed that some progress was finally being made, another hitch developed. This problem surfaced during the course of a routine "clearance" required of government agencies. The research RFP had directed the contractor to make use of data being collected under a temporary contract with one of the educational laboratories. Proposals were in fact written on the assumption that these data would be available. But the data collection effort encountered a serious setback when, in the fall of 1976, the Office of Management and Budget (OMB), while it was reviewing the data collection instruments, questioned the desirability of such a study. Now the RDU staff found themselves trapped in an unpleasant dispute between OMB and NIE that transcended the RDU program itself.

Two parts of OMB eventually became involved in the review. Some members of the "forms clearance" section expressed concern that the RDU evaluation overlapped a study on change agents that was just being published by the Rand Corporation. The Institute's defense was that by giving schools technical assistance, RDU was filling an important void in the Rand data, since Rand's study dealt with neither implementation questions nor with large-scale R & D outcomes; only locally originated programs were considered in the Rand study. The OMB "budget office" then entered the dispute. Apparently RDU had slipped by them during the budget process, and now they were trying to rectify the oversight by raising a basic policy issue—namely, whether NIE should be involved in an expensive technical assistance/service delivery program such as RDU, which seemed only remotely connected with the Institute's research mission. OMB is a prestigious and influential agency (see Dershimer, 1976; Hargove, 1979), and it had explicitly objected to the provision in the legislation that had transferred responsibility for dissemination to NIE. Notwithstanding NIE's legal position, and convinced that dissemination belonged to OE, OMB was determined to cut large-scale dissemination activities. It was OMB's position that NIE was intended to be a policy analysis shop whose purpose was to keep the Office of Education on target, and *not* to run operational programs that service schools.

This quandary was never fully cleared up, but it faded away as a result of changes in the research design deliberately calculated to create a low profile for RDU. No further effort was made to revise the OMB instrument submission prepared by the Far West Laboratories on behalf of NIE, and all immediate plans to collect data requiring OMB approval were halted. Case studies and other methodologies that did not fall under federal forms clearance regulations were substituted. The debate over whether the RDU study would duplicate the Rand Study was also put off by changing the label for the research from a "study" to an "evaluation" on the grounds that an action research program as large as RDU deserved to be "evaluated," regardless of whether the study would duplicate others or contribute to general knowledge about program implementation and problem solving. This change of labels did not affect the RFP or Abt Associates' winning proposal, but it did later create confusion among NIE Project monitors and Abt Associates' researchers about the functions and purposes of the research reports.

What is most important to us here is to note the inadvertent but nonetheless critical impact which the politically motivated intervention of this oversight agency (OMB) had on the research design. The intervention was prompted by a dispute with the agency rooted in history, which had little to do with RDU. However, the effect was to tip the balance of intellectual and political forces in favor of one research strategy (case studies) over others. The incident also helps illuminate the ability of an agency to maneuver around political and administrative obstacles when its staff is committed to an objective. Even though the research component was not the highest priority of the staff, they were determined to fulfill their research mandate.

Related Political Issues

In addition to the key actors at NIE and OMB, some other shadowy figures were rumored to be involved on the fringes of the controversy. For example, some persons close to the program suspected that some adversaries of RDU had tried to influence OMB. While these rumors cannot be fully substantiated, they were a part of the social climate prevailing at NIE at the time and deserve mention for that reason.

It is important to understand that in 1975 the Chief State School Officers' Organization was rebelling against the burden of extensive data collection at state and local levels. OMB relied on a committee from the group, the Committee on Evaluation and Information Systems (CEIS), for advice on the forms clearance review process. While the CEIS committee as a whole was laudatory about the evaluation design, there were reports that some of its members became upset when RDU proposals from certain states were turned down; this dissatisfaction about RDU might have prompted some of the questions raised about whether RDU was duplicating existing data. There was also some veiled maneuvering from some directors of a competing program who claimed that the state chiefs were displeased with RDU. In addition, an evaluator of a competing OE program was inadvertently involved when OMB asked her to comment on any overlap between RDU and other programs. Her candid answers were then used by OMB against RDU. The extent of these and other rumors is indicative of the volatile climate that existed at NIE during this time.

Choosing the Research Contractor

The "evaluation" RFP was finally issued in the summer of 1977 in the middle of the OMB crisis. Millsap proceeded to convene a panel to evaluate the proposal. The panel was composed of NIE program directors, representatives from three of the operating RDU projects, and an evaluation coordinator from OE. To help maintain the independence of the research components, and because of Hutchins's informal ties to one of the bidders, Hutchins did not participate in the review, although other RDU staff members did. The question can be asked about why project representatives were included on the panel. The answer appears to be that only the projects were uniquely qualified to: (1) determine if the bidders understood the program; (2) interpret how proposals from different bidders might affect them; and (3) assess whether the proposed research would be useful to them. In addition, NIE hoped to gain the confidence of these project representatives, who would then endorse the study for their colleagues. This was a move that seemed essential to ensure full cooperation. Subsequently, the project directors seldom complained about the burdens of the study and they were confident that the information being collected would be meaningful. RDU staff deny that this close cooperation with the projects ever threatened the integrity of the research findings. However, dangers of subtle bias are inherent in such arrangements. Whether it is called evaluation or research, there will always be questions and viewpoints that may prove uncomfortable to the parties being studied.

Only two proposals were submitted in response to the RFP. A $1.7 million contract was awarded to Abt Associates Inc (AAI). The winning proposal turned out to be more than an evaluation of what was already taking place. Some informants believe that it helped clarify aspects of the program and helped shape the way people thought about it; others doubt this. What is relatively certain is that after making some visits to the project sites, the proposal writers had concluded that some critical aspects of the program were being overlooked in the RFP. It was the Abt Associates' proposal that for the first time stressed the importance of the roles that linkers had been playing in the program. The proposal described the program with greater clarity than had been achieved up to this time.

The research effort was to concentrate on three distinct but related issues (Chabotar et al., 1978):

(1) The school level study was to investigate the processes and the outcomes involved in the use of external resources by schools.

(2) The linking agent study was to examine the use of linking agents in the process of managed change.

(3) The project study was to look at the effectiveness of the different types of networks that were set up and the services that were delivered by each project.

The overall goal of the research component of the program was to examine different approaches to knowledge utilization and problem solving within the common framework of the linkage model, and thereby develop knowledge and information to be used in future school improvement efforts.

However, Hutchins was not fully satisfied with the Abt Associates' proposal. He had anticipated ongoing, interim or "formative" research reports that would provide project directors with a continuous flow of information which they could then use to make mid-course corrections in their projects. Instead, Abt Associates chose to withhold the school-level information until the end of the project.

Effects of the Delay

Did the delay in launching the research make any difference? At the very least it altered the relationship between the program staff and the research contractor. It is probably unreasonable to have expected the research design to be in place before the projects were selected. This was not a "planned variation" experiment, and in any case, few agencies manage to exercise that kind of control. However, as a general question about federal programs, the possibility is worth considering. It would have been possible to select proposals on the basis of their appropriateness for the research design. Without this guide, the projects were selected from a variety of criteria, and they subsequently varied along no known dimension. On the other hand, however, the fact that the projects were already in operation made it possible for the research contractor to produce a design that reflected the program's realities rather than one relying exclusively on visionary plans.

Perhaps as important as the delay itself was the fact that the delay was produced by unresolved controversies and questions that can impact other programs. For example, who should control such research, and whose interests should it serve? Can an action research be simultaneously useful to project directors and to Washington program managers, as well as to the top management of an agency like NIE who must decide between competing programs in this agency? The problem is that when program managers, whether in Washington or in the field, do not control the evaluation, the information is likely to remain inaccessible to the people making program decisions who could readily use it. But if they do control it, the study can become self-serving, or at least risk an apparent conflict of interest that could destroy the credibility of the results.

The methodological issue that surfaced over the efficiency and utility of case studies, as compared to more quantitative data collection procedures, was resolved with a compromise. The Abt Associates' contract included the case studies but much of its resources and effort went into the survey approach. In addition to the technical questions that were involved about how to aggregate data from case studies, there was a pragmatic consideration supporting the compromise—case studies provided the RDU managers with an acceptable way to avoid the OMB instrument clearance procedure. There were also some ideological overtones concerning the relative power and legitimacy of different traditions of research. And, beyond that, there was an intriguing political question that was never fully exposed. Regardless of whether or not it is *technically* possible for a group of idiosyncratic case studies to add up to a program evaluation, the fact remains that case studies can be used to legitimize a program, that is, to give the symbolic appearance that the program is being studied impartially, when in fact the sites control the research. Those who believe that Hutchins was reluctant to expose the new program to an "outcomes" evaluation were hinting at the possibility of a symbolic evaluation (Louis and Corwin, 1982).

SUMMARY

For six months the program incubated as the staff set down on paper the rationale for the program and a tentative outline for its design. Writing the request for proposals (RFP) had proved to be a trying experience. The staff struggled through seemingly endless revisions as they debated how much emphasis to give to the consumer information and technical assistance approaches and whether the primary objective was to promote R & D products or to help schools develop the capacity to solve even those problems for which R & D products were not relevant. These issues were never fully resolved, and consequently some critics sniped at the vagueness of the final RFP. Those whose ideas had prevailed, however, regarded the RFP as little more than a flexible guide.

Some of the political issues that were to plague the program surfaced during the proposal review process when two members of the review panel protested being excluded from the critical decisions. Then, a government hiring freeze left the program shorthanded in Washington. Several of the projects were late in getting started. And, most importantly, the major third-party research component called for in the design was delayed for nearly two years by a combination of circumstances—most notably by (1) internal conflicts among the RDU staff to control the research design and methods and (2) a power play from OMB intended to squelch the entire program. RDU was indeed off to a rough start.

NOTES

1. However, it should be noted that the concept paper was not a blueprint. It was a position paper designed for criticism and revision.

2. Awards were made to four state education agencies, two educational consortia and one professional association.

3. All of the RDU staff, except Hutchins (and Raizen), were civil service employees.

4. The contract was awarded to the Far West Regional Educational Laboratory.

Chapter V

Working with the Projects

The people who ran the local projects were pleased with the way they were monitored from Washington. They reported that the program officers carried out their responsibilities conscientiously and with attention to administrative detail. We turn then to a consideration of how the Washington staff carried out their duties.

PROGRAM MANAGEMENT

For the most part, the operation was centralized in the program director's (PD) office. Hutchins, who was devoting more time to the Consumer Information Program, had turned over the management of the project to an associate. (Hutchins would soon turn his attention to creating still another program.) To reassure project directors who were concerned about the burdens of the external evaluation, the program director wrote in a memo to the projects, "I think you need to know that I have been battling very hard internally to maintain a clean line of authority running from NIE to the projects. I have insisted that communications to you from anyone other than your project monitor be cleared with me first. Memos to you from other persons outside of my staff will bear my initials." Moreover, PD seems to have extended this tight control over the program officers on his staff. They in turn observed the local leadership structure when they contacted people in the projects. In only a few instances were some minor complaints expressed from members of a project about receiving inconsistent advice from the PD's office.

Each program officer was responsible for only two or three contracts. Each also had many other responsibilities in addition to monitoring contracts, but it was still an enviable workload when compared to monitors in other programs; it meant that the projects could be monitored closely. Theoretically, project officers had enough time to become familiar with each project and, even more importantly, they became personally identified with their projects. Consequently they developed a personal interest in helping their projects achieve success. Their interest was so great that they were sometimes accused of not being objective enough about the projects they were monitoring. The monitors tended to play down their contract management responsibilities, and sought instead to establish *collegial* relations with the projects. They strived to be facilitative rather than directive. They did not provide much direct technical assistance, but several project officers thought that NIE had been very supportive and flexible toward requests for changes in the budget, procedures, allocation, and so on. When some project directors had difficulty locating some items listed in the NIE R & D catalog, the project officers scouted around for them. They secured waivers for some NIE regulations which seemed unnecessarily burdensome to the projects. They honored linkers with site visits, promoted training sessions, and organized conferences for linkers and resource persons. They also devised a simplified, unburdensome progress reporting form, provided opportunities for program directors and linkers to visit one another's projects, and provided ways for them to share materials. The PD kept projects informed of developments at NIE with a monthly memorandum. But what the project directors seemed to find most useful were the quarterly meetings held for all project directors. These meetings provided a way for the projects to stay in touch with each other and with their project officers. The NIE staff conscientiously solicited ideas for meetings from the projects and maintained flexible agendas. Despite these efforts to remain responsive to the interests of the projects, however, some project directors perceived that NIE insisted on controlling the meeting agendas.

Program Officer Roles

Any program officer must assume several types of responsibilities for the projects that are being monitored. Chapter IX will deal more fully with the three types of roles that program officers typically carry out (Corwin, 1982): the contract management role, the advisory role, and the technical assistance role. It will be helpful to see how each of these responsibilities was carried out by the program officers who were responsible for managing RDU.

The Advisory Role. When acting as an advisor, the program officer, in an effort to help members of a project interpret policy, criticizes their procedures, and recommends ways they can improve their performance. To act in an advisory capacity, a program officer must first develop a collegial, facilitative relationship with someone in a project. Thinking of his relationship with a project as a collaborative effort, for example, one program officer operated on the assumption that he could learn from the project staff. He participated in two training projects with local linking agents, as though he were a linker, and he was proud of the fact they treated him as a colleague rather than as a superior who was "snooping around."

An advisory relationship in RDU sometimes developed when project directors asked for permission to change their plans, which usually required shifting line items of a budget. These requests were seldom denied. The program officer would discuss their plans with them and advise them about what they needed to do to get their proposals processed. If there was a question about the feasibility of a request, the monitor would look for a loophole in the contract or find some other way to meet the request.

Advisory relationships more typically arose spontaneously in informal ways. For example, in one instance a program officer attended a training session. When he was later talking with the project director about what had transpired, they jointly agreed in the course of their conversation that the same training contractor should not be used again, and that the curriculum procedures should be changed in a certain way for the next session. In another case, a program officer was part of an audience at which a project director spoke. When the program officer sensed that this speech was not going over very well, he tried to act as a facilitator by raising questions. In addition, program officers routinely read drafts of reports and raised questions or suggested ways to rewrite passages in order to clarify them or to achieve more balanced treatment.

Technical Assistance. In order to provide effective technical assistance, program officers must be more than colleagues. They must act essentially like employees or consultants and assume the role of specialized experts who are responsible for carrying out certain details of a project. Technical assistance can assume one of two forms: (1) implementing project activities in substantive areas, such as working out an evaluation design, identifying the resource pool, planning training programs, setting up a management system and the like; and (2) acting as advocates on behalf of the project, such as buffering a project from federal regulations by "cutting red tape," or acting as an advocate for a project when it is attacked by an adversary.

In RDU, program officers did not provide much technical assistance of the first type in substantive areas of the project. Most of them were transferred from OE and had backgrounds in diverse areas. They did not have the kind of experience and training that would have prepared them to confidently offer technical assistance with the dissemination problems that were encountered by the knowledgeable directors of these seven projects. However, the program officers did provide the second type of technical assistance in administrative matters, by acting as advocates on behalf of the projects when conflicts arose with the contracts office.

In government agencies, authority for legal and financial matters is lodged in a unit that functions independently from the operating programs. The relationship between this "contracts office" and the RDU staff became tense soon after the program was initiated. As the Institute's liaison with the projects, the program officers were on the organizational boundaries; they were caught in the middle between the NIE policies and the pressures coming from the projects. They had become sensitized to the needs of the projects and to the constraints under which they were operating.

There is nothing surprising in the fact that the relationship between the RDU program staff and the contracts office grew bitter. There are some generic reasons for such tensions. Contracts offices are insulated from people in the field and they are concerned with formal audits that carry legal sanctions. They use government-wide procedures and schedules which are typically, and often arrogantly, indifferent to the needs of individual contractors. "Federal time" is organized around fiscal year schedules which can conflict with the academic school year calendars that bind projects. School districts usually plan a year in advance and hire ahead of time, but contracts officers are under no obligation to defer to these constraints.

However, according to some informants, the actions of the RDU staff aggravated these generic tensions. As one person recalls, RDU insisted upon some unusual changes and concessions. Even before the RFP was written there had been altercations with the contracts office. The program staff wanted RDU to be approved as a contract, not as a grant. The contracts office maintained that the program did not qualify as a contract, since (according to an informant) this instrument is reserved for those cases where an agency purchases a product or service, and RDU did not constitute a request for a service to the Institute. In addition, the RFP was not specific enough about what products were being "purchased." However, the program staff were determined to force through the RFP as a contract because it could take over a year to obtain approval for a grant. The RDU staff won the skirmish, but the relationship was off to a bad start.

Contracts officers next objected to the fact that the program staff had not provided adequate budgetary detail about how much money would be required for travel. The RDU staff maintained that it was not possible to provide this kind of detail before each project had identified its local sites. They then went to the contracts office for a clearance that would honor some precontract expenditures that had been incurred by some of the projects. After that, during the first year of the program, the program staff negotiated with the projects to take more responsibility for the locally developed case studies than they had originally contracted for. This required changes in the budgets and scope of work. And then, during the third year, it was learned that all of the projects had underspent their budgets and wanted "no cost" extensions. To a contract officer all of these changes might have been a nuisance. The project officers saw it differently. They complained that even when they had gone to the contracts office ten months in advance of the contract deadline with a request for an extension, the contracts office took no action until the deadline neared, which put the project officers in a state of panic about whether to hire, fire, or lay off staff as the impending deadline approached.

These problems were compounded by the fact that five different contract officers worked with this program at various times during its short history. Complications developed from conflicting advice received from different contract officers. The head of the contracts office overruled some of his subordinates, and it is possible that the contract officers were not always able to visualize precisely what they had agreed upon until they encountered a specific instance of it. In addition, perhaps project officers were stepping on contract officers' toes when they made pointed suggestions to program directors about which budget items to add or cut. And all of these instances were magnified and exacerbated by occasional emotional outbursts that occurred between particular project officers and contract officers.

Since the contracts people bore the brunt of all of the extensions, amendments, and additions, they understandably did not look upon this program with special favor. But it is not clear how all of the hostility might have affected the program. It is true that the friction created some delays and added to the consternation of the project directors as they stood on the brink of bankruptcy while these struggles were going on in Washington. And all of this confusion and indecisiveness took time and energy; some project directors estimated that it took one to two months of their time to justify one request for a six-month extension. Nevertheless, the NIE staff became closer to people in the projects precisely because of their mutual difficulties with the contracts office.

The Contract Management Role. Whether they liked it or not, however, there were occasions when project officers found themselves acting as monitors while exercising their contractual authority over projects. Because the contract management role includes responsibilities for monitoring and enforcing contractual requirements, it often requires project officers to assume a directive relationship with the projects as well.

For the most part, these instances were confined to issuing routine reminders, as on the many occasions when monthly reports were late. But there were some more serious instances. In one case, it was learned that the key members of one project had all retired from their parent organization. Without success, NIE attempted to get more active personnel assigned who might carry on the project after funding was terminated. In another instance, the monitor was concerned because linkers in a project were being spread over too many sites and devoting too little time to their project responsibilities. This situation was eventually corrected.

And one time a project officer investigated a complaint that a project was not tailoring the information it was disseminating to the needs of individual schools. After discussing it with the project director, a solution was reached.

One notable case of intervention occurred when a project officer persuaded officials in a state education agency to correct some problems with a project's leadership by reorganizing the leadership structure and management procedures. The project had gotten far behind schedule, due in part to the fact that the state was slow to authorize the project to spend federal money. Concerned about the delinquent monthly reports and a negative evaluation from a team of consultants, the Institute nearly terminated the project. It was then salvaged by the Institute, however, when the state agreed to reorganize the management team by creating a new position.

The Project Officer Roles in Balance

Each of the three project officer roles entails some problems. The contract management relationship can be particularly uncomfortable since it requires that a project officer assume a supervisory position for extended periods of time over colleagues who possess comparable training and backgrounds. Moreover, while project officers can sometimes use a diffuse "moral authority," they have little direct leverage over a project that has been funded. They can threaten to terminate it, or hold up money until compliance has been achieved, or reward good performance with still more funds. The first two options can only hurt an agency, as they announce failure, create more work, reduce the scope of the agency's program and budget, and create political enemies in the field. The third option is even more confining because it commits the agency to spend more money on old programs at the expense of starting new initiatives.

The advisory and technical assistance roles can be compromising. When providing assistance, the project officer tends to ally himself with the project and consequently becomes identified with it. If the advice she or he gives is used, there is a risk that the program officer will be predisposed to see only the favorable results. The consequent conflict of loyalty can be detrimental when the same person has responsibility for evaluating the very components that she or he helped to design. Furthermore, it is often difficult to draw the line between giving "assistance," trying to control the project, and being co-opted by the project. It is sometimes difficult to tell whether a person is forcing himself on a project, or whether a project is attempting to appease and assimilate the person in order to gain influence in the agency.

SOME UNINTENDED EFFECTS OF MANAGEMENT DECISIONS

During the process of managing the projects, some actions were innocently taken by managers at each level of NIE that had unintended effects on RDU. Three examples will be cited here: a decision at the program level, a decision at the division level of NIE, and a decision by NIE management.

The Site Visit Snafu

There is one point at which the contract management responsibility proved to be particularly irritating for several of the projects. The RDU director organized a series of site visits by a consultant team that made some negative comments about some of the projects in their report. The stated purpose of these visits was to:

- assess how closely the R & D Utilization program management was sticking to the "battle plan" set for the RDU;
- assess the extent to which educational change was being effectively supported by the strategies employed by the projects;
- make recommendations for short-term improvements in project operations, data gathering and NIE project management; and
- make recommendations to help shape the RDU program after December of 1978.

The project directors interpreted this to mean that the major purpose of the site visits was to monitor the progress of the overall *program* and provide evidence to support the third year of funding; they believed that the major purpose was *not* to evaluate the merits of particular projects. This latter possibility hardly seemed feasible on the basis of a short two- or three-day visit by a group of outsiders who had little previous experience with the program. Some of the consultants made some negative statements about project operations which reached the project directors. Some project directors became alarmed, and relationships with NIE were strained for a while.

Engendering Competition Among the Projects

The evaluation by the consultant team merely accentuated the growing competition among the projects. At one point NIE began to plan for a possible fourth or fifth year, and the budget being considered made it clear there was no prospect that enough money would be available to extend all seven projects. This information made projects defensive. As one project director said: "Because of the limited resources at NIE, we play it close to our chest.... The uncertainty at NIE tends to play us off one-on-one, rather than working as a group." Perhaps all directors did not feel as strongly, but there is reason to believe that the project directors treated each other with gentle ambivalence. While they all faced similar problems and could benefit from an exchange of information, it is difficult to see how the existing competition would have given them much incentive to communicate openly about certain topics.

Fall-out from the NIE Reorganization

The numerous reorganizations at NIE must also be mentioned here. Some members of the projects complained that the inordinate amount of time that the NIE staff had to spend at meetings and in writing internal reports made them less accessible to the projects and less able to respond quickly to reports and requests from the field. At one point, the PD despairingly wrote to the project directors: "I appreciate the fact that several of you have called to inquire whether we are still in business. The reorganization, as it affects us, has been very slow in unfolding, and there have been several unanswered questions." That was a masterful understatement.

Perhaps even more important than their inaccessibility was the toll these re-organizations took on staff morale, time, energy, and enthusiasm. With the Institute in flux, there were numerous reassignments of monitors. One project was assigned three program officers and four contract officers during a three-year period. Even with a relatively light case load during this period, it seems unlikely that the prospect of being reassigned would have provided much incentive to a project officer to become deeply involved in any particular project.

SUMMARY

Generally speaking, the program ran smoothly. The program officers developed a personal interest in helping their projects. They played down their contract management responsibilities, seeking instead to establish collegial relationships with the projects. They tried to be facilitative rather than directive. They did intervene in a few instances, but typically they confined themselves to an advisory role. The technical assistance they provided was largely in the form of buffering the projects from the sometimes demanding technical requirements of the NIE contract office. As a result of this active intervention, several incidents occurred that stirred up bitter strains between the RDU program managers and the contracts office.

Despite their zealous efforts on behalf of the projects, the program managers made some minor mistakes. Some project directors were temporarily upset because of a misunderstanding over the purpose of a site visit, and some individuals associated with the projects felt that NIE had inadvertly put the projects in competition with one another for limited resources. But most of the management problems were no one's fault. They grew out of the demands that the NIE reorganizations had made on the time, energy and morale of the managers and the numerous reassignments of monitors.

Chapter VI

Accommodation

Early in this chapter four ways in which program designs can become accommodated to the realities under which programs operate are identified. The remainder of the chapter is devoted to descriptions of discrete events that occurred in the course of RDU that serve to illustrate each type of accommodation.

It is commonly recognized that programs are seldom implemented precisely as planned (Bardach, 1977; Pressman and Wildavsky, 1973; Bailey and Moser, 1968; Jones and Thomas, 1977; Lazin, 1973; Murphy, 1971; Smith, 1973). The process of reconciling intention with reality has been variously termed "successive approximation," "progressive specification" (Eveland, Rogers, and Klepper, 1977), and "mutual adaptation" (Berman and McLaughlin, 1977). "Mutual adaptation," in particular, has received much attention. This term refers to the process through which users make goals and methods concrete as they acquire the skills appropriate to the innovation (McLaughlin, 1976:168). In McLaughlin's (1976:169) language, "It involves modification of both project design and changes in the local institutional setting and personnel during the course of implementation." The key is that although the program design is modified to meet special conditions, the program continues to resemble the basic plan. The fact that the key ideas continue to guide actions suggests that this concept is still closely allied with rational models of planning and policy analysis that are premised on the notion that the core concepts are understood and measurable. But, as Williams (1976:275) notes, "What we are finding over and over again is that program objectives are often so illusive as to be difficult to determine at all, much less define rigorously. Moreover, as we

71

move from broad objectives that are subject to many interpretations to rigorous ones that are not, the likelihood of disagreement
rapidly increases."

Since it can be difficult to adapt detailed program designs to a
variety of conditions, some program designers shun the single
"best" approach (with its detailed plan and instruction) they pre-
fer broad, flexible guidelines which can be worked out amid the
forces of the marketplace, that is, competition, self-interest, incentives, etc., (Williams, 1976). Such designs are deliberately left
vague and responsibility for specification is delegated to lower
levels of the federal system.

The fact that such a variety of terms and distinctions has been
proposed suggests that the accommodation between plan and
practice occurs in different ways, and that it might be fruitful to
explore a typology of accommodations. At one extreme, some
writers appear to operate on the assumption that (1) there is a
coherent plan which (2) is being *deliberately* modified (3) during the
course of *implementation*. However, the opposite conditions prevailed in the RDU program—namely, alternative approaches included in the design produced *tensions* that were *inadvertently* reconciled during the course of the program. The *design* was the
source of the subtle modifications evident during implementation.

It seems possible to distinguish at least four types of accommodation. The following typology rests upon two considerations:
(1) the degree to which modifications are deliberately calculated

Figure VI.1   Types of Accomodation between Design and
                Implementation

TYPE OF DECISION		
STIMULUS	Planned: Mutual Adaptation	Inadvertent: Slippage
Obstacles in Field	Progressive Specification	Reconciliation
Design Ambiguities	Successive Approximation	Mutation

(as compared to occurring inadvertently) and (2) the extent to which they are necessary because of obstacles encountered during the course of operating a project (as opposed to actions required because of inconsistencies and ambiguities in the original design). (See Figure VI.1) These dichotomies are obviously oversimplifications, since the categories shade off into one another. Nevertheless, they can help to illuminate some real differences in the accommodation process.

MUTUAL ADAPTATION AS ADJUSTMENT AND REVISION

The term mutual adaptation is used here in a very specific way that refers to deliberate efforts *calculated to adjust a design* to specific situations. It can occur either through:

1. "Progressive specification," involving *adjustments* through which the original design concepts are elaborated or fleshed out in greater detail during implementation, or;
2. "Successive approximations," through which the design itself undergoes step-by-step *revisions* as the program is tested.

Eveland, Rogers, and Klepper (1977) view innovation as a process of gradual specification of operational details—that is, a movement from a general idea to specific forms of behavior. They apply the same term, specification, to both alterations in the way the innovation is applied and to successive approximations or revisions in the innovation itself. However, I have used different terms to distinguish between accommodations in usage and in design.

Progressive Specification

Both specifications and approximations are calculated, but in specification the design continues to guide action, while successive approximation is calculated to correct design flaws.[1] The need for specification has been anticipated in the design in recognition of the fact that variable and changing *circumstances* will be encountered at different locations. In other words, a basically adequate design is adjusted to fit a variety of specific circumstances.

Successive Approximation

But successive approximation requires revisions because of "errors" made when designing the program and, in particular, because a project does not have the *capacity*—that is, staff capabilities or resources—to meet the requirements of the design.

SLIPPAGE AS RECONCILIATION AND MUTATION

The term slippage is used here in reference to the inadvertent transformations that creep into a design over the course of a program. These modifications accumulate from the unintended actions and decisions of a wide range of people as plans and policies filter through levels of government and organizations. Slippage can occur in two ways: (1) "reconciliation" resulting from *resistance* to features of the design by the people involved in implementing it; and (2) "mutation" due to *reinterpretation* of design concepts. Both transformations are *evolutionary outcomes:* existing options are selected, rejected, or merged as advocates for different alternatives struggle to protect their philosophies and interests.

Reconciliation

Reconciliation is a product of resistance, and resistance, in turn, implies conflict among groups that support different options. Reconciliation can produce different types of results: the survival of one option over others, a realignment of priorities, and/or a compromise among several options. The options can be proposed in the design itself, or they can be opposed to it. In the first instance, opposition is exemplified by a group of teachers who refuse to comply with some provision of a program. In this case the source of the obstacles is found in the situation in which the design is being implemented. In the second instance, inconsistencies or competing options are incorporated into the design itself, and the source of conflict is, in fact, the design (in conjunction with the situation).

Mutation

Mutation refers to new design concepts that emerge from novel interpretations of prevailing practice or from a creative synthesis of previously sovereign options. Mutations are products of new perspectives and visions as well as cross-fertilization of approaches. The potential for mutant forms to develop is always present in a program design because of the necessarily abstract language in which designs are expressed. Even well-defined concepts can sometimes be interpreted in different ways, and often they are not even expressed in operational terms. However, while the design is thus a source of mutations, they are not predictable from the design. And while they include elements of existing approaches, they are hybrid syntheses that consist of existing options.

CAVEATS

In short, accommodation takes several different forms. It is sometimes deliberately calculated, but it often seems to creep in inadvertently and virtually unnoticed. Unplanned accommodations are not necessarily detrimental, and indeed they can result in more effective programs; designs are sometimes purposely left vague with this assumption in mind. The primary obstacles to a program can sometimes be found within the situations where the plan is being tested; in these cases successful implementation hinges on correcting the situational factors. The obstacles are often inherent within the design itself, however, because the design is (1) so ambitious that major revisions eventually must be made, (2) so contradictory that priorities must eventually be reconciled, or (3) so vague that alternative interpretations are permissible.

I caution again that these differences are matters of degree. The forms of accommodation identified can operate simultaneously, or at different times within the same set of events. In practice it is often difficult to isolate calculated negotiations from unintended consequences. Similarly, it is not always easy to distinguish between tinkering with a basically adequate design, in order to fine tune it for a given situation, and making wholesale revisions, because the people involved do not have the necessary skills and resources. Nevertheless, these distinctions point to some important differences. Some changes are made routinely as a standard installation procedure. Others reflect inherent deficiencies in the design itself. Designs sometimes contain contradictions and ambiguities that are in turn responsible for changes made during the program. I will therefore try to be cautious in my use of this simple typology, but I will use it as an organizing framework for the following discussion in which I will attempt to illustrate how each type of accommodation occurred in particular aspects of the RDU program.

PROJECT MONITORING AS A SPECIFICATION PROCESS

The instances of adjustment through specification that were most obvious in RDU were typically confined to contract renegotiations while the program was in operation. For example, at some sites classroom teachers eventually became frustrated with the staged "decision-making model" that prescribed a sequence of activities that teachers were supposed to go through before deciding to adopt a particular curriculum or practice. On paper it had seemed to be a reasonable model, but the NIE project officers, as well as some of the people within the projects, concluded that the diagnostic phase was taking too long, and as a result NIE agreed to establish a one-year limit on needs assessments.

In some cases, the decision model was adjusted in recognition of the interplay that was occuring between the available products and the way teachers were defining their problems. The projects had been instructed by NIE not to inform teachers about the available products until they had first defined their problems. Decisions were to be made in a logical sequence, which meant that teachers needed to clearly understand their problems before they began to consider available products. But this linear model proved to be too restrictive and difficult to enforce. For these reasons, teachers were sometimes allowed to identify problems in terms of the products they already knew were available (i.e., "our problem is that we do not have [a particular] math program").

After the program began, NIE renegotiated a "case study" activity that was required of all projects. The new scope of work extended the effort required for this activity, and therefore projects were permitted to request additional resources. In still other instances, as their ideas about the project evolved, project directors asked to reopen their contracts so they could modify the "deliverables" they had originally agreed to provide NIE. For example, they asked NIE to consider special reports their staffs had written for other purposes as part of their final contract obligations. They also obtained funds to help them undertake management responsibilities that were called for in the contract but that they subsequently found they could not provide without assistance.

Not all of these examples are pure instances of specification as I have defined it. One could take the position that they are instances of successive approximation, in that NIE had overestimated the capacity of some projects to meet certain provisions of the design. But in the final analysis the changes were matters of detail and compatible with the original design.

DEVELOPING THE KNOWLEDGE BASE AS AN INSTANCE OF SUCCESSIVE APPROXIMATION

During the course of writing the RFP, a major controversy had divided the NIE staff as they considered how to identify the "eligible pool of R & D products." It was proving difficult to identify R & D products worthy of publicizing. The staff could agree on neither how the product pool should be identified, nor on who should be responsible for identifying it. And yet the entire justification for the program was premised on the existence of quality R & D products that would be of use to schools. The capacity of both the R & D system and the NIE staff to identify these products had been grossly overestimated.

Identifying the Product Pool

Part of the original rationale for RDU was that NIE had products worth promoting. The RFP leaves little doubt that the NIE-sponsored products were to be given serious consideration. After noting that NIE did not intend to advocate any specific product, the RFP goes on to direct proposers to include among the alternatives they would consider for their product pools all relevant products and practices "produced under NIE sponsorship."[2] Proposers were advised to send for the list of NIE products immediately, and if it were not already clear enough, the RFP goes on to state that

> contractors must obtain, analyze, review and report on products and other program materials produced by NIE in the problem area—proposers should identify which of the NIE products are to be reviewed once the project begins, or provide a plan for selecting and reviewing NIE products together with outcomes from other sources.

In spite of this directive, from the beginning some staff members had expressed serious reservations about the ability of NIE-sponsored products to meet the needs of local practitioners. By the time the proposals were submitted, the dissemination staff had entirely backed away from this strong desire for NIE-sponsored products, largely because of comments from practitioners and consultants who had reacted to the concept paper. Pushing for NIE products had perhaps been a management concern at an earlier stage; indeed, it is possible that the stress on NIE products helped get the RDU RFP through the government hierarchy. The program staff, however, was not inclined to hold their colleagues in the field to such an obvious promotion of their own products.

One might consider this shift a simple instance of reinterpretation of priorities that occurs as policy filters through the hierarchy (i.e., "slippage") if it were not for another consideration. The fact is that the NIE knowledge base was not in good shape. While a "catalogue" was available that described the products sponsored by NIE, the ambitious plan to publish "consumer information packages," which would synthesize information on different types of R & D products and would be written in a popular style for lay persons, had bogged down. The original thought was that RDU could become the conduit for delivering this information, and, in fact, the concept paper had promised that a common pool of products available for all projects would be compiled by NIE. But the Consumer Information Synthesis Project was never completed, in large part because NIE did not have the resources or access to the capabilities needed to organize a centralized knowledge pool. NIE's capacity had been over-estimated, and consequently the delivery technology (RDU) was in place before the substance (the products) was.

The Quality Control Issue

By the time the RFP was written there was no recourse except to shift responsibility for the product pool to each of the seven projects. There would not be one but seven different, partially over-lapping data bases assembled from different criteria. But this left unresolved two questions: Should the Institute establish quality control *guidelines* that projects would be required to follow when making their selections of eligible products? Or, should projects be given the discretion to establish their own criteria for their own product pools? The ensuing debate opened a host of questions about what constitutes an "R & D product," and more fundamentally, what constitutes a *good* one.

A controversy surfaced over whether NIE should take steps to assure that the products being considered had been tested and screened. The pertinence of this suggestion was underscored by the fact that an active panel of experts from OE and NIE had recently passed judgment on the quality of numerous R & D products in education. Hutchins was a member of this joint review panel.

But the OE-NIE joint product pool was never seriously considered. It seemed to Raizen, Hutchins, and others to be too narrow. For one thing, it included only federally funded R & D, and Hutchins had come from a laboratory with a support base and interests that were broader than federally funded research. It also seemed to him presumptuous for a federal agency to prohibit state and local education agencies from using products that other practitioners had found useful just because "experts" had not "validated" them.[3]

The NIE catalogue had included products which the federal monitors considered to be only "defensible," and many of them were not officially "validated." Both Hutchins and Raizen had taken a firm stand that RDU would differ from NDN on this point; whereas NDN used only products validated by the Joint Dissemination Review Panel, RDU had a broader conception of what could be disseminated.[4]

Each project was assigned responsibility for developing, and then monitoring, the specific criteria it would use to select its product pool. Each project was also to establish its own procedures for assuring that the quality control issue would be addressed. A project's only responsibility to NIE was to describe the products, the criteria, and the quality control procedures used. There was no provision for NIE to formally review, and certainly none to evaluate, these criteria and procedures as part of its monitoring responsibility. Furthermore, no provision was made at either the program or project level for monitoring the fate of the products that were adopted.

Rethinking the Meaning of R & D

In a dispute that was to have great import, the quality control issue resurfaced after the projects were underway. The irritating question that kept popping up was whether the R & D products included in the pool should have been developed through systematic "research." Might they, for example, include "promising practices" endorsed only by testimonials from some practitioners? This issue was raised by a formidable professional association that wanted to circulate some teacher training materials that had been neither developed nor evaluated by research procedures. Learning that only a dozen or so of the available training materials this project proposed to use had any connection with research, NIE decided to permit the use of untested materials. According to informants, this was all that was available; the very fact that this material was being used by teachers was sufficient validation of its utility. And besides, the project had already been funded.

In sum, the program was conceived on the premise that there was a pool of high quality products developed through research and about which practitioners were not well informed. The concept paper proposed that NIE would identify them, but when it came to locating these products, it was necessary to defer to the practitioners. Despite the rationale that had originally justified the program, NIE was never able to clearly identify the knowledge base that some of its staff were so convinced existed. Then the Institute decided to skirt the issue by delegating the decisions to the projects. If the illusive pool of products did exist, it was not readily apparent, and in any case, it had not been packaged in time for such an ambitious dissemination effort.

There is no reason to assume that this redirection was in any way "worse" than what might have occurred if the program had been implemented faithfully according to Hutchins's first tentative ideas. Certainly, it is doubtful whether anyone associated with the RDU program would regard any of these shifts as serious violations of the original vision. The point is that what eventually developed was markedly different in certain respects from what Hutchins had first contemplated when he joined the Institute and circulated the concept paper. The program was taking form one step at a time. The course that developed grew out of successive approximations that were calculated to test and modify some preliminary notions. In trying to reconcile the realities, the designers traded off some desired benefits for some more realizable ones.

Because of the program, practitioners were now sharing information which exposed them more directly to whatever relevant practices were available, and perhaps, with group decision-making processes, they were making better judgments as well. But there was a price: a set of overlapping pools of products that were only loosely validated in different ways. This does not add up to impressive evidence in support of the original argument that a pool of good R & D products was going to waste. What the scenario does suggest is that the capacity of the knowledge base and the capabilities of NIE and the projects were grossly overestimated. Much of the subsequent history of the program can be understood as successive efforts to compensate for these original miscalculations.

RECONCILING ACTION RESEARCH

As the idea for RDU first took shape in Hutchins's mind, he seemed to be thinking of a model consumer information program complete with a technical assistance component. This would provide a real service to the projects and to participating school sites during its brief existence, and this would leave a residue of useful experience for others to follow. The program would be a demonstration of how to deliver a service to schools and of how to link the schools more effectively with the products and the people associated with educational R & D. In addition, of course, such a program could certainly provide rich opportunities to learn more about designing and delivering a consumer-information program. In any case, Hutchins quickly realized that a research component would be *necessary*.

At this time Congress was still prodding NIE to distinguish itself from the Office of Education, which had traditionally housed the service delivery programs for education. And Congress had made it clear that NIE was not the place for operating programs. (ERIC was an exception, but Hutchins had not been able to make successful connections with that program.) Research would be necessary to put the program in line with the Institute's mission. However, research was never the driving force behind RDU.

Action Research

The rationale was to create a new approach for the purpose of learning about it, with the hope that the findings would eventually be used in other long-term service delivery programs. This kind of research is called "action research." Action research can be placed on a continuum between natural variation at one extreme and planned variation at the other. In the natural variation model, the investigator studies what already exists in its natural state. In the planned variation model, the investigator creates cases that reflect systematic differences in a particular characteristic or treatment. Action research is a combination of the two. The investigator attempts to influence a natural setting enough to produce some variation; typically, however, there are far more known and unknown variables (most of which cannot be controlled) than in a planned field experiment. Action research has the added advantage of providing a direct and immediate service to practitioners in exchange for their cooperation during the research.

For the Institute, action research provided a welcome approach through which service could be delivered within the framework of research. It offered the hope of eliciting immediate cooperation and support from professionals in the field in a way that long-range research seldom achieves. But there are also enormous hidden costs in this kind of research. For one thing, action research is a mixture of two sovereign strategies—a practice-driven program and a research-driven program—which do not blend well. It is difficult to maintain an equilibrium between service and research because each has different requirements and the two types of activities therefore compete for resources. For example, a research-driven program would seem to require a staff with research experience, a focus on issues which are generalizable, a commitment of staff time to participate in the research, and a program that is sufficiently stable to permit implementation of the research plan. In contrast, a service-driven program requires a staff with backgrounds as practitioners or consultants and a problem-solving focus, and tentative findings are used immediately to make continued readjustments in the program design and procedures. (See Weiss and Rein, 1970). The fact that RDU was sold to practitioners on the basis of the services that would be delivered placed the research in a marginal and vulnerable position with respect to securing the time and effort of practitioners. Even at NIE, where the staff was undoubtedly clear about the priority of RDU's research mission, the critical third-party research component was delayed for almost two years. Although some data were being collected by the projects, research was not a major focus.

As action research, RDU also got caught within the contradictions of its own claims. Judged as research, it could be criticized for not being as demanding as planned variation (an approach that the associate director for Dissemination was convinced was impossible). Judged as a constituency building exercise, the program probably did not provide much payoff for the Institute. It was a centralized intervention that was designed and operated for the express purpose of serving the Institute's needs, and it involved only seven projects. By comparison, for example, the State Capacity Building Program eventually provided less restrictive grants to forty-three state education agencies, which could use the money with more discretion since they were not part of a coherent plan administered from Washington.

The dual objectives also left action research vulnerable to the vicissitudes of managerial turnover. When RDU was initiated, the leaders then in the "front office" at NIE thought that action research was a splendid idea. But managers came and went, and priorities changed. The director who was in office when RDU wound down favored planned variation, and the rather meager political benefits that it seemed to him could accrue from RDU were hardly sufficient to justify its loose design.

Organizing for Action Research

These problems might have been minimized through a different management system (Williams and Evans, 1969). Research and service both seem to require independent structural support which simply was not provided by NIE at the time that RDU took form. The program managers controlled both facets of the program, and in the process of mobilizing and operating the delivery service component they were repeatedly tempted to compromise the research. Some of the staff were never clear about whether Hutchins thought of the program as a research project established to *test* research hypotheses, or as a *demonstration* project that would illustrate the validity of the assumptions on which the program had been designed. The program director and project officers who were responsible for RDU did not have research backgrounds. One must ask then, what are the guarantees that a project director who possesses the kind of missionary zeal required to fight for a new service delivery program, will be equally dedicated to the protection of long-range knowledge production goals?

The persons who perhaps placed highest priority on the research component—the evaluation coordinator, the associate director, and the evaluation contractor—were isolated from the program operations. One can assume that this structural isolation helped protect the integrity of the research, although it is equally possible that as a result of its marginal status, the research was allowed to languish for two years.

Beyond the loose integration between the research and service components within the RDU program, there had been and continues to be, a larger schism between dissemination and the research programs at NIE. The marginal status of dissemination has isolated it from the core activities of the Institute with the consequence that the dissemination staff has had little access to the research skills available throughout the Institute.

NIE has since created an independent evaluation unit within the dissemination program which is on a level comparable to the programs it is responsible for evaluating.[5] This new structure may help to support the research activities, but it still does not reconcile the impossible demands placed upon program managers and project directors who must act simultaneously as missionaries and political negotiators with equal dedication to the missions of service and research. The inherent structural problems generated by action research, it seems, can be reconciled only through the day-to-day decisions that arise in the course of operating such programs.

However, this is not meant to imply that the research component must always come out second best. The outcome depends on a confluence of factors, many of which were operating in RDU. Remember that RDU was originally conceived as a means of building a constituency for NIE. The individuals who were most instrumental in designing and managing the operation were committed to the importance of providing service to practitioners. The persons who placed highest priority on the research component had only marginal authority over policy decisions and were structurally isolated from the program's leadership. Moreover, program managers must consider the adverse effects of publicity about negative findings, and they are often in a position to exercise subtle control—by selecting trustworthy evaluation contractors, by delaying research schedules until the findings can no longer impact funding decisions, by focusing the research on individual cases rather than evaluating the overall program, by insisting that the study should be useful to practitioners rather than to policy makers who fund the program, and so forth. These conditions are not necessarily inherent to action research, but they do often seem to prevail in action research programs.

RECONCILING PRODUCT ADOPTION WITH ORGANIZATION DEVELOPMENT

In a bold effort to include the strengths of different approaches within the RDU design, the designers opted for multiple objectives and mixed strategies. However, the delicate task of meshing approaches based on divergent philosophies remained to be worked out during the course of the program. From the beginning, there was a conflict within NIE, and in Hutchins's own mind, between the priorities of a "top-down" consumer information approach (CI), which focuses on products, and a "bottom-up" organization development (OD) approach, which trains practitioners to use group decision-making methods that will enable them to solve their own problems.[6] The question was, should the success of a project be measured by the number of products adopted, or by how carefully decisions had been made? The RFP had acknowledged that the solutions to many problems do not depend upon adopting R & D products. Some of Hutchins's staff and his own consultants as well as his severest critics in the Institute maintained that a central objective of the program was to "improve the capacity of schools to make decisions," even if that goal might divert attention from products. The implication of this view was that groups of teachers should be encouraged to sit down at regular intervals and talk about their problems and to consider possible solutions, including, but certainly not limited to, available R & D products.

Actually, either approach might be justified depending upon how one reads the RFP. The problem was how to effectively mix the strategies in practice. It was a question of priorities, and given a fixed number of resources, in the minds of many it came down to a conflict between a "product orientation" and a "client orientation."

A Shift in Priorities

While Hutchins subscribed to the OD approach as a means of assisting schools with adopting R & D products, he never intended to concentrate primarily on interpersonal relationships as the way to solve all sorts of problems. He held a less global view of the problem-solving process, one that relied heavily on informing potential users in clear language about the nature and advantages of various materials and products that were available. The RFP clearly reflected this position when it called for proposers to provide services to schools that would help them "to implement and use existing research and development (R & D) outcomes." Contractors were sought who could increase educators' knowledge of the existence, nature, and utility of research and development outcomes and who could help schools implement R & D outcomes as the means of solving the schools' problems.

However, as a committee product, and after thirty revisions, the RFP had become permeated with organization development terminology. Indeed, OD could now be interpreted as a major objective of the program, although it was still not on a par with product adoption. The first sentence of the RFP reads, "The National Institute of Education (NIE) has a requirement to solve educational problems in the schools." The idea continues on the second page:

> each project must go beyond the dissemination of information about R & D outcomes and provide necessary support to adoption and adaptation activities. Local needs must dominate the decision process, however, and the application of R & D outcomes should occur when they are clearly the best available solution to the problem addressed.

Group problem solving was mentioned in the RFP as the initial step in a four-stage adoption process; the other stages mentioned were: the identification of an R & D knowledge base; the selection of an R & D outcome at local sites, and the installation of R & D outcomes.

The RFP acknowledged that "a legitimate project outcome could be the conclusion that... there is no R & D outcome that represents an acceptable solution." But this does not appear as a major theme. Hutchins never advocated that the program should be judged on the basis of the number of products adopted, but there was a definite expectation that the sites would begin to adopt more products as a result of participating in the program.

So what began in Hutchins's mind as a consumer information program had reconciled the ideas of OD advocates by the time the RFP was issued. The concept paper had embraced a technical assistance component, but primarily because it was deemed necessary to help schools use the products. In the RFP writing process this technical assistance thrust had been translated into organizational development concepts. Then too, most of the winning proposals had included even more concrete OD approaches.

This part of history represents what I call "mutation." The point to be noted here, however, is that tension between the product orientation and problem solving was growing more acute and still had to be reconciled. After the program got underway, the balance of effort and concern continued to shift from products to helping schools develop the capacity to make decisions more effectively. In comparison to the energy expended on matching products with problems, projects devoted an increasing amount of time and resources to managing interpersonal relationships, organizing decision-making groups, conducting needs assessments, and other management techniques. The RDU staff were becoming more convinced that unless these management requirements were fulfilled, the R & D products selected would have minimal impact. Schools received enthusiastic encouragement from NIE to form "local action teams" consisting of committees of teachers and administrators at each school, who were assigned responsibility for managing the problem-solving process. These local teams were not explicitly mentioned in the RFP. However, they emerged early in each project as part of its strategy.

Reasons for the Shift in Priorities

What accounts for the growing prominence of organization development approaches? Several forces can be readily identified. First, after his discussions with practitioners throughout the country, Hutchins himself began very early to gingerly back off from an exclusive reliance on consumer information to do the job. He learned that educators were themselves calling for more personal assistance to identify and adopt R & D products. Their requests for help were later reinforced by advocates of OD both in the seven RDU projects and within the Institute, who chastised RDU for being a "product-pushing" effort. The question they asked was, "Are we in schools to help people, or to push products?"

These initial pressures were later reinforced when it became evident that in some schools teachers were having serious difficulties defining problems that were relevant to existing R & D products. It was taking them much longer to identify, adopt, and install products than had been anticipated. (See also Yin, Gwaltney and Louis, 1980). Clearly, they needed help with the decision process. If quick adoption of R & D products was used as the only criterion, RDU would surely be judged as a failure. Both NIE program managers and project staffs were adjusting their views of the project's objectives in light of these circumstances.

Finally, the shift in priorities was, at least in part, a function of the personnel involved in the seven RDU projects. In most projects, primary responsibility for working with schools was delegated to "linking agents." These individuals were selected for their skills as facilitators, and not because of their substantive expertise in areas covered by the project's knowledge base. Thus, they tended to emphasize the OD approach in their field work, and their communications with project staff also reinforced a preference for process over products.

These forces, then, help to explain how a program that was conceived as a way to inform the public about R & D products gave progressively more attention to helping schools set up problem-solving mechanisms and to providing them with technical assistance for problems that often extended well beyond the available R & D products. The point is not that this shift violated the original design, which had, after all, provided for multiple objectives and mixed strategies; the emphasis on OD materialized within that framework. The point is rather that the *balance* between strategies shifted in favor of OD. Slippage was fostered by the design itself. The multiple objectives produced tensions that were eventually reconciled in a way that could not have been predicted from either the design or the original rationale for the program. What developed was the outcome of a struggle among essentially competing alternatives that had been included in the original design and were then chosen on the basis of circumstances that arose during implementation. The original emphasis on products was eclipsed by what came to be seen as an even greater need for organization development.

This scenario was produced by an intricate set of forces within the design itself. On the one hand the design established the *constraints*—the available options and tensions from competing priorities. At the same time, the incompatibilities in themselves permitted persons to exercise their own discretion. Thus, while the incompatibilities were responsible for some of the problems, they also allowed the flexibility needed to reorder priorities in the face of particular circumstances.

THE ROLE OF LINKERS AS A CASE OF MUTATION

Inconsistencies in the program design were, then, important sources of the type of slippage I call "reconciliation." Design ambiguities also played a major role in another form of slippage, namely the "mutations" that emerged in the form of new design features. The evolution of the linker's role from obscurity to prominence as the RDU program evolved is a case in point.

Both in the concept paper and in the RFP, the RDU program was portrayed as a combination of two broad approaches: (1) it would provide technical assistance to schools in identifying, adapting, and adopting R & D products; and (2) it would help existing agencies work together to identify and implement the most promising R & D outcomes. The latter approach was referred to as "linkage" strategy. With the exception of a reference to developing "linker agent" skills (training) that was mentioned in the concept paper, there is nothing in the background materials to suggest that "linkage" would be confined to an exclusive reliance on the individual "linkers" that each project had assigned to act as liaisons with schools. Hutchins was using the term "linkage arrangements" as it was commonly used in general systems language. RDU would show that *agencies* can act together in ways that do not depend on particular individuals. The particular persons performing extension-agent roles were presumably of minor importance, since individuals in such roles cannot do much in a complicated system like education.

Reasons for the Growing Prominence of Linkers

However, as the idea of linkage took hold through a confluence of events, the term came to be interpreted almost synonymously with the linker's role. There were several contributing factors occuring at various times. For one thing, the importance of inter-personal influence was being proclaimed in the educational change literature, and a study had recently been released by Sieber, Louis, and Metzger (1972) that raised hopes for this approach. Most of the project directors were familiar with this literature, and in fact one was in the process of writing a paper on this very topic. In addition, the interpersonal approach was being advocated early on by several speakers who were invited to a conference that was convened to discuss the concept paper. Some RDU staff members had made known their favorable predisposition toward the use of specialized linking agents. Finally, at this time a member of Congress was insisting that NIE should explore the possibility of using "educational extension agents" modeled after the agricultural extension agent system.

For all of these reasons, then, linkers had a central place in most RDU proposals.[7] In addition, Hutchins's unit funded a book developed by the University Council for Educational Administrators on linkers' roles, and a training project for linkers was sponsored jointly by the NIE labs and centers. All of these materials were available to the projects at the first RDU directors' meeting.

Add to these circumstances the nature of the dissemination field itself. In working with schools, state education agencies had long used individuals who were called "curriculum coordinators," and the NDN program was exploring a similar approach in its use of "state facilitators." Therefore, the existing structure of SEAs and LEAs made it relatively easy for them to accommodate linkers. By comparison, there was little precedent, and not much clear guidance, for establishing the so-called system level linkages that were intended for autonomous institutions such as universities, R & D centers, and the like. And then, when it became apparent that schools were taking too long to work through the problem-solving process on their own, the case was cinched. The schools obviously needed the kind of help that linkers were prepared to provide.

Abt Associates was another key actor in this episode. The Abt Associates proposal was engineered by Karen Seashore Louis, one of the researchers who had investigated the experimental use of linkers in a three-state pilot project. She and her associates brought a perspective and a sensitivity that had never before so thoroughly highlighted the critically important responsibility that linkers had assumed in most of the RDU projects. Abt Associates' evaluation design virtually guaranteed that henceforth no aspect of the linker role would escape unnoticed. No one could ever again overlook how important the linkers had become.

In sum, a vague and multifaceted concept called "linkage," which was central to the original design, was winnowed down and eventually transformed into one peculiar form of linkage through a process of interpretation and through a confluence of events. There is no doubt that RDU gave this interpersonal strategy a real test. But during the process, the original sweeping vision of knowledge transfer as a social system function requiring many types of linkage among an entire network of institutions and organizations was eclipsed by the rather commonplace social psychology of interpersonal relationships within schools.

INSTITUTIONALIZATION: AN ABORTED MUTATION

There was some controversy about whether the program ought to be extended beyond the original three-year period. It is doubtful that anyone in NIE management intended for it to continue for a longer period, given its complexity and cost. The RFP did mention the possibility of a two-year renewal for projects at the end of the third year for the purpose of disseminating results and studying any long-term effects that the program might have had on the projects. But while this left an opening for continuation, it never seemed to be a serious NIE commitment.

A Drift Toward Institutionalization

The question of renewal was tied to a vision of the program that was espoused by a few persons—namely, that certain aspects of it could live on permanently in the seven projects even after federal funds had been withdrawn, if the projects were given some time (and money) to more fully embrace it. The advocates of this continuation were hoping for "institutionalization," which technically means the incorporation of a set of practices into the structure, routines, and traditions of an organization.

This notion of institutionalizing program components into the projects was mentioned in some of the project proposals as part of a general process of "building institutional capacity." Such references in the proposals prompted some of the NIE staff to anticipate a long-term impact on practice from this short-term action research program. As the program progressed this originally remote possibility grew more attractive to several individuals. Some persons who were running the program were even beginning to believe that if it was helping the seven participating projects, it would be desirable to extend it to more states.

In the second year of the program, the PD began to encourage project directors to think about how to institutionalize something concrete from their projects before the program ended. He requested project directors to make periodic reports on the progress they were making toward institutionalization. Project director meetings held in the spring and fall of 1978 were devoted to this topic, and papers on institutionalization were solicited from outside consultants and project directors. Another project officer at NIE posed questions to project directors in a way that encouraged them to suggest how state Department of Education personnel might be trained to take over some projects on a permanent basis.

All of this activity conveyed the impression to project directors that, in order to transfer the projects onto a more permanent footing, the program would probably be extended for at least another two years. The PD wrote in May 1978: "It (institutionalization) is a topic about which our leadership has much interest." In September of that year he added: "The FY 1979 and 1980 program plans apparently have some flexibility, but we need to present a logical plan to complement and take advantage of the work of the three operational years of RDU.... At this point the initiative is in our hands."

There was in fact little basis for this optimism. It was already too late. The $800,000 he had vainly proposed for the two-year extension had already been slashed in half by his superiors. Then, unknown to the PD, the remaining $400,000 had disappeared entirely from the budget during the summer of 1978. This occurred even while the PD was in good faith encouraging project directors to look forward to an extension. Both Hutchins and the associate director for dissemination had left the Institute, and a new boss had been recruited who was, at best, skeptical about the whole plan. At about this same time the contracts office wrote to all project directors advising them not to request any future extensions.

Undaunted, the PD launched his own information campaign. Going over the head of his new supervisor, he invited NIE managers to accompany him on visits to some of the project sites. He also invited a guest consultant to talk with an audience of NIE managers about the advantages of institutionalizing RDU.

The Extension Ordeal

Even while promoting the hope of obtaining new funds, the PD was deadlocked with the contracts office over a proposed "no-cost" program extension that would permit the projects to use all of the money they had already been authorized to spend. It seems that all seven projects were behind schedule, which left them with appropriated money that they had not yet spent. The plan was for projects to apply for permission to use these unexpended funds to extend their work for another six months to a year. Most of the seven proposed extensions were in the $10,000 to $40,000 range, but two had not gotten around to spending well over $100,000 and they had only one month remaining in the projects.[8]

NIE had not expressed much concern about this underspending. Late in the second year, the PD wrote in a memo to the directors:

> Based on early expenditure information from several projects, as well as many years of experience in looking at project budgets, I would be very surprised if most of your projects did not turn out to be significantly underexpended at this stage of the game. Please be assured that we do not look upon this with great alarm or as a sign that your project is failing.

The program director understood the operational problems faced by the projects with far greater clarity and sympathy than the contracts office or the NIE management. "We are aware," he wrote in a memo to project directors, "that complex programs like RDU take time to gear up, and that original budget estimates are usually compiled without benefit of much experience. We antici-pated the need for budget revisions." Most of the projects had accumulated money because of start-up delays. Now they wanted to use the money for a six-month extension that incidentally would keep them alive while NIE was deciding to refund some of them for two years.

The contracts office resisted. The PD wrote in another memo at a later date:

> Much to my chagrin, I have to report that the six month extension process is still bogged down in our contracts office, which is again insisting that the documents be submitted to a sole source review board. There is no cause for alarm with respect to the extension actually happening, but I confess I now cannot predict when the final solicitation will reach you. I will con-tinue to push from this end.

The final decision was not handled routinely. In an uncustomary move, the budget extension requests were passed up to the NIE director for final judgment. Six of the projects were given more time. But PD never succeeded in his quest to revive the proposal for the two-year extension needed to facilitate institutionalization.

Images of a Bureaucracy

These unsuccessful moves to extend the program can be seen as an aborted mutation. The quest for extension was an effort to create new meanings and to reinterpret the scope and mandate of the program. The efforts failed in this case, but if they had work-ed this three-year *program* (operating from Washington) might have been transformed into seven permanent *projects* (operating in the different states). And, beyond that, the PD was even hoping to build a long-term program in Washington that over the next decade would permit all of the states to eventually participate in an RDU project on a rotating basis. As it turned out, these muta-tions did not materialize, and most of the informants were not surprised. RDU was, after all, only a short-term project that was slated to terminate, and it did. Nevertheless, it may be worth considering some of the other reasons the program did not survive because, under slightly different circumstances, the slippage might have worked in the other direction—the program *might* have survived in some form.

One consideration mentioned by some of the informants as a matter of conjecture was that a program like RDU provides a power base for its managers, and their competitors tried to undercut them by scuttling their programs. However, even in an entrepreneurial bureaucracy it seems unlikely that such decisions are made on a personal basis. There were more fundamental group pressures at work.

Group conflict plagued RDU from its conception. Hutchins argued with other program directors, with OMB, with the contracts office, and with his own staff. There were bitter controversies over the evaluation, over the objections of the NIE staff to the proposal review process, and over the ceaseless revisions in the RFP. As one informant put it, RDU simply did not have the "smell of success" from the beginning because of these intraorganizational rivalries. Some of the first problems to reach the desk of the new NIE deputy director when he assumed his duties were OMB's objections to the program and the contract office's complaints about the underspending and the requests for no-cost extensions.

However, while these internal arguments perhaps caused management to take a harder look at the program, other considerations seem more important. There were, for example, pronounced discontinuities created by the recurrent succession of managers. When his supervisor left, the PD lost what little support he had for continuation, and he was faced with two new supervisors, neither of whom had reason to be sympathetic toward the program. A new manager in this type of agency typically makes his or her mark by taking fresh initiatives which can justify expanded budget requests, and not by propping up programs carried over from a previous administration. This is nowhere more true than in the director's office. When the issue of continuing RDU arose, a new NIE deputy director was looking for some discretionary money to support a proposed dissemination initiative, and the unspent money in RDU was an attractive option, especially in view of the rate at which the projects were already underspending. The leftover money also hurt the case for the additional $400,000 request.

The question of continuation had unavoidably gotten mixed up with the priority changes in the Institute. The NIE management was turning its attention to other things, and RDU did not fit well into the new plans. It did not, for example, stress minority populations in urban areas, one of the Institute's top priorities. While ardent supporters claimed that the bulk of RDU schools was in low-income neighborhoods, none of the projects was operating in the problem-ridden urban centers, even though Raizen said she repeatedly encouraged RDU staff to move in this direction. In addition, the dissemination program was shifting its funding strategy: large, federally administered action research programs had now lost favor.

However, even with these marks against it, the program might have been renewed had it been able to muster more external backing. But the initial impetus from Congress had diminished. Not one question was raised about dissemination in the 1979 congressional budget hearings; the sense of urgency about disseminating R & D products had subsided. Nor had the program attracted a constituency within the Institute or among the chief state school officers, professional associations, or other groups. Little pressure had been applied on behalf of the program. Even the RDU program staff at NIE were being assigned to additional projects, and this split them up into different regions of the country. But more important, the program had lost its most essential base of support—namely, the endorsement of the NIE administration. That RDU was not pushing NIE products was of little consequence now. What was decisive was the program design. RDU had simply not impressed the NIE management in power at the time as a well-planned experiment that would be likely to yield useful and policy-relevant information.

And, even if that assessment turned out wrong, there was, as yet, no systematic *evidence* that the program was effective. The Abt Associates studies had been started too late to be of use now. True, research data at this critical juncture *might* not have made much difference: after all, how often are essentially political decisions guided by scientific information? But the fact remains that NIE managers were calling for hard facts, and whether he knew it or not, research evidence was the PD's last hope. The RDU study is not unique in this respect. As Bernstein and Freedman (1975) observe, few evaluation studies have been completed in time to influence the short-range decision process of policy makers. But it seems not a little ironic that the RDU research component was never given the level of priority called for by the Institute's mission. Without systematic information there could be no case for institutionalizing the program in this erratic and inconstant environment. The program was once again trapped by its own history. The designer's grand ambitions for the program were dashed by the very events that had haunted it for four years—the nagging ambiguities and contradictions and the euphoric ambitions that were built into the program design itself. It is ironic that the program managers never supported the evaluation at the level of priority called for by the Institute's mission, because it was this fateful set of decisions that proved to be the program's final undoing.

From still a larger perspective, however, institutionalization was never the really critical issue. RDU was simply a three-year program that was dragged out for nearly four years; why should it be surprising then that the program was not institutionalized? What is puzzling, however, is that no concrete provision was ever made for putting the findings from this effort into use. For example, had RDU been more closely linked with OE, the findings from the program might have been fed directly into parallel service delivery programs operated by that agency; or OE might even have taken over RDU; or provisions might have been made to incorporate the RDU findings into other dissemination programs at NIE. But due in part to the stormy relationships with those programs at the beginning and in part to the federal structure, no explicit provision was ever made to provide for such information transfers. Not until RDU was in its final stage were some steps considered to merge it with the State Capacity Building Grants Program and to disseminate results to a group of laboratories; by this time it was probably futile to try to reshape these projects which were now so far downstream.

Finally, plans might have been made for some of the states or other dissemination programs to build on the RDU experience, and a few of the projects did make concrete efforts in this direction. But it was not until the project was tottering on the brink of its own demise that much thought was given to *how* this might be made to happen, and NIE never did take the bold steps that were needed to assure that it would happen; it was an after-thought. In short, no one had thought to include in the original program design specific mechanisms that would *facilitate* the transfer of knowledge produced by RDU into other dissemination programs. RDU was always a program in search of an audience.

SUMMARY

In sum, four ways in which program plans and practices become accommodated can be identified: (a) two forms of mutual adaptation—progressive specification and successive approximation and (b) two types of slippage—reconciliation and mutation. These different types of accommodation depend upon whether the changes are planned or inadvertent and whether they are responses to obstacles encountered in the field or from difficulties with the design itself.

Specification involves fleshing out the details implicit in the original design and making the appropriate adjustments in project procedures. A number of such instances came up in the course of routine monitoring. In some cases contracts with the projects were renegotiated to adjust schedules and budgets.

Successive approximation is a different story. In this case the design itself undergoes a series of transformations, one step at a time, as it becomes obvious that the capabilities of the parties involved were originally miscalculated. For example, the program was premised on the existence of a national pool of high quality, research-based products that were not being widely used. But in practice NIE was never able to either identify them clearly or to assess their quality systematically. The Institute even equivocated on the importance of a demonstrated research base. Unable to establish a national product pool, the Institute relied on the seven largely autonomous projects to identify overlapping knowledge bases. Many of these products were not based on R & D and no uniform assessment procedure was established. These developments differed substantially from the original tentative concept. However, the result was not necessarily inferior. The point is that the program had taken form in successive steps.

Reconciliation comes about when some of the people responsible for implementing a project resist certain aspects of the design in favor of other options. A realignment of priorities or compromises often result. In some instances competing options are suggested in the design itself. For example, the fact that this program attempted to tie the research to a demonstration project exacerbated tensions between groups of people who placed different priorities on research and service. RDU could not satisfy the requirements of a planned variation field experiment, and yet given the costs, its service impact was limited to relatively few school sites. Moreover, the research component was repeatedly delayed as the immediate problems of implementing the demonstration component took precedence.

Another set of tensions was generated from the dual requirements that the projects should provide technical assistance on problems the schools identified as well as providing information about available R & D products. What if a school were to identify a problem that could not be solved with the available product pools? Should priority be given to introducing products to practitioners or to helping them with their problems? It remained for the persons responsible for the project at each site to resolve the issue.

Mutation refers to new design concepts that emerge from novel interpretations of prevailing practice or from a creative synthesis of previously sovereign options. For example, through a confluence of events the abstract idea of "linkage" was quickly winnowed down to one particular form of linkage, the "linker agent." While the concept of linker agent had been present from the inception of the program, this one form of linkage eclipsed all other options.

Another precipitant mutation was aborted, but the case is nonetheless instructive. Although RDU was planned as a limited three-year program, some key actors attempted to extend it and ultimately to institutionalize it as a long-term operational program. That these ambitions were not realized can be explained in large part by the time line in the design. But in addition, it is important to note that RDU never had a strong base of support in the Institute. From the beginning it was isolated and plagued by intra-organizational rivalries and disputes; the priorities of the Congress and of the NIE managers had changed; and ironically, because of excessive delays in awarding the research contract, systematic evidence of the program's effectiveness was not available when it was needed by the NIE managers.

While the instances that were used to illustrate each type of accommodation are by no means "pure" or conclusive, the typology does seem to illuminate some valid differences. Thus, it might be profitable to give further consideration to what it really means to "implement" a program. That is the subject of the next chapter.

NOTES

1. Revisions take place either with or without a corresponding change in the local setting. McLaughlin (1976) calls instances where the design is modified without a corresponding change in the local setting, "cooptation."

2. However, in addition to its own products, NIE has always assumed the responsibility for disseminating products developed elsewhere.

3. Hutchins did not personally believe that the federal government should be involved in validating products at all, on the grounds that there are no external criteria for determining whether a product can be made to work in a *particular* situation.

4. One might speculate that if the problem-solving position prevailed, with products being viewed primarily as a means to help schools help themselves, there would be less need to worry about the validity question.

5. In the fall of 1977 the senior staff met to reorganize the office. A research and evaluation unit was part of the resulting plan. The unit would have the budgets and responsibility for evaluation. Informally the unit was operating at least by December of 1977, shortly after the Abt Associates contract was awarded. The unit was subsequently formatted in the Institute-wide reorganization.

6. The term "organization development" has a variety of meanings. Here it refers to a mixture of problem-solving (P-S) and social interaction (S-I) strategies. The P-S approach is based on a group decision-making process that stresses the priority of local needs, goals, conditions, and resources and relies upon local initiative as opposed to outside resources, directive assistance, and standardized materials. The idea behind S-I is to form networks of people drawn from inside and outside the system who will share information, skills, and other resources. Neither strategy places much stress on using R & D products to solve problems, although this is one option. In RDU, these strategies were combined in the local action teams or committees from each school site that worked with consultants ("linkers") from the project offices.

7. With dubious but revealing logic the PD writes, "Since a 'system' cannot interface with a local school, it was essential to have an individual (linking agent) to carry the ball at the local site. The winning projects did not seem to have much trouble interpreting this from the RFP" (personal communication).

8. Project budgets ranged from $835,000 to $1.4 million.

Chapter VII

Beyond Mutual Adaptation

When Berman and McLaughlin (1977) proposed that implementation is a process of "mutual adaptation," it struck a responsive chord because anyone familiar with complex social programs knows that putting an idea into practice is more complicated than filling a recipe. And yet, policymakers—and indeed, many evaluation researchers—have continued to insist that a program should be weighed against, and then held faithfully to, the original program design. Clearly this "program-fidelity" approach does not properly recognize the need to adjust initial plans to given situations.

IMPLEMENTATION AS INSTITUTIONAL DRIFT AND GROUP CONFLICT

However, in retrospect, the mutual adaptation approach is only one step removed from the idea of program fidelity. For all of the commotion that it created in some circles, the notion of mutual adaptation still did not illuminate the variety of ways in which accomodation takes place, nor did it sufficiently stress the features of program design itself that create the need for adaptation. It was taken for granted that the core notions of a design would be resilient enough to guide the adjustments necessary to implement them, and that perhaps while the original federal intent is being chipped away, program managers know what they are after and do their best to salvage the original vision. However, in fact a federal agency often does not know what it wants because it speaks with so many voices. Designs grow out of conflict. They are

both conflict strategies and products of a conflict process. Consequently, at best they create vague, inconsistent, and often unrealistic expectations. *Programs seldom run smoothly because the compromises that are necessary to bring them into existence become the constraints
that continue to shape them after they are in operation.*

A paper by Attewell and Gerstein (1979) reports one of the few
studies to date that have attempted to link the "failure" of local
efforts to conflicting demands embedded in governmental policy,
as government agencies attempt to co-opt or placate interests hostile to new policy directions. Although some investigators have
acknowledged the imprecision inherent in program designs, few
have examined the dynamics within federal agencies which are
responsible for the ambitiousness, the ambiguities, and the inconsistencies that creep into designs. As a consequence, an important
point tends to have been obscured—namely, that designs are
products of ongoing conflicts between groups at the federal and
local levels, and between groups within federal agencies themselves. The modifications that must be made in an entrepreneurial bureaucracy in order to create a program continue
to haunt it, sometimes to its very demise.

An outsider can be easily deceived about the integrity of a
federal program. From a distance (i.e., from reading an RFP) it
may appear to be a cohesive, forceful plan of action that has the
full backing of the sponsoring agency. Indeed, we often speak
innocently of "federal" programs, policies, and goals as though
they were of one piece, when in fact they include much rhetoric
and myth, which hide the internal maneuvering that brought
them into the world and mask the compromises that continue to
shape their destiny.

The critical dimensions of the implementation process include:

- the strategic nature of design as an institutional myth that
  masks disputes among the pluralistic set of actors who had a
  hand in shaping it;
- the openendedness of federal policies governing operating
  programs;
- the unplanned, inadvertent character of much of the
  compromise.

All of this means that one can never be sure who is "adapting"
what. In recognition of these problems, some writers have come

to think of implementation in still a third way—as an "evolutionary process" (Farrar et al., 1979; Fullen, 1981). I believe it is. But evolution can be an impersonal, bloodless process of automatic development based on mechanistic laws—namely, variation, competition, selection, and survival (see Aldrich, 1979). Hannan and Freeman (1977) have extrapolated the assumptions of this view to their ultimate. They take issue with what they call the "adaptation perspective" which presumes that managers of organizations (or dominant coalitions) scan the relevant environment for opportunities and threats, formulate strategic responses, and make appropriate adjustments. It follows that the way organizations are affected by their environments depends upon the abilities and tactics of the leaders in buffering or exploiting relevant aspects of the environment. They dispute that and challenge the assumption that the structural variability of organizations can be explained by the actions of their *members*. They propose instead that variations can be better explained by impersonal processes of "selection." That is, features of organizations which are compatible (isomorphic) with their environment will be reinforced and preserved by the *environment*. For example the decentralized administrative pattern characteristic of construction firms is due to seasonal variations in demand. Firms with improper (incompatible) administrative styles have been "selected out" (not survived).

But while they can help explain certain phenomena, such evolutionary approaches often bury the human decisions and moving dramas that shape programs. I think that the power of an evolutionary approach could be increased by distinguishing between two interacting but distinct sources of evolution. The first type of evolutionary development is *institutional drift*. Drift follows in the wake of policy actions that accumulate in an unplanned manner. There are many reasons why plans can go awry: they need to be interpreted; people lose sight of goals in the press of day-to-day problems; outside pressures constrain and deflect the organization; the sovereign actions of members, seeking to cope with fluctuating outside demands, often unintentionally commit programs to new lines of action; and perhaps most importantly, entrepreneurial bureaucracies often lose their memories in the wake of turnover at the policy level and due to the premium placed on new initiatives.

The second type of evolution is a product of *group conflict*. Programs are driven by incessant struggles for influence and control among individuals and interest groups, both within and outside of federal agencies, who seek to uphold their principles, advance the goals of their organizational units, and aggrandize their own philosophies, values, and self-interests. Instead of thinking of "program design" and "implementation" as different stages of a linear development, it is more useful to see them as parallel, overlapping aspects of a larger, continuing conflict process among competing groups in a pluralistic environment.

THE ROLE OF LEADERSHIP

This distinction between drift and conflict leaves room for the possibility of leadership influence even within the evolutionary model. While programs are in large part molded by impersonal institutional forces beyond the control of leaders, within the parameters set by the design flaws and other constraints, leadership can play an important part in creating a program and giving it form and direction. In the case of RDU, there were numerous instances when the actions of the principal actors were decisive.

In fact, two different types of leadership commitments were evident at different stages of RDU. Selznick (1957) once distinguished between "institutional leadership" and purely organizational leadership. The actions of institutional leaders are calculated to benefit the public (in this instance, practitioners), rather than to exclusively serve the interests of their parent organizations. Institutional leadership in RDU was exemplified in the decision not to push NIE products, in fact, in the decision not to push R & D products at all (even though that might have been in the interest of the agency), but instead to provide technical assistance to the people who said they needed it. Through these decisions, it was determined that RDU would serve broader purposes. However, once the program was under way, a new leadership, faced with making the program work, turned its attention to organizational detail. Over time program managers in Washington and project directors in the field grew to appreciate how dependent they had become on one another and, as the end approached, they turned their attention to the survival of the program. The leadership had necessarily become preoccupied with organizational maintenance as well as with the program's broader purposes.

But the story of RDU also demonstrates that one should not

overestimate the role of the leaders. If program designs are imperfect, it is not because federal program managers are too inexperienced and unaware of the real world to set up and monitor workable programs. Perhaps more information would help, but as the biography of RDU vividly demonstrates, programs are shaped by power as well as by knowledge. If a program *begins* from compromise, no amount of visionary leadership will turn it into something more coherent. The stark fact is that program designs often *cannot* be formulated coherently, even if that were desirable. Programs are strategic political compromises in a pluralistic environment. Their results will be as mixed as the motives that brought them into existence in the first place.

When in 1973 I was attempting to understand why another federal program, the Teacher Corps, evolved as it had over a five-year period, I came to the conclusion that: the same battles that had seethed within the Congress during the legislative process were continuing to be played out in the local projects long after the program was in operation, and its friends and enemies struggled to gain control over its operating policies, just as they had formerly contested with each other over the design. Farrer et al. (1979) came to the similar conclusion that all implementation is a continuation of policy development. Program design perhaps sets pliable zones of tolerance, but within those parameters programs are free to evolve in directions that are determined by the outcomes of power struggles.

This brings us to the end of this story. But the key actors, and their discretionary programs, live on in Washington. The disinterested observer has reason to wonder what it all means for the nation's classrooms, and I suspect that these programs will never reform education. But they do provide a breath of fresh air for the often hidebound and old-fashioned federal bureaucracy, and they manage to engage small groups of citizens in some intriguing schemes. If they help only to revitalize the imagination of the nation, that might be enough.

Part III

*Patterns of Federal-Local Relationships in
Education*

Chapter VIII

The Experimental Schools Program

In the study of RDU reported in Part I our attention was riveted on the internal workings of NIE as an entrepreneurial bureaucracy. But federal programs also bring federal agencies into contact with other institutions in the course of implementation. Some insight into these complex relationships can be gleaned by examining the various ways in which government employees monitor the progress and quality of projects financed with federal money. In direct contact with state and local governments, school districts, and other recipient institutions, their responsibilities put them in a position to exercise a vital influence on the nature and quality of federal-local relationships.

The subject of project monitoring has been barely introduced thus far, but now with the context established, we can profitably turn to consider in greater detail the types of roles performed by the program officer. For this purpose, it will be useful to describe another NIE program, the Rural Experimental Schools's Program (ES) where program officers assumed several different types of roles.

In 1970, the United States Office of Education introduced ES to provide large, five-year block grants to selected school districts interested in implementing locally developed plans for "comprehensive educational change." The program was a response to growing concern in the late 1960s that federal assistance had become too fragmented, lacked overall coherence at the local level, and provided little room for local initiative. The ES program was designed to rectify these shortcomings through its focus on com-

109

prehensiveness and locally designed plans for change.[1] With an anticipated budget of $190 million over eight years, the Washington ES Office held three separate competitions between December 1970 and June 1972 to select eighteen projects for long-term funding—for eight urban and ten rural school districts (Figure VIII.1). This report considers only the rural districts.

Figure VIII.1. Dimensions of the Rural Experimental Schools Program

Program recommended by President Nixon, March 1970   Program started operation, December 1970
Total number of local projects (urban and rural): 18
    Number of rural projects: 10
Total anticipated budget for ES program (eight years) $190 million
Total funding (eight years) for ES program (approx.): $53 million
    Funding for ten rural projects (approx.): $6.4 million
Contribution of ES as percent of local budgets: 10 to 15%
Total number of program officers employed during course of program: 17*
Maximum number of program officers at any one time: 5
Maximum total staff at any one time: 17
Fewest program officers at any one time (prior to June 1976): 3
Lowest total staff (prior to June 1976): 4
Minimum program officer load: 2 projects
Maximum program officer load: 7 projects
Typical program officer load: 3 to 4 projects
Number of projects assigned to four different program officers over course of program: 3
Number of projects assigned to three different program officers over course of program: 4
Number of projects assigned to two different program officers over course of program: 3
First Program Director's tenure: December 1970 to December 1974
Second Program Director's tenure: December 1974 to December 1975
Third Program Director's tenure: December 1975 to 1978

*This figure does not include five persons assigned to program evaluation responsibilities.

BACKGROUND FOR THE RURAL ES PROGRAM[2]

The Rural ES Program passed through three phases: a selection period, a one-year planning period, and a three-year period of implementation.

The Selection Period. An announcement was mailed to all school districts in the U.S. having fewer than 2,500 pupils in March of 1972. Interested districts were asked to prepare a "letter of interest" describing the district's readiness to undertake a project of *comprehensive* educational change. Approximately 320 letters were received. Each letter was read and rated by ES/Washington staff members and five regional panels (see Herriott, 1979; Kane, 1976). Two groups of school districts were eventually selected for some participation in the small schools project. Six districts were awarded one-year grants in order to plan a five-year project of comprehensive educational change, with a "moral commitment" that subsequently they would be funded for four additional years. Six other districts received one-year planning grants, but with the understanding that long-term funding would be conditional upon the results of their planning process.

The Planning Period. Shortly after the process of site selection was completed the ES program was transferred from the Office of Education (OE) to the newly-founded National Institute of Education (NIE). Herriott (unpublished) notes that:

> At the time the planning grants were awarded, the administrative leaders of the ten rural ES school districts were not aware of the very active role which ES/Washington staff members would play during the planning period of these projects. There seemed to be within the National Institute of Education a sense that the substantial grants to those school districts for the planning year, and the fact that the districts would subsequently be awarded large *multiyear grants,* made it essential that the federal government exercise a responsibility to insure successful launching of the projects. Over time, there also developed within ES/Washington a concern that its survival as a federal program depended upon the ability of these school districts to produce plans which would reflect well upon their capabilities. Given the limited planning expertise which existed in most of these districts at the time they were awarded their planning grants [and the increased vulnerability of ES/Washington within NIE noted later in this report], ES/Washington increasingly found it necessary to play a very active role in the local planning process. See also Herriott, 1979, pp. 58–59.

The expectations which ES/Washington had for these school districts during this period were communicated in several forms:

- A formal Grant Document was prepared by the contracts office of the U.S. Office of Education in June 1972 and subsequently accepted by the Board of Education within each ES district. The document made explicit the number of dollars available to the district during the planning year and discussed more generally the purposes for which those dollars could be spent.
- Appended to the Grant Document was a set of conditions for the preparation of a Formal Project Plan.
- A federal program officer was assigned to oversee the grant relationship between the federal government and each ES school district. Such monitoring took a variety of forms and occurred through visits by ES/Washington staff members to the school district, visits of school district staff members to Washington, D.C., periodic telephone calls, and letters and memoranda (pp. 59).

The Washington ES office required a Formal Project Plan spelling out project goals, details of comprehensive changes to be made, procedures and resources. It was stipulated that ES/Washington must approve budget requests and all professional staff. Local districts were required to submit written drafts of their proposed plans at periodic intervals for review and suggestions for revision from Washington.

The Implementation Period. ES/Washington's expectations were communicated principally through the negotiation and subsequent signing of a contract between the National Institute of Education and each of the ten school districts. Discussions of long-term funding began early in 1973 with the review of draft Formal Project Plans submitted during the negotiation period and, for most of the school districts, continued on into the summer of 1973. Herriott (1979) observes:

> While the funds for the planning year had been awarded as *grants* to the school districts, ES/Washington was required by NIE to *contract* with the school districts for the implementation of the Formal Project Plans. The budget levels were to be negotiated between the NIE contracts office and the local ES project leaders. As in any contract, both parties would bind themselves to perform: ES/Washington to pay out funds at agreed levels and at agreed times, and the school districts to produce comprehensive

educational change that had been locally planned and described in detail
in the Formal Projects Plans (p. 62).

The typical contract document consisted of approximately ten
pages; the formal expectations of ES/Washington were spelled
out through a series of sixteen "special provisions," the most
important of which incorporated the Formal Project Plan of each
school district into a "scope of work" statement calling for the
implementation of that plan. A series of "deliverables" was also
called for, consisting of a final revision to the Formal Project Plan,
a series of Quarterly Progress Reports, a series of Quarterly Financial Reports, and an Interim Project Report.

The Aims of the Program

Each local project was to be unique. There was no intention of
replicating any project exactly in other school districts, nor of
disseminating specific products. Rather, the aim was to see if it
was possible to produce change through a few basic strategies,
including locally initiated designs, participation of lay citizens,
provision for comprehensive changes that would affect the total
district at all grade levels of all schools, intensive and systematic
evaluation (budgeted up to 25% of the total program cost), and
long-term planning with the understanding that at the end of the
funding period the district would continue to support the changes
it had made. In the words of an official announcement, the program was to test the hypothesis "that significant and lasting improvements in education, beyond those made possible by piecemeal innovative efforts, are more likely to occur if comprehensive
changes are introduced into all elements of a school system" (National Institute of Education, 1974, p. 38).

The program was also designed to test and demonstrate the
feasibility and worth of approaching school districts in a less directive, more personal and supportive style than is typical of the
traditional federal bureaucratic approach to school districts. The
originators hoped to aid districts where possible, to have a larger
visible impact on local projects, to avoid bureaucratic snarls that
result from time lag and misunderstandings, and, at the same
time, to hold districts more "accountable" for their use of federal
funds and for the programs they were supposed to implement.

The Realities of the Program

In general, the program as it was implemented approached these aims, but certain differences between the vision and the reality must be understood to fully appreciate the program officers' role. First, the title "Experimental Schools Program" proved to be a confusing element. In fact, it was not a well-planned social experiment, but a loosely conceived approach to funding a few selected school districts. ES was conceived and backed by several powerful sponsors who disagreed on the nature of the program. Herriott (1979:21) writes, "even before it had properly been started, the program had become a part of various power struggles, within the executive branch, within HEW, and within OE itself." ES shared with other demonstrations a sense of confusion over whether this was primarily a research project, a grant in aid, or a demonstration. This ambiguity eventually had a chilling effect on the program officers who, on the one hand, had a visible impact on the projects, and yet on the other hand were never sure whether it was appropriate for them to provide technical assistance, even when it was requested by the local communities.

Secondly, the program was very ambitious and not well planned. It seems inconceivable that the $6 million allocated to ten rural school districts could have been expected to produce the extensive reform anticipated. Moreover, the overall program was launched immediately after funds for it were appropriated, which left little time to recruit personnel, select local projects, or formulate guidelines as well as job descriptions for program officers. This forced the program officers to assume responsibility for shaving down the broad and vague policy goals into something more feasible.

Finally, a transfer of the Experimental Schools Program from the Office of Education (OE) where the program was conceived to the National Institute of Education (NIE) proved to be traumatic. It inevitably introduced pressures on the program officers to adopt a particular style of project monitoring. The new agency was required to assume existing OE programs, which left it with little discretionary money to initiate its own new programs (Herriott, 1979). Experimental Schools became defined as an "old OE" program. The significance of this development can be better appreciated when it is recalled that NIE was created *because* Congress was convinced that OE had failed to fulfill its reserach function (Summerfield, 1974).

The effect of the transfer was twofold: (1) it intensified competition for discretionary funds controlled by ES, which middle-level bureaucrats prize as a source of power; and (2) it centralized decisions about ES, thus reducing the ES director's discretion and subjecting the program to higher-level political pressures (Corwin and Nagi, 1972; Summerfield, 1974). The first ES director was personally inclined to defy the bureaucracy (see also Sproull, Weiner, and Wolf, 1978:4–5, Chapter 6). But that was at best a short-term strategy. For, as a new, middle-level bureaucrat with little prior government experience, he had not yet cultivated a clientele through this program. Therefore, the most viable route to the power required to accomplish his objectives was to satisfy the interests of his superiors. This meant adjusting to severe pressures to accommodate this program to the NIE research priorities and demonstrating that research rigor and fiscal accountability could be brought to the program. OE is an old-time service agency; NIE is a new and vulnerable agency seeking stature through its research programs. The first NIE director was very critical of the lack of experimental rigor in the ES program. The research component appeared to be secondary to the heavy social action mission of the program. It was acknowledged, in fact, "from the participant's perspective [ES] is primarily a problematic social action rather than a research effort" (Budding, 1972). The difference that the local districts and NIE attached to the research and social action priorities was bound to be a fundamental source of tension and confusion.

There were also concerns about the loose fiscal accountability implicit in the "no strings" guaranteed grants that OE was perceived to have given to the districts. In view of the relatively large size of this program within the total NIE budget, and management's skepticism, it is understandable that the NIE management could see better uses for the funds.

One program officer conjectured that, "There isn't anyone in the structure of HEW, OE, or [NIE] who wants to believe the Experimental Schools' people know what they're doing." The Experimental Schools' managers were obliged to prove otherwise and to demonstrate that their program could be a credit to NIE.

In retrospect, perhaps, they exaggerated, even contrived, the "research" aspect of the program. One program officer stated emphatically, "No one has believed in the research design from the beginning. When I say no one, I mean no one." The Experimental Schools director was, one source observed, now compelled to "prove to somebody that he is being rigorous."

At least one respondent felt that NIE was deliberately attempting to destroy the program:

> NIE imposed additional restrictions on the program, in an effort to kill it, which the first program director then passed on to local projects in an effort to save it. For example, there were a number of requirements that the local projects essentially should be able to "demonstrate an impact" which was not understood in the beginning.

THE NATURE OF THE STUDY

What follows are some of my personal observations and reflections about one facet of this program, the relationships that developed between the federal program officers and the ten rural communities participating in the program. The data come largely from the following sources:

- ten program officers who completed questionnaires and were interviewed in person by the author;
- eight school administrators, representing eight of the ten rural school districts in the program, who were interviewed by telephone by the author;
- ten social scientists who were employed by Abt Associates Inc. (AAI), and assigned to live as observers in the communities to study and evaluate the local projects, and who submitted to me materials and comments regarding this study;
- site visit reports and correspondence available in files of the ES/Washington office.

In addition to the data sources, administrators and practitioners from a teacher training institution, a federal agency, a private foundation, and a university department of political science have examined a draft of this report, and critiqued my interpretations.[3]

Design Limitations

It should be kept in mind that this is an exploratory case study, and, as the data sources suggest, relies primarily upon qualitative rather than quantitative modes of inquiry. I often found myself working in the mode of a "site review" team member who visits local research and development projects to assess their progress and quality of work. I was looking for some crude *patterns,* insofar as they could be detected in a single program composed of a wide variety of local projects, each with its own history. I have tried to be sensitive to this variation and to the limited data base while calling attention to some salient factors that might be more generalizable—wherever there was a hint of a more general problem. While I have tried to document my conclusions, this was sometimes difficult, and therefore some interpretations can and probably should be challenged.

A major limitation forced on the design by severe, unpredicted budgetary constraints was my inability to visit the ten local projects as originally planned. The study therefore relies heavily on information supplied by the ES program officers themselves and from ES files in Washington. However, I have tried to check the sources in several ways: by reporting, in many instances, more than one independent source of an observation, by identifying the sources of opinion expressed, by including some modest data from telephone interviews with most of the local project directors, and by checking particular facts and interpretations with the on-site observers employed by Abt Associates.

Thus, my conclusions are informed by data, even though they are not grounded in either first-hand knowledge or statistical tests. They are based largely on my own speculations, formed as I reflected upon the data and the issues for several years. I have operated on the assumption that using qualitative modes of inquiry would be better than no inquiry at all. My objective was simply to "make sense" out of a complex situation that, to my knowledge, has not been studied previously. To the extent that this is research, it is exploratory and in the tradition of hypothesis-generating work rather than theory validation.

A second limitation in the design is that it concentrates on only one unique federal program. It would be a mistake to draw final conclusions about the general issues addressed here without further study under more diverse conditions. The traditions and the constituencies of various federal agencies and programs make a big difference. As will be shown, this program had to overcome the reluctance of the government to take risks with new ideas, funding delays and cutbacks, inadequacy of funds appropriated for monitoring and support services, a traumatic transfer to a new agency about which Congress was already dubious, and the strong inclination on the part of Congress to support local officials over federal employees. Moreover, what the ES program officers were trying to do, namely to provide program assistance, was not supported by the NIE administration. Consequently, the authority of the program officers to render the services they were offering within the scope of this program was generally in doubt.

A study of ES probably does not adequately test whether it is possible to carry out effectively the different program officer roles within a federal agency, because the way these program officers functioned cannot be regarded as typical of federal agencies. Their tendency to become actively involved in local projects as advisors and their readiness to provide technical assistance with specific problems, although not without precedent, are exceptional. Each ES program officer monitored only two or three contracts, whereas program officers in some other parts of HEW monitored as many as ten to fifteen contracts or twenty to thirty grants. Consequently, the ES program officers had more time and opportunity to become familiar with the details of a few local projects than is true of many federal agencies. Moreover, the majority of the officers in this program were term employees drawn to Washington specifically to work on this particular program. Most were not career civil servants with broad government experience.

Nevertheless, some facets of the ES Program do parallel the procedures used to monitor certain large research and development centers, and at least a few large-scale domestic programs sponsored by OEO, HUD, and CETA. Under some circumstances, most agencies are probably tempted to provide the services offered by the ES program officers; it seems very likely that at least a few program directors in Washington would like to provide more consulting advice and technical assistance to local projects. To some extent, this program is an extreme case that serves to highlight both the potentials and the hazards of labor-intensive federal program assistance.

Overview

The subsequent discussion unfolds as follows. Three types of roles played by program officers are described and analyzed. One of these roles, contract management, is the one for which program officers typically are held responsible. This study is primarily concerned with the effects and feasibility of two more active roles, namely, the provision of advice and technical assistance to local projects. While these two roles are not unprecedented, they are far less frequent than contract management. Several ways of combining all three roles are also considered, together with some reasons for the stylistic differences reported among program officers. The ways in which program officers had an impact on local projects are then reviewed, and several reasons are offered for the wide variations in impact that occurred over time and from place to place. The ways in which program officers differed among themselves are also considered. Finally, some conclusions are drawn about the advantages and disadvantages of federal assistance, as well as some conditions that affect the ability of a federal agency to provide it in a large program such as ES.

SUMMARY

This is an exploratory case study of the roles carried out by federal program officers in the Experimental Schools (ES) Program. The study relies upon qualitative rather than quantitative modes of analysis. The conclusions are limited by lack of prior research on this topic, the nature of the data that could be obtained for this study, and the unique features of the program as outlined in this chapter. Nevertheless, the topic deserves attention, and in fact, given the dearth of information currently available, exploratory inquiries such as this are entirely appropriate and urgently needed. Government agencies should give more attention to the problems faced by program officers in order to help them improve their relationships with local communities. For, as communication links and mediators between federal and local circumstances, program officers can make or break the federal-local partnership.

The next chapter sketches the backgrounds of the ES program

officers and describes the complex set of roles they attempted to play.

NOTES

1. This report makes an important distinction between the terms "program" and "project," with the former referring to an organizational unit at the federal level and the latter to that at the local level. Organizational units within projects are referred to as "components."

2. The following description relies heavily on numerous published and unpublished reports of Robert Herriott and his associates.

3. I am grateful to the following persons, who read and commented upon early versions of this study: Daniel Griffiths, Dean of the School of Education at New York University; Terry Saario, Program Officer at the Ford Foundation; Randall B. Ripley, Chairman of the Department of Political Science at Ohio State University; and Michael W. Kirst, Professor, School of Education, Stanford University.

Chapter IX

The Program Officer:
A Three-Dimensional Portrait

Despite a growing literature on the implementation of inter-governmental policy (Jones and Thomas, 1976; Smith, 1973) the role of the federal program officer has not been the subject of much serious analysis. Yet, it is commonly recognized that program implementation typically involves a substantial amount of "slippage" between the level at which decisions are made and the level at which they are applied. Lipsky (1976) and Weatherly (1979) have stressed that typically the people at the lowest level of organization exersize substantial discretion in translating policy into action, and therefore one cannot understand the policy process without understanding in detail how the street level bureaucrats who work directly with recipient clientele perform these jobs. They were referring to the service delivery personnel in local agencies, but the same proposition is equally applicable to the agencies that fund local programs. Clearly, much of the responsibility for interpreting decisions must be delegated to program officers, who as bureaucratic employees have the power to resist or distort policies according to their personal philosophies (Downs, 1967; Mechanic, 1962; Selznick, 1948; Van Horne and Van Meter, 1976). As communication links and mediators between the norms of the federal bureaucracy and the values of the community and institutions with which they work, they must play many different roles as programs evolve. In their direct and visible contact with the public, they are under severe pressures from various sources to compromise these norms (Bar-Josef and

Schied, 1966; Katz and Danet, 1973). And yet, for the most part, the functions of project officers have been only informally defined (CPI, 1977). They typically learn their jobs through experience and they are associated with a wide diversity of programs.

INTERGOVERNMENTAL RELATIONS AS A BALANCE OF POWER

All kinds of targeted federal programs intended to stimulate change and improve the quality of local services have multiplied in recent years (Bailey and Mosher, 1968; Reagan, 1972), and account for up to one-fifth of local and state revenue. Reagan (1972) estimates that the federal share of domestic direct expenditures exceeds the share assumed by the states or the local levels of government. With specific reference to education, during the decade of the 1960s the federal share of expenditures increased from 4.4 to 7 percent. This amounts to about a $2 billion increase, although local expenditures increased even faster (by almost $12 billion) (Kirst, 1973).

Recently efforts have been made to reverse these trends, but the long term increase in the federal role raises the spectre of federal control that haunts many Americans who fear the regimentation of civil life. Nowhere is the struggle to maintain a working balance between national and local interests more sensitive than in the area of federal aid to education, especially in rural areas (Bailey and Mosher, 1968; Berke and Kirst, 1972; Murphy, 1971). This was once a rural nation which continues to jealously guard the autonomy of its local institutions in the face of prevailing nationalizing influences, including the mass media, residential mobility, and regional disparities in wealth and in social problems. Noting that authority for education in this country has traditionally resided with the states and with local school boards, critics charge that federal regulation has increased disproportionately to the federal dollars received. A statement by Cronin (1976) addresses itself to that point, and he concludes:

> Most of the signs point to an increasingly centralized system of national education policy. This trend may, in fact, increase certain kinds of education opportunity while diminishing the traditional options of local and state governments. The junior partner is taking over the firm through sheer aggressiveness, while the senior partners fret about additional paperwork but graciously accept the extra income (p. 501).

Other observers, less nervous about federal domination, maintain that all levels of government must cooperate, not only in formulating policies but in implementing them (Reagen, 1972); that federal agencies are only one element in the total picture; and that federal influence can help equalize resources, expertise and induce local governments to perform services they could not carry on unassisted. Moreover, even as federal taxes increase, federal agencies sometimes relinquish some of their control by turning to mechanisms which in effect "debureaucratizatize" their authority, such as subcontracting and cooperative agreements with local institutions, block grants to states, reliance on citizen committees for developing policy, and so forth.

Whether further centralization of power is inevitable, and whether if it occurs, such centralization would necessarily undermine American values remain open questions. Although federal government agencies participate in many areas of local life, the programs are not generally operated by federal employees. In many instances, the power of local governments to resist federal pressure, co-opt federal agencies, and force modification of proposed guidelines is great enough to cause some observers to wonder if the federal government has perhaps lost control of its programs (Lazin, 1973; Lowi, 1969; Nagi, 1976; Van Horn and Van Meter, 1976). Indeed, where local autonomy has prevailed, it has often accentuated economic disparities, paralyzed broad-scale attacks on local problems and served as a bulwark of racial and economic oppression (Riker, 1964).

It is, thus, a matter of empirical investigation to determine who in fact holds the balance of power in any given program and with what consequences (Grodzins, 1966). This balance hinges partially on how contracts and grants are administered. As the representatives of the federal government in contact with local officials, the program officers can tip this balance and literally forge the shape of the federal-local partnership. Perhaps inadvertently, they have been thrust into positions of enormous responsibility. Yet very little is known about these people, the issues they face, and how they carry out their responsibilities. The Experimental Schools Program (ES) offered an opportunity to study various roles played by federal program officers and to gain some insights into the nature of federal-local relationships.

After a brief discussion of ES program officer backgrounds, we shall turn immediately to consider how they described their work with the ten rural school districts. Of course, all of their views cannot be accepted at face value, but I have relied heavily upon their statements when they made sense within the sociological frameworks that I have been able to apply. I have tried to avoid using statements that were not expressed by at least two sources.

The framework employed here was developed in the following way. The program officers were asked in interviews to describe both their primary responsibilities and their "styles" of working with local projects, and to elaborate by describing specific incidents. After a careful examination of the interviews, it seemed to me that the responsibilities they described clustered into three distinct roles, which I have labeled *contract manager, project advisor,* and *technical assistance specialist.* While there is always a danger that such labels will be misused as stereotypes, it seems to me that in the structure of the federal government the contract manager role is primary, the one that program officers usually *must* fill. The advisory role also may be appropriate at times, but it is less well institutionalized and not as well understood. The technical assistance role, while not unprecedented, is novel and therefore warrants much of our attention here.

After having identified those three roles in a preliminary way, I drew upon my general knowledge of the sociological literature pertaining to interaction in social systems for a set of concepts that could be used to analyze each role in more detail. While there is no one source for the four concepts that I selected, they are widely regarded by various sociologists as basic components of any social system (although not necessarily the only components). The four concepts, referred to here as "role components," are discussed later in this chapter: *intensity of role involvement, type of communication, basis of authority,* and *scope of influence.* Identifying role components in this way can help to anticipate potential role conflicts that arise when the roles are combined, and (as will be seen in Chapter X) to pinpoint conditions that must be present for these three roles to be adequately performed (Chapter XI).

THE PROGRAM OFFICERS' BACKGROUNDS

The program officers came from a variety of backgrounds, which seemed to affect the way in which they worked with the local projects. Their modal age (for five of the ten) was between 35 and

45 years. Three were 50 years old and two were between 28 and 34. Typically, they had earned a master's degree (six of the ten), but two had earned doctorates and two had a bachelor's degree or its equivalent. Only four of the ten had majored in education while in college. Others majored in humanities and social science, communication, and public administration.

As a group they were relatively inexperienced with education. Five of them had no prior teaching or school administration experience. Only two of the five who had taught mentioned prior experience with experimental educational programs. Three reported over six years of teaching experience and two reported over five years of school administration experience.

Most of the ES program officers had held jobs outside the field of education and six of them had at least a few years of experience in some specialized area such as research, planning, evaluation, or budgeting. Five had come to their positions very recently (within 12 to 18 months prior to this study). Only two had been assigned to this program for as long as three years.

In short, several of the ten program officers had little prior experience with schools or with the sensitive relationship between school administrators and school boards, and several had no training in education. Few possessed much formal knowledge of, or personal experience with, rural communities in different regions of the United States. Others had at least some experience in schools, if not with rural communities. All these individuals were thrust into demanding situations, calling for a level of expertise that could justify being treated as colleagues of experienced school administrators. Most important, they were all attempting to carry out the responsibilities of three quite different types of roles.

THREE PRIMARY ROLES[1]

I have labeled the three ways that program officers seemed to be defining their relationships with the projects as "the contract manager role," "the project advisory role," and "the technical assistance role." These roles are based on different types of authority and yield differing degrees and types of influence for the program officer. They lead to different degrees of involvement in local projects and different forms of communication. Moreover, when combined in various ways, the roles spell out at least four very different "performance styles" or distinctly different ways of relating to the projects. Each of these dimensions will be considered in sequence in the following discussion.

The Contract Manager Role

All ES program officers assumed management and supervisory responsibilities. This role is far more typical of what program officers traditionally do than the other two roles. One program officer refers to this responsibility as a routine "watchdog" role:

> I see [it] pretty much as a rote type of thing. The things that are specified in the contract . . . are carried out; the financial reports get in; the progress reports get in; the money is enough, but not too much; they request equipment when they're supposed to; and they do it in the way they're supposed to. So that's pretty much a paperwork type thing.

Speaking of this role, another program officer observes:

> . . . it's my responsibility to see that the school district does what they said they were going to do. There've been some procedures set up for that: monitoring how they are spending their money, reviewing quarterly reports, other documents that come in from the project and, from time to time, requesting documents or things that have been developed from the project, and then occasionally visiting the project to see if those things have been done. Also, requests for changes in what they want to do, and particularly when they result in changing some line item in the budget, are funneled through this office and then on to Contracts and Grants.

Types of Responsibilities. This role seems to involve two different types of responsibilities: (1) *monitoring,* which means securing information and exercising general surveillance over the project; and (2) *enforcement* of the contract provisions through corrective action where necessary, including termination of a contract or part of it. Both these responsibilities apply to the two major dimensions of any federal program: fiscal matters and program content. The program officer shares fiscal responsibilities with another federal employee, the contract officer. While the latter assumes the primary legal responsibility for all fiscal aspects of a contract, the program officer must monitor expenditures to certify that they are related to the program goals, authorize or disallow purchases, and see that the program is spending on schedule. It is his or her responsibility, as one program officer expressed it, "to make sure that what they say they're going to do in the plan is in fact given strong consideration, if not carried out."

In the ES program, each local project was required to provide for its own systematic evaluation of the project, and an outside research firm (Abt Associates) was contracted by ES/Washington to undertake systematic evaluation across all ten communities. This information potentially provided a more systematic way for ES to monitor the projects than is usually available to federal agencies through periodic reports and occasional site visits. However, for this very reason, the local school districts feared the evaluations, since an evaluation report could publicize or distort certain things and jeopardize local personnel and projects.

The contractual nature of the relationship was used by ES program officers as the basis of their enforcement responsibilities. A program officer who had prior government experience as a contracts specialist noted that once a local project is under way, it should not be allowed to change plans before they have been adequately tested and assessed:

> One of the biggest problems with educational research is that the school system would get into something, and about half way through they would decide that they really wanted to do three other things and they went off into those directions, and you never found out what happened to the first things and you ended up with nothing. You had no data that correlated. But we did not determine, unlike most federal programs, what the sites were to do. With the contract only determined the procedure that they were to use.

The contract provided some protection to local communities as well. The same program officer went on to say:

> It had the benefit to them of being a bilateral agreement. We could not unilaterally change the terms of that agreement, unlike a grant, which is a unilateral agreement on the part of the government and can be withdrawn or altered at will. Now the grantee can also refuse to go along with it and get out of it, but there is not a lot of negotiation there. A contract is much more difficult to terminate for convenience than a grant.... We didn't want program officers saying, "Instead of putting in a reading program, why don't you try math?" We both got benefits. We got the discipline, and they got the protection.

But this protection applied only to those matters which were explicitly treated. Actually, the communities agreed to several key provisions that were not well defined. For example, in principle they agreed that the project should produce "comprehensive" change, but as one program officer admits:

> We didn't necessarily think it through, as a group, and come to some sort of consensus on what the behavioral manifestations would be of what we expected. I mean, what did it actually mean to expect a comprehensive plan or expect community involvement, and how would that translate into our behavior on site?

Another source complained about the awkward position in which this placed the program officer:

> I was responsible for going over their drafts and criticizing them from some basis, which really wasn't specified—something to do with "feasibility," and whatever "comprehensiveness" was.... I looked for obvious failure to see how elements in the plan would connect with each other ... but I thought that some of the kinds of things that were vetoed by the staff here were arbitrary. And I found that I was in the middle of the situation; that I really couldn't explain to a local community why things in their plan weren't acceptable. I found that the most difficult, because I didn't think there was a firm guideline to give them.

Organizations with a hierarchical structure but an egalitarian philosophy find it difficult to innovate. Similarly supervisors in all types of organizations encounter tensions trying to reconcile their responsibilities for "initiating structure" (being a stern taskmaster) with the "consideration" role (showing a humane interest in the morale and well-being of one's subordinates). One way to resolve these tensions is for the organization to assume that the participants will simultaneously "discover" the plan of the decision makers (Kirst, 1973). One program officer gave the very strong impression to a community that it would not be funded until it independently stumbled into what ES/Washington had in mind all along. This officer gave the impression to local administrators that he knew exactly what was wanted but adamantly refused to say what it was. For example, the program officer required the community to rewrite the entire proposal, to direct it toward a local rather than a professional audience. One school board member responded, "You are the one who is going to write the plan. You know you are. Just tell us what you want. If you want it in red ink, we'll write it in red ink. If you want it in green ink, we'll write in green ink."

Importance. This managerial role was viewed by the originators of the program as important. Given the large federal commitment to this program in time and dollars, it was argued that "an unusually rigorous project monitoring system" was required (Budding, 1972). However, there was also a concern expressed that the monitoring not become a license for federal intervention, and that project support be guaranteed subject only to "gross-malfeasance in the use of public money or total abandonment of the particular attempt" (Budding, 1972).

The program officers reported numerous instances in which they found it necessary to enforce their management responsibilities, especially as the program matured. While they seldom reported taking steps to ensure contract compliance during the selection stage, such steps were reported in one-half of the situations during the negotiation and implementation periods (Appendix C, Item 1).[2] Disapproving formal requests also became very frequent (Appendix C, Item 3). Several of the program officers also report that they often advised school administrators that they were using inappropriate procedures (Appendix C, Item 2) and that the plans they were considering probably would be disapproved if submitted (Appendix C, Item 4). Although conceding that this is the conventional program officer role, most of the federal employees in this program did not really enjoy these duties. As one lamented:

> I guess I'm almost operating in the traditional program officer fashion, where you pick up the phone and say, "Your quarterly report is due"; and "Get your 5140s in"; and "You made a mistake on this form"; and that kind of crap. Well, it's fine. I have no particular quarrel with that, except I don't want to do it.

His comment suggests that this is a highly routinized role which in effect limits the program officer's discretion. However, the fact that it is a routine role does not minimize the power an officer can bring to bear on a community which fails to comply with the terms of the contract or with administrative procedures.

This underlying element of power was awkward for some program officers to deal with as indicated in the comment:

> I am uncomfortable in... that kind of authority position that some of them perceive us to be in. I don't like that feeling. I am not used to it I guess. I used to work with superintendents all the time, always working for them and that's how they viewed it and it was a good relationship. Here, I am not working for them and that's clear, they know that. It's difficult to develop that kind of relationship with those guys. They don't want to lose control, they don't want to lose power, they don't want to appear weak to us.

The Project Advisor Role

But in the ES program, management was only one aspect of the program officer's position. As one commented, "we tried to work toward a different concept of monitoring—an expanded concept." As one aspect of this new concept, the program officers felt a responsibility to help projects to be as successful as possible. In the words of one:

> ... my function is primarily to... work with the school district and insure that they come close to fulfilling that plan.... And doing that means ... serving as a gadfly at times, trying to stimulate them and pique them, and keeping them from becoming complacent, by looking at the district— through their reporting cycle and from site visits—finding areas of weakness and pointing them out to the project people.

As another explained this role:

> [It] actually involves closer contact with the district in a more aggressive way; building relationships with people within the project; digging into what they are doing—more than just a sort of surface monitoring.... [Instead we] ask questions, like "Why did you choose to do it in this particular way?" "Had you ever thought about this or that?" "What other alternatives did you consider?" and that's not always in retrospect; that's in advance of decisions being made.

Raising pointed questions may be an important part of this role:

> Trying to see whether questions had been asked about how receptive a group of, say, teachers, would be to a change; or whether there were facilities for carrying it out, or some kind of back-up; just generally,

whether it was practical, and whether it was an obvious attempt to meet existing needs that were kind of piecemeal and fitted together without going to the first stage of developing a rationale.

One program officer described the role in this way:

> Well, let's take this problem... 30% of the children in the elementary grades are not reading, writing and spelling and doing arithmetic at grade level, at the end of grade six. Then we come up with some goals and we then say, "Five years from now, all the children in the elementary grades will now have improved. We teach now in a self-contained classroom, so we are going to put in team teaching. And in five years the school will all be changed." Well then, the role for me was to say, "How are you going to do that? Doesn't the change take 12 years?" So that you become involved in the way they planned.... That is, "If your budget permits only x number of aides and x number of technical assistants, what could you seriously accomplish in five years' time?"

Sometimes, the "advice" amounted to little more than providing encouragement to local officials to follow up their own tentative ideas:

> I don't know that these are really recommendations on my part. These are things that I pick up, either from visits or from reports, that they would like to do. For example, with the library [component]... what I did was simply to write them asking questions: "How is this coming along?" "Are you still interested in it?"

Types of Responsibilities.   This role is obviously very complex. A key to the difference between it and contract management is that the program officer becomes more directly concerned about the *substance* of the local project and tries to assist in shaping its direction and working out its problems. This requires greater personal initiative and discretion on the part of the program officer. In the words of one program officer, the role "can range from serving as a sounding board for what they're thinking about to suggesting some things that they need to do or consider in terms of the plan that they have spelled out." Or, it may mean, "holding a mirror up for them to see, or holding their feet to the fire if that's the case. Or, in some cases it's persuading them to back off from a process they're using or a direction they're going." Another program officer thought of it as *interpreting* the government's interest in the project to the local community, to remind them of the original objectives, and to encourage the project personnel to consider more than one way of proceeding. But to simplify, it seems to include at least four different types of diagnostic and prescriptive responsibilities:

- *Interpretation,* that is, translating the language used in the contract into operational criteria, for example, determining whether or not a reading program for only three grades satisfies the requirement that the change must be "comprehensive";
- *Challenge,* or prodding local officials to justify their plans and actions and to provide a rationale;
- *Criticism,* or finding fault with particular aspects of the project and making judgments;
- *Recommendations,* that is, proposing one or more alternative courses of action to be considered.

Importance. As the program matured, the program officers became more aggressive about suggesting solutions to implementation problems and exerting influence on specific implementation procedures (Appendix C, Item 10). However, this influence appears to have been limited to implementation procedures. They rarely claimed to have proposed a component of the project plan that was later implemented (even though they may have participated in the discussions) (Appendix C, Item 13). Perhaps aside from a few instances, they also denied having had much influence on the design or goals of local projects (Appendix C, Items 11 and 13). Moreover, they reported that, as the program had evolved, local administrators typically came to them for advice (Appendix C, Item 14). Except during the selection stage, they felt free to offer criticisms and advice whether it was solicited or not (Appendix C, Item 30), and typically they believed that administrators tried to implement their advice (Appendix C, Item 12), apparently even when it was not solicited.

The program officers generally enjoyed this role and considered it to be very important. As one summarized, "We came [to ES/Washington] because that was to be our role. [We were] to be active persons working with the sites." One program officer saw his role as:

... a major step toward eradicating this traditional "dragon" of federal relationships with the local people. What I mean by that is that by being more visible and more accessible to them, especially the community, it would allow for their looking at the federal government with other than a jaundiced eye. What I'm talking about here is that there must be an authentic relationship forged between the local people and the federal government. Because most of what I have seen has been a kind of inauthentic role in that the federal government... to most people represents a pot of money; and a community can't understand, for example, why we can't just give out the money and then leave.... I think by being out there often, being visible and letting them observe what you are doing, telling them what your role is all about, they begin to see that there are different kinds of governmental relationships with the private sector. It begins to dispel some of the myths about federal procurement [in the minds of] local people.

The Technical Assistance Role

In the advisory capacity, the program officers were generally concerned about project *design*. The problem remained that, even if the program officers' advice were accepted in principle, it could not be *implemented* properly unless the local community had the necessary technical capacity. If either the local officials or the program officer doubted this capacity, he or she might offer (or be invited to provide) some of this assistance. Thus program officers became involved in *implementation*. As a former ES director explained, "What's a program officer supposed to do? One argument is that he is supposed to respond to the call for help." A program officer confided, "Having had experience with schools my whole professional career, I can't help but see some things that I'm interested in where I've got some expertise, and I really don't hesitate to offer it if I'm asked, and in some cases even if I'm not."

One of the persons interviewed described his role this way:

[Suppose] they had decided what they wanted to do. But they said, "Say, I am not sure how; what would be the things we would have to do in order to do that?" Then we would all sit down and roll up our sleeves and take a yellow pad, and we'd sort of brain storm and maybe come up with a strategy together. At least in my case, all the deciding would be theirs.

Another, who spent much of his time in this role, explained:

> ... my role became that type of a program officer who came in and actually rolled up his sleeves and went to work with the project, to examine plans that they were developing and to look over the data that they had gathered and make suggestions and serve as a kind of a "friend of the court."

When the program officers assumed this role, they thought of themselves as colleagues, or partners in a common enterprise. One refers to it as an "interactive" role:

> I take my role to be a partner in an experiment, and while I may be a silent partner in a sense that I don't actually do the work, I certainly am involved in the project.... I stay out of the actual decision making, in the sense that the operation of the project is theirs; it's not the federal government's and they're responsible for delivering the product or contract. But nevertheless, if I see, in my judgment, that they're putting themselves into jeopardy, I consider it my responsibility to point that out. And if they continue to do it, then fine, that's their decision.

Types of Responsibilities. At least three types of responsibility seem to be part of this role:

- Actually working on *implementation;* for instance, interviewing candidates for jobs on local projects, or modifying an evaluation design;
- *Brokering* for technical advice, that is, acting as a go-between to suggest consultants whom the local project should hire to provide certain types of advice;
- *Advocacy,* or in other words, occasionally representing the local project's interests to the federal bureaucracy; that is, intervening in a dispute between a local community and the federal contracts office to support the project's request to purchase a questionable item or to deviate from established procedure.

Regarding the latter responsibility, after the projects became operational, most of the program officers reported having helped local administrators obtain approval for changes in their contracts. As one program officer recalled:

We spent a lot of time... trying to identify some of the areas in which the bureaucracy could, in fact, get in the way [and] hinder the involvement of a smaller school district who didn't have years and years of experience of dealing directly with the federal government. I'm sure [the local officials]... didn't understand it because they didn't see all... the interference that had been taken care of before the fact. In fact, one program officer thought of herself as a "double agent."

Importance.   The technical assistance role became more prominent as the projects became operational (Appendix C, Item 5). In fact, it was typical. Most program officers reported that they often performed this function. In about half of the instances during the implementation stage, their help was solicited, but in many cases there was apparently no clear invitation (Appendix C, Item 13). Much of their assistance was to help local administrators formulate or clarify their plans (Appendix C, Item 7).

Not surprisingly, some program officers devoted a large portion of their time to technical assistance:

[The largest part of my job] is being on the phone (I'd say maybe three hours a week) with the site, talking with building principals; for example, discussing the degree of implementation... trying to find out what areas they need help on, or if I can get somebody to help them with their technical assistance.

In one case, recently, I was talking to somebody who's developing a native American program, and I have been trying to put him in touch with people, giving him references to materials and that sort of thing; and then also with the central office in helping them to prepare financial budgets and to do financial planning for the year and the quarters individually... so, I would say that technical assistance is the largest aspect of my function.

But, while most of the program officers might have enjoyed this role, and some of them spent much of their time on it, at least one had reservations about its legitimacy; "I enjoy the idea of technical assistance, of just sitting down and rolling up my sleeves and getting into it, but I don't see that as much as a legitimate role."

ROLE PROFILES

Each role described in the preceding section contains the potential to forge very different federal-local relationships. Exactly how different can be more fully appreciated by comparing the "components" of each role. I have identified four components which seem to differentiate among roles: type of communication, intensity of involvement, basis of authority, and scope of influence.[3] They are not entirely independent, but it will be useful for our purposes here to consider each component separately.

Type of Communication

The *management* role is based on, and circumscribed by, the *contract* which formally defines rights and obligations in a hierarchical relationship.

By contrast, the *technical assistance* role casts a collegial relationship which is less explicitly formalized and circumscribed than the managerial role. It permits the program officer to exercise much more discretion in determining how his or her influence will be exerted. Decisions are made on the basis of feedback and mutual adjustment. Accordingly, the program officer's actions will be less predictable.

The *advisory role* overlaps with the other two roles, blending the *contractual* with the *collegial* styles. Therefore, responsibilities in this role shift fluidly, and the parties involved often are confused about their respective rights and obligations.

Intensity of Involvement

The degree to which the program officer becomes involved with the details of implementation also differs among the roles. Remote forms of supervision suffice for the managerial role, for example, periodic review of progress and adherence to standard schedules. This supervisory style seldom provides the program officer with enough detailed information for him to provide much assistance with implementation.

At the other extreme, technical assistance requires the program officer to collect detailed knowledge about the day-to-day operations of the project, which puts him in a position to affect local planning.

To be an effective critic and advisor, the officer needs more information than is typically available to a manager, but less than would be required to provide adequate technical assistance. In

Figure IX.1 Types of System Linkage:
Communication and Intensity of Involvement

Type of Communication	Intensity of Involvement With Implementation	
	High	Low
Contractual	Contract Specialist*	Contract Manager
Collegial	Technical Assistance Specialist	Project Advisor

Note:
*The Contract Specialist type of linkage was not present in the ES program. However, it can be found in the large "hardware" oriented programs, such as in NASA where very detailed specifications govern the relationship. The Contract Specialists in such programs oversee specific components which they must understand in detail; yet they are not able to have an impact on program implementation once the specifications have been established.

combination, these first two dimensions begin to describe the four roles portrayed in Figure IX.1.

Basis of Authority

The authority of the program officer to *manage* the contract is inherent in his or her *formal position* in the federal bureaucracy, which is in turn governed by legislation and standard administrative procedures. But for his *technical advice* to be accepted, the program officer must convince local officials that he or she has the necessary training and experience, that is, *technical competence*. Again, the right to act as an advisor overlaps with the two roles. To some extent this right is inherent in the position, but it also presumes a necessary level of technical competence. And again, this role can be confusing in particular instances, especially if the program officer does not have the necessary competence.

Scope of Influence

Having the authority to exert influence, however, is not the same thing as actually *being* influential. One may have more or less influence than either the position or one's competence might warrant. Influence differs from the other components mentioned in that it is not inherent in particular roles. Influence is a product of many forces in addition to one's role, including the individual's initiative and the other person's will and ability to resist. A program officer can be influential in any of the roles, but the role does circumscribe the *scope* of his influence, that is, the number of different aspects of a project the program officer can affect.

As a contract manager, a program officer can virtually control whether the project will survive, or whether the contract can be altered. Such decisions can affect the entire project. By contrast, because the capacity of program officers to give competent advice is limited by their own specialized backgrounds, they tend to concentrate on particular components of a project when they act in an advisory capacity. Their advice is therefore likely to affect fewer aspects of a project than their actions as contract managers; as managers they are responsible for seeing that all components of a project are successfully completed, even those for which they do not have expertise. The scope of influence afforded by the advisory role is therefore indeterminant, and probably depends to a great extent on the program officer's interests and competence.

The same logic applies to technical assistance. But because technical assistance is even more time-consuming than offering ad-

Figure IX.2. Types of System Linkage: Scope of Influence and Basis of Authority

	Basis of Authority		
Potential Scope of Influence	Formal Position	Position and Competence	Personal Competence
Broad	Contract Manager		
Intermediate		Project Advisor	
Focused			Technical Assistance Specialist

Figure IX.3. System Linkage Profiles

Role Components	Linkage Roles		
	Contract Manager	Project Advisor	Technical Assistance Specialist
Intensity of Role Involvement	Low	High	Very High
Type of Communication	Contractual	Collegial and Contractual	Collegial
Basis of Authority	Formal Position	Position and Competence	Personal Competence
Scope of Influence	Broad	Intermediate	Focused

vice, program officers advise on more components of a project than they can possibly take the time to work on in a technical way themselves. The scope of their influence in this role is extremely limited.

By combining these two components, authority and scope of influence, the three roles can be further specified as indicated in Figure IX.2. The blank cells in the figure suggest some potential conflict situations. For example, a contract manager whose authority resides in his official position might expect some criticism if he or she seems to be preoccupied with one aspect of the project to the neglect of its other features (the Formal Position—Focused Scope cell). And a program officer's credibility as an expert will be questioned if that person acts like a "jack of all trades" by volunteering advice about too many components of a project (the Personal Competence—Broad Scope cell).

The three roles can be summarized in terms of the profiles outlined in Figure IX.3.

BACKGROUNDS RELATED TO OPINIONS AND ROLES

In view of the differences in their backgrounds (noted at the beginning of this chapter) it is not surprising that program officers express widely different opinions about some aspects of the local projects and about their own roles.

Differences in Perceptions and Opinions

On the question of whether local administrators were well qualified to direct the projects to which the program officers had been assigned, their answers ranged from "strongly disagree" to "agree" (see Appendix C, Item 18).[4] On the question of how frequently they had been helpful to these local projects, their answers ranged from "seldom" to "very frequently," but typically they judged the situation as "mixed."

There were comparable variations in the priority the ES program officers gave to the various roles. Two program officers reported that they seldom exercised their management responsibilities, but several others said they often found themselves in this role. Then, too, one program officer reported providing technical assistance very frequently and two others provided it often, whereas another seldom provided it. The others reported mixed situations.

The frequency with which they provided advice that influenced implementation varied from "seldom" to "often," but typically the situation was "mixed." They seldom advised on goals, but there was at least one exception; one program officer said that he often gave advice on goals. One program officer said that he was often solicited for advice or technical assistance, but several others said that they were seldom asked.

Relationship of Backgrounds to Roles

These differences can be explained to some degree by the backgrounds of the program officers. Though respondents are few in number, some crude correlations among their responses provide clues (Appendix D summarizes the measures used). There was a tendency for those who had taught longer to believe that they had been more helpful ($r = .91$), and for those who had spent more time in specialized work to have a lower estimate of their helpfulness ($r = -.82$). Those with more teaching ($r = -.75$) and more administrative experience ($r = -.84$) also had lower estimates of the competence of the local administrators to direct this kind of project.

Those who had taught in more schools tended to stress the technical assistance role (r = .62) and to neglect the managerial role (r = −.85). It may be significant, however, that teaching experience did not seem to be related to the amount of advice given about either implementation or goals, and if it was related to specialized work the correlation was negative. Nor was any of these roles related to the type of degree a program officer held or her or his major field in college. One reason may be that when some of them were hired during the early years of the ES program, there was no plan for them to offer technical assistance.

Each of these two-variable relationships was graphed for the eight program officers who supplied all requested information. A careful examination of these graphs revealed that the one program officer who provided the most technical assistance also had several years of teaching experience and had taught in several schools; it is also clear that the two who provided the least assistance had little teaching experience. But these graphs also revealed something that seems equally significant. At least one program officer who frequently provided technical assistance had little teaching experience; likewise one with teaching experience provided little assistance.

The individual who provided the most technical assistance also paid the least attention to the managerial responsibilities, but for most of the program officers this trade-off was not quite so extreme. The two persons who placed the most stress on the managerial role both had several years of teaching experience.

The relationship between teaching experience and technical assistance paralleled what has been said about the relationship between experience and implementation. However, one person did have far less influence on implementation than would have been predicted from his behavior in the technical assistance role.

The program officer who had the most influence on implementation also had the most influence on goals; similarly, at the other extreme, one person ranked low on both of these measures. But another individual who had a high degree of influence on implementation reported very little influence on goals; in still another case, this pattern was reversed.

SUMMARY

The ES program officers expressed varied opinions and held somewhat different perceptions about their relationships with local officials. They also came from a variety of backgrounds. Some had prior experience as employees of local school districts, while others did not. Few were well prepared to work with the type of rural communities involved in the program. They were all thrust into demanding situations in which they were attempting to carry out the simultaneous responsibilities of three different types of roles.

Those program officers who had taught longer and in more schools tended to believe they had been more helpful, whereas those who had spent more time in specialized work tended to have a lower estimate of their helpfulness. Those with more teaching and more administrative experience also had lower estimates of the competence of the local administrators to direct their projects. Some of them also tended to stress the technical assistance role and to neglect their managerial responsibilities.

It may be significant, however, that teaching experience did not seem to be related to the amount of advice given about either implementation or goals, and if it was related to specialized experience, the correlation was negative. Nor was any of these roles related to the type of degree a program officer held, or his academic major in college.

One way to gain better insight into the roles, now that they have been described abstractly, is to speculate about how a program officer might respond to a local project that is behind schedule and having difficulty implementing some of its components. One can imagine three different scenarios corresponding to the different roles available to the program officer. Let us say, for example, the project has not been able to develop an adequate evaluation plan as called for by its contract. As a contract manager, a program officer might respond like this. First, the program officer might remind the local project director of the original deadlines, and then perhaps call for an investigation. Subsequently, the officer might either negotiate new deadlines or terminate the project. If he or she ventures any recommendations, they probably will be limited to the parameters of the contract itself, for example, that the project scale back its goals, increase its staff, or request funds to provide for more outside help. The officer also might be inclined to entertain a request from the local project director to reduce the scope of work statement or increase the size of the budget. In all of these respects, his or her posture remains rather remote from the details of the project itself.

But in the advisory role, the program officer becomes more aggressive and concerned about finding the source of the project's problems so that they can be corrected. She or he will try to become more familiar with project activities, staff capabilities, and any constraints that might be present within the school district. With this information, one might volunteer advice about how the project could cope with its problems. S/he might evaluate the materials being used and suggest the names of consultants who should be called in. The officer might recommend that the school district should reassign personnel or hire new personnel. He or she might help them to reinterpret the meaning of evaluation in this particular situation, or to elaborate on what does and does not meet the agency's requirements. S/he might evaluate, criticize, and challenge the project plans, pointing out weaknesses or unfeasible designs. In short, the program officer takes an active interest in the substance of the project, recommending alternative courses of action.

In the technical assistance role, the program officer becomes even more involved with the details of selected project activities. He or she may spend days working with local project members helping to redesign a component or to develop new materials; he may help the district locate and interview new personnel, or may procure technical consultants for the district and, if it seems advisable, work out the details necessary to increase the scope of the contract. If it is necessary to renegotiate the budget, the program officer might help the district with that task and then take the case to his superiors, acting as representative and advocate for the local project.

The complexity of these roles can be better understood by considering the several components of each. It was shown that differences among the roles are matters of degree and that they differ in at least four respects: the intensity of the program officer's involvement in the project, the type of communication with the project, the basis of the program officer's authority, and the scope of his or her influence. Each role consists of a profile of these four component variables. When these components are considered one by one we can begin to anticipate role conflicts that could arise when components are combined in inappropriate ways and identify the conditions that must be present for each role to be performed adequately.

But of course, we have thus far been describing analytic distinctions. In practice program officers combine these roles in various ways. The way they mix the roles determines their *performance style,* that is their manner of working with local projects. The various styles they used will be illustrated in the following chapter.

NOTES

1. Portions of this section have been adapted from Corwin (1982).

2. Occasionally throughout this discussion, reference is made to the way program officers answered some questionnaire items. All items referred to are listed in Appendix C. The percentages cited are based on the number of *observations* they made, not on the absolute number of program officers. This is because several program officers completed a separate questionnaire for each site for which she or he was responsible. The percentages reflect the number of observations made by the ten program officers at each stage of the ten projects. Note too that different program officers were usually involved at different stages of the project.

3. Distinctions are being made here among influence, scope of influence, and intensity of involvement. *Influence* refers to the probability that directives or suggestions will be carried out; if that probability is high it can be called "control" rather than influence. The *scope* of influence refers to the number of different aspects of a project that are affected. By comparison, intensity of involvement implies the (1) *potential* to influence (2) *specific* aspects of a project. For example, providing technical assistance in the area of evaluation, a program officer *can* influence the evaluation plan (if his advice is accepted). But if that is the only aspect of the project that he affects, his scope of influence remains limited.

4. Between two and four program officers answered items specific to each site. For purposes of this analysis, the responses of program officers were summed and averaged for each site. Also all project stages have been combined. However, one officer assigned to two sites did not answer this portion of the questionnaire.

Chapter X

Performance Styles

Given the range and complexity of the three roles, ES program officers could use their own discretion in deciding how much emphasis should be given to each of their various responsibilities. They adopted very different performance styles, depending on the way the roles were mixed. To simplify, I will concentrate here on only two stylistic features that help to account for some of these differences:

- The amount of directiveness exercised by the program officer;
- The program officer's involvement with, and sensitivity to, the local project's problems and values.

These two dimensions identify four types of styles outlined in Figure X.1.

FOUR STYLES

The Uninvolved and Directive Style

This style evolved when managerial and advisory roles were combined. The program officers felt uneasy with this style, but acknowledged that they did use it. In the words of one program officer:

Figure X.1. Performance Styles

Involvement in Project	Directiveness	
	Directive	Nondirective
Involved	Involved and Directive	Involved and Nondirective
Uninvolved	Uninvolved and Directive	Uninvolved and Nondirective

> I have had the experience where it has been a strictly very formal type of relationship. I'm "the government," and I come in and they have to listen; and they know that; and they do. But they don't go any further than that.

Another program officer observes:

> There are [program officers] who are strong interventionists, and who have a fixed idea about the projects and what the projects should achieve, and who set out to make them do that. That's certainly one school of project monitorship. And they may have more immediate effect. [But] I don't believe that that kind of thing is going to contribute to long-range change in the district.... A design is imposed on a community, and... at the end of the fourth year of that project, I find people rebelling and saying, "For Christ's sake, this isn't our work—this is ES coming in here and imposing the design on us."

The Involved and Directive Style

Program officers might also adopt a very different style by combining the managerial role with the technical assistance role. When they did this, they could remain directive, even over project operations, but they operated from a better knowledge base, and hence greater sensitivity to local interests and concerns. One program officer's comments suggest some elements of this style:

When something wasn't working well, I would say, "Look, that particular component just hasn't got off the ground! Why is that?" Then he would volunteer a few things, and I would say, "Well, okay; do we still need that component, or is that just something on paper in the plan? If you still feel it is a worthwhile component, then you had better get some specific objectives. So, why don't we do that? Together we'll think through that, and then you submit to me a management plan by such and such a date...." There were times when I did give directions: "You will by such and such a date have interviewed the following; by such and such a date you will have selected your local evaluators, or else we cannot release the funds." But I never felt I was threatening or hostile.

One source reported that a fellow program officer:

... often found himself siding against the superintendent in front of the board.... I am not very comfortable with [his] type [of intervention] where you go into the school board and fight for what you think is right.

In one long, hard bargaining session, the above program officer was determined to cut items out of the budget but the director of the local project fought hard to keep them in. The program officer's position was that because the school system was having difficulty passing budgets, it should start scaling down its expenditures years in advance of the end of federal funding if voters were ever to pick up the costs. When two instructional leaders left their jobs, the program officer insisted that their positions should be eliminated. After long negotiations, one position was eliminated, despite the resistance of other school officials.

Note that "directiveness," in this context, means only that the program officers had a point of view and a clear idea about the preferred outcome. They could be directive in very subtle or even unintended ways. One program officer who referred to his style as "Aristotelian," suggests how pressure can be subtly applied:

I rarely give a direct order to the projects. I rarely give a long monologue unless I am really moved to, and I rarely do that. I usually try to arrive at things through questions, asking them questions, leading them. And I know that's what I am doing, and I have to assume that they know that too, leading them down a particular path. I usually have an idea of where I want them to end up.

Even more frequent were instances when a program officer's

suggestions were interpreted as being directive even if that was not the intent:

> And you may say something that you don't think is directive at all, and it may be taken that way because, in fact, you're a representative from Washington.

The Involved and Nondirective Style

This is the interactive, collegial relationship that most program officers idealized. It is the epitome of the technical assistance role, often mixed with certain responsibilities from the advisory role. One respondent described this role as she recalled how a colleague had worked with local communities:

> And she was able to give some very concrete, helpful, suggestions. But she never force-fed anybody. She would not say, "I think you should use this approach." It was much more, "Have you looked into this? And have you investigated this kind of curriculum?" My experience with her was that... she tried very hard not to tell people what to do.

Another program officer explains that he approached a project like this:

> If I spend time talking with the building principals, I try to find ways to encourage them to get involved with the project, because I really think that when you get to be a building principal in a community like this, there's very little incentive to bring about change. And I've worked with them, asking them, "Would you go to this meeting and then tell me what happened," and "Why don't you invite people into the schools, parents to come into the schools, and visit with you?" I think that I've had some significant impact.

Local people in one community reputedly appreciated one program officer who was regarded as being very honest, not pulling any punches and "calling a spade a spade." He had high credibility in a part of the country that traditionally respects that kind of behavior.

Program officers often stressed the importance of becoming sufficiently involved with the project to understand the community's power structure and to become sensitive to its problems and values. One source emphasized this quality as he favorably described a colleague:

[She] was quick to pick up the nuances that made small schools different from suburban and city schools and to play, not on their weaknesses, but to play on their strengths.

But for various reasons program officers sometimes failed to live up to this ideal. For example, one program officer was described as extremely "aggressive, officious, and threatening." Some principals reported they were outraged when she visited with teachers in a lounge without first notifying the principal that she was in the building.

One program officer is very critical of a colleague who was insensitive to local norms:

She tended to be kind of an abrasive, liberated kind of a woman. And she used foul language, and in that community, their women don't talk like that. They may be ranchers and farmers and miners, but they don't expect to hear that kind of thing. ... Basically, she tended to be domineering, demanding and "I the government." "You must do this because I represent the government." She was very condescending to the people, and generally they felt that she was looking down her nose at them.

In another instance:

[One community] has a luncheon counter. That's it. If you want to eat out, you go there; it's a little diner. And it was run by this woman and her husband, and evidently this program officer didn't feel that she was being served properly, and started yelling at the woman about sexism; about how she was waiting on all the men first; and she not only yelled at the woman, but went back in the kitchen and lectured her husband. That left a lot of bad feelings. Not only in the schools themselves, but in the communities.

Another program officer concluded more generally that:

With [two] exception[s], there was no one [among the program officers] who ever really knew rural America. There was an outpouring of feeling, a sincerity of interest; there was even a high degree of romanticism; but I don't think these people understood the environment and mores of the communities. They were just out of the mainstream.

The Uninvolved and Nondirective Style

By carefully selecting only a few aspects of the advisory role, program officers could sometimes remain both uninvolved and nondirective. Elements of this style are reflected in one program officer's comments:

> I never tried to force a district to do anything. I figured that if we can't talk about it and work out the directions between us, it probably shouldn't be done (whatever it is) because it's their district anyway.

Another elaborated:

> This is a design that's locally initiated, and I consequently do not like to put extraordinary amounts of pressure on them from Washington. I don't like the idea of Experimental Schools sort of seeming to be an imposed project and to bat them over the head with it. I think that's self-defeating, and I think it also interrupts the research design that we are theoretically trying to test.

In at least one case, this style was carried to its logical extreme, as reported by a program officer who didn't like it:

> There was another style, which was to simply do nothing. The practitioner of that style has now left the office. And that is just as bad, in my estimation, as the strong interventionist. Because in the one site where this was the case, that site was not visited for a year; and the reports weren't read; and they weren't critiqued; and we had absolutely no understanding of what was going on at that site. As a result now, in my estimation, that project is nothing. I don't even think there is a project.

VARIATIONS IN THE USE OF STYLES

Particular program officers were closely identified with one or another performance style. But these styles represent more than descriptions of individual behavior. They denote types of behavior that vary according to a number of conditions other than personal inclination including: (1) the persons in the district with whom the program officer was working, (2) the program officer's expertise, (3) the type of community, (4) the changing political context of the federal program, (5) support within the federal bureaucracy, and (6) the type of legal relationship.

The People Involved

There are indications that the officer's style depended upon the issues and the local people with whom he or she was working. For example, one program officer reported that when the issue concerned a district-wide component, she tended to be more directive with the school principals than with the superintendents, because principals were used to taking directions (from the central administration) about district-wide matters. However, she was less directive with the same principals when the issue was specific to the school, where they were used to some autonomy. The relationship then became more collegial because the principals felt more self-confident in these matters.

The Program Officer's Expertise

A program officer who felt particularly competent in an area might be more inclined to intervene:

> The first time I saw any of the products, I was really taken back, because I thought they'd gotten bum advice from a consultant.... So I discussed this with the superintendent and criticized much of what I saw in the way of the [materials] the teachers had developed. The superintendent went back with this consultant, reworked in-service and spent maybe the last year in trying to improve the quality of those things. I think they're making some progress.... I suppose that if I had never had any experience with [this material] myself, I wouldn't have known a good one from a bad one.

Sophistication and Values of the Community

Some program officers said that they deliberately used different styles with different types of communities. Several factors were involved. One was the community's prior experience with federal agencies:

> The fact that came out very strongly was how much relationship the districts had had with the federal government before and how they felt about it. It seemed to absolutely color relationships from the beginning, and a lot of times that was the major thing to change or to work with.

Another person elaborated:

> There's something that's really different about my experiences with the rural districts as compared to working with the street academies, for example. For the street academies... know that whatever I say is only suggestion, and half of what I do say they discount anyway, I think. They're urbanized, and they're used to dealing with the federal government. A lot

of the rural people really aren't. There's a constant fear out there, I think, that I control the budget, that I control their money, and therefore, that they've got to pay attention.

He adds that:

Some rural communities also are more sophisticated than others about the government. I have one project in the North, one in sort of mid-America and one in the far South, and the degree of sophistication rises the further north you get. [The northern community] is just a much easier place to deal with, because there aren't so many other agendas going on, it seems. We can speak much more plainly. They can say no, flat out and not worry about it. In [the southern community], on the other hand, just about everything I say, they try to do something about.

Another program officer concurs:

Each site is different in the way you go in and the way you work. I don't think I'd try to be nearly as strong in _____ as I am in _____. In [the latter community], they'll challenge you more. That's good. I enjoy that.... In [the other community] you don't always know whether they've thought it through, or are only doing it because you seem to want it.

Another factor was the program officer's sensitivity to the local value system. Some communities seemed to take more pride in their small size and rural traditions than others. Some of the Westerners, in particular, seemed especially suspicious of the "bureaucrats from the East" (see Messerschmidt, 1979). In some instances, local officials were more resentful toward what they regarded as the federal officer's abrasive, condescending, or insulting attitudes than specific disputes that arose over money or procedures.

Another important factor affecting performance style is the assumptions the program officer made about the community's expertise. In the absence of a clear sense of what "comprehensiveness" meant, for example, local officials were forced to assume the burden of defining their project as they put it into operation. When a community did not have planning specialists who were prepared for this responsibility, the program officers became more directive in trying to fill the void. Nor did they believe that most local administrators involved were well qualified to direct a comprehensive change effort (Appendix C, Item 18). Even during the later implementation stage, in less than half of the observations made by program officers did they fully agree that local people were either committed or qualified to undertake it. And typically they were divided about whether local people agreed on objectives and procedures (Appendix C, Items 15 and 16):

> The weakness is that a lot of those communities knew the right words, knew the right way to put it all on a piece of paper, but they had no idea (even if they believed in it) of, say how you develop a curriculum. You don't do it in the summer, you don't do it overnight, you don't do it in a workshop, you don't do it over a weekend. That may be a three- to five-year process, and I'm not talking about the whole curriculum—I mean a piece or a subject area or a grade level.

Someone else, a program officer with extensive experience in contract management, adds:

> Basically, the systems themselves didn't have any facility, or expertise, for pricing. With possibly two or three exceptions their books are kept by women with open ledgers. Some of them are little old ladies; some of them are young girls. They don't have any sophistication whatsoever. They keep their books by object line, often for entire districts. Most of them felt they were terribly put upon.

This individual blames the legal structure in public education for this situation:

> I think it's because they don't have to be accountable. Who are they accountable to? They all work for lay school boards who don't have any way of judging whether they are getting more or less education for their dollar. They certainly don't have to be responsible to the general public, the taxpayer. How do they know what's happening? They elect the board, right. The board doesn't have any way of judging. So who are they accountable to?

One source lamented:

> They may have some ideas... but... they just don't know how to get them out on a table, gain consensus, and put them down in objective form; [or how to] develop activities to accomplish them, and to work out a budget to deal with them.

But lack of experience and expertise were only part of the problem. The plain fact is that the program officers and local officials were often suspicious of one another's motives and commitment to the project. During the early stages of the program, few program officers considered the local officials to be highly committed to comprehensive change (Appendix C, Item 17). The program officers probably had some reason to be suspicious. Federal officials often complain that local officials are interested in federal money, but not in the programs (Pressman, 1975). Local officials tend to use ongoing projects as a means of financing new or recurring concerns that are only loosely related to the original plan. This lack of trust was an important factor in how the program officer chose to (or could) deal with the project. One officer, for example, felt compelled to keep a close watch on a project because that school district often would pretend to be implementing a reading program, for example, when it was actually using some of the money to repair the basketball court.

One program officer expressed her suspicion that:

> The federal money to most school systems is the goal, OK? They write in and get their money, and they take it and they do what they want, and nobody ever holds them accountable and nobody ever comes in and checks to see if they spent it well or badly or whatever.

Another made demands on a local project for documentation because of his lack of trust:

> For the most part [we have to assume] that the potential is high that everybody may burn us, and we had better safeguard against that rather than the reverse.

One source elaborated:

> ... The superintendents come into the projects with different reasons than we attribute to them. Because, we are operating from this end and they're operating from that end, and consequently what they see is their needs. What they see as legitimate and moral and ethical ways to spend money may not coincide with ours, and may not coincide with our legal ways.

Some of this mistrust was apparently reciprocated by local officials, who it seems may have had reason to doubt federal officers. One person who was interviewed laments:

> At the moment, there is almost no reason for the local community to trust the federal government. They're confused about our inclinations; they're

confused about our staff assignments; they're confused about our organization; they're confused about personnel; they're confused about direction. We present a chaotic picture.

As Etzioni (1961) has stressed, the members' level of involvement in a program will influence the type of control exercised. If local officials are morally and emotionally *committed* to the program objectives, a nondirective and involved style may work effectively. On the other hand, if they are hostile or *alienated* from the program, the program officer will probably be more inclined to use, say, a highly directive and uninvolved style. But in many cases the local officials are simply being *calculative,* that is, participating in the program for the financial and other benefits to be derived. In this case the program officer will feel compelled to exercise close surveillance (involvement) over the contract and to become very directive in order to protect the agency's interest.

The Political Context

There seems to be little doubt that the program officer's choice of performance style reflected changes in the prevailing political climate in Washington. In response to the suspicion and criticism that, as noted previously, was being leveled on ES by NIE Managers, it appears that the first Experimental Schools' director became more suspicious and demanding of local projects and more directive in his relationships with them. He challenged his staff to uncover potential problems to head off possible criticisms, and they in turn became aggressive toward local officials. In the course of all of this, the director reportedly became hostile towards officials in several communities, humiliating them on more than one occasion when he perceived that they were not fulfilling their obligations to the program. Firestone (1979) reports that:

> At one point, the first director's abrasive questioning of the school board member about technical jargon buried in the district's plan reduced her to tears. After that day, the superintendent and the counselor sat up most of the night trying to revise the plan (p. 23).

Forced by the climate in Washington to reinterpret the original guidelines and maintain close surveillance over the local projects to assure outcomes that would justify the program, the first ES director described the bind in which he found himself:

The early arguments were... give the money to the communities. That's it. And if they burn it, or blow it, have a big party, or whatever they do, it's their money. However I think it's fair to say that in 1970 the emphasis of the federal bureaucracy was on carrying out some explicit program... not being creative.... Be sure that you're successful.... You go into it with the idea that it was experimental, but that's a concept that I'm learning is impossible to sell to an elected official, who must go back afterwards to his constituents after his second year and say, "Yes, I didn't waste any money." And somebody says, "Well, what about the $600,000 that they blew in _____?... What did they do with that money?"... So, the idea of "experiment" was ludicrous. The experiment was only that by the time [the community] got through all the hurdles to get the money, the experiment was going to be successful; that was the last criteria. That's why you were funded, because you would look like a winner, and not (which I think is more correct) if you get one out of ten winners, that's not bad.

When the program officers were directive, it was often because they themselves were being supervised this way. Speaking of the director, one officer observed:

He was viewed as a person who felt that it was important that these projects succeed, and you had to have either some answers or explanations, or at least a thought about what the difficulties were in the projects and how you could help them overcome them; or how, or what types of things could be done to get them to overcome some of these difficulties and move forward.

When asked whether the program officers at that time agreed with this style, or instead just went along because of the pressure, one replied:

Well, they never fully agreed with it.... Program officers were pretty much straightforward with the districts, except when they were directly told, "This is going to be your agenda when you get on site." Then, there was no way to avoid it without being insubordinate.

But the first director was backed into a corner. For, it was not possible to lean on the communities for long without trespassing on local control and provoking the wrath of local school boards. Perhaps partly because of the complaints from local officials in several communities, he was replaced in December 1974. The new director allowed the program officers more autonomy to adopt the style that was most comfortable to them personally; that is, to the extent that some program officers had been forced to be directive in order to satisfy the administration's anxiety about project failures, they were now free to become less directive. One program officer summarized the situation:

> But I think after [the original director] left, a period of transition took place. The program officers were left by themselves. _____ was acting director, but he was pretty loose. It was [the program officers'] project; they had to see the thing through and they couldn't expect a whole lot of direction from their superior. So yes, I would say the transition period occurred after his departure.

Economy, Congressional and Administrative Support

Political machinations and personalities aside, however, there was another, perhaps overriding factor, which affected the program officer's behavior. The technical assistance and advisory roles are labor intensive. To do a good job the program officers had to concentrate on relatively few projects, which were costly, in terms of the staff needs and travel money required for frequent site visits. For a combination of reasons, there was not sufficient administrative support. There were drastic reductions in the travel budgets, and program officers were not replaced when vacancies occurred. Within one period (several months), the number of program officers declined significantly.

While most program officers at first felt they had received adequate support from the ES/Washington office, in the later stages they more typically reported only inconsistent backing. One lamented:

> The government has a strange way of saying, "Do something and do it well, particularly do it with quality. But we're going to have to reduce the staff, and we're going to have to reduce a lot of things.

Another source comments:

> I think the bureaucracy is such that... this problem [to provide staff for technical assistance] is not going to receive any attention. It's not going to be discussed at any levels that will effect the kind of change that we'd have to have to make it fit. Now it's almost idiosyncratic, a group of us who are probably at the lowest echelon of any of them; people who are out there in the field. And, the people who make all the decisions, you see, all they have

to do is cut you dow.1 on your travel and you're dead. There isn't any way to carry that out effectively, if you can't get on site.

The argument has been, and still is, that it costs too much money to operate that way. But I think that's penny wise and pound foolish.... You spend fifty-five million dollars on a program and then not put the support behind it that it requires to get good clean data. I think it's ridiculous.

Type of Legal Relationship

The legal instrument used to award funds also seemed to affect style. As one program officer explained:

> ... there is an important difference between *contracts* and *grants,* in that you have more leverage with contracts. That is, contracts spell out pretty closely what these people are going to do by such and such a time, and if they're not delivering, then you can step in and call it to their attention. With grants (basically what is called a "donative award" or gift), you can only probe up to a certain point. If they choose to ignore you, they can. So that right from the start, I think the program officer has to understand that you have certain legal limitations, and know what those are.

This difference, in fact, was believed to be so important that the program was converted from grants to contracts when it was transferred from OE to NIE. An ES specialist in fiscal matters explained:

> ... Generally speaking, you get very low fiscal accountability with a grant. You can't control them.... So if I went to them and said, "Where am I on spending on this grant?" all they could do was tell me, as of the end of the last quarter, which was two and a half months ago, what that grantee had actually dispersed—not obligated, but dispersed, which means actually written a check for. So I had no idea where anybody stood, and I had no idea what they were spending the money on. I just knew that they were spending money. And that really wasn't very satisfactory.... They [NIE] just didn't have any grant documents that allowed me to put any restrictions on the sites that I wanted to, so we changed them all over to contracts.... So it changed the role of the program officer, in the sense that he could control the program more under a contract than a grant. It gave him a greater legal way to insure that the contractor delivered what he said he was going to.

However, the Washington fiscal agents and the local school administrators had very different conceptions of the Formal Project Plans, which NIE suddenly decided would be the basis of the contracts. The fiscal officers thought they were purchasing "deliverables" described in the plans; but, at the time that school administrators submitted them, they had regarded them merely as proposals, that is, guidelines which could be altered at their discretion as implementation proceeded. This difference of opinion put the program officers in the middle. The managerial role is more compatible with contracts than with the grant review mechanism, but they were nonetheless convinced that their advice and technical assistance were needed more than managerial supervision.

SUMMARY

This chapter identifies and illustrates four types of performance styles based on the priority program officers gave to each role described in Chapter IX. These styles are differentiated by the extent to which the program officer becomes involved in the local project and his or her directiveness in dealing with project personnel.

For example, a program officer's directiveness, and in some instances that person's inclination to intervene, seemed to *increase* where:

- the program officer felt particularly competent in a substantive area of relevance to the local project;
- the program officer worked with school principals on district-wide matters;
- local community officials had prior unfavorable experience with federal agencies, did not themselves have local expertise and/or did not seem to be committed to the project;
- the community's values were alien to the program officer's own experience;
- the federal agency responsible for the local projects was being closely scrutinized and held responsible for rigorous contract management;
- there was little backing for federal assistance from the federal bureaucracy;
- projects operated under contractual agreements.

With these performance styles in mind, we are ready to consider some consequences of each style, including some of the conditions that seemed to affect the style which a program officer chose to use. This is the topic of the following chapter.

Chapter XI

Types of Federal Impact

What are the consequences of each of these diverse roles and performance styles on the local projects and on the program officers? It was not possible to obtain enough information, within the scope of this study, to arrive at a conclusive answer about the *amount* of impact from each role and performance style. However, the program officers provided some crude estimates (see Appendix C), and it is possible at least to *illustrate* various *types* of impact that occurred.[1]

In combination, the ten program officers estimated that they exerted a major perceptible influence on the ten projects a total of 73 times (at various stages of the program). They also estimated that in an equal number of cases they exerted a minor but still perceptible influence, and, there were perhaps another 50 times when they thought they might have had a subtle or almost imperceptible influence. This means that on the average, a site might have been subject to 20 different influences from program officers, although of course, some sites received more influence than others.

More influence was reported on operating procedures than on conceptual design (a ratio of 2:1). Procedures became more subject to influence as the projects became operational, and the minor and subtle forms of influence increased from one project stage to another. Project design was more subject to perceptible influence during the planning period than during the early or latter stages, but some influence on design—both perceptible and subtle—continued during the implementation period.

As the program matured, program officers became more convinced that this relationship with local school administrators was productive for the administrators (Appendix C, Item 27). However, the program officers would like to have had even more influence both at the planning stage and in the implementation of the projects.

Any of the roles and work styles described can have an impact. As one program officer observed:

> It's a myth that the program officer isn't going to have some effect on a project. I don't give a damn how; he's going to have an effect. He's a representative of the federal government. By God, he's going to be an important person when he walks on site, and there's no way to get around that. And how that project views him makes a hell of a lot of difference in how it behaves.

One program officer estimated that she had succeeded in getting local projects to change about one-fourth of the items that she had questioned. Her influence:

> ... took the form of putting absolute stops on the plan; questioning other things [requiring] involvement of groups in the community; [and making] suggestions in governance; ... and personnel selection [specific individuals].

VIEWS OF SOME LOCAL PROJECT DIRECTORS

Local project directors representing eight of the ten school districts, expressed widely divergent opinions about their program officers. Their views differed according to the particular program officer under discussion, but also reflected the unique history of each project. The following selection of statements provides a good sense of their feelings.

> *Director A:* This was the best-run program that I have encountered in forty-one years of administration. [The program officers] were apt, capable, understanding and helpful. ... They provided some expertise that the community needed.
>
> *Director B:* [One program officer] was dedicated and competent. She would answer questions and come out to help. ... By contrast, [another program officer] would not communicate through the superintendent, but instead worked directly with the board. ... This raised questions in the board's minds about my competence. [Another program officer]

did not know his place.... He only complained a lot. He considered himself to be an authority on everything, and was very opinionated. He didn't contribute anything.

Director C: [One program officer] tried too much to determine what the program should be.... [She] pressured the community to push community schools.... She was very directive, both about content and procedure, and she turned off people. ... However, she did know her job from a technical point of view.... In the final analysis, she did not have very much influence on the program, because it happened that we had our own ideas. However, she could have had a big impact had she been working with another community.

[Another program officer] was easy-going and not pushy, but he did not have the field experience either in schools, or in Washington. He was too theoretical, and consequently, not credible.... He would take it upon himself to talk to people in the community and try to turn them against the school district. [The program officer] was very directive and would not compromise. He was primarily watching out for the federal dollar, but he was very hard to deal with.

Director D: [One program officer] related to the community more as a consultant than as a program officer. He would give advice directly to the school board and staff members and attempted to influence school board decisions without going through the superintendent. He would even have individual meetings with school board members without me or my staff present. My leaving the district was a direct result of his impact.

By contrast, [another program officer] was much more helpful. She asked what the school district wanted to do, and then tried to suggest some options, without advocating any particular one.

[Another program officer] was very dogmatic and enforced the contract too literally. And, more important, she was too insistent on incorporating her own ideas, to the point where it limited the districts' options.

Director E: Our experience with the first program officer was bad. Part of the problem stemmed from her arrogance, but in addition, she kept insisting that we rewrite the entire proposal. And, when we tried to make the changes she suggested, they were rejected by ES.

Then [another program officer] took over and raised specific questions and then got the proposal adopted. She was always available and provided written answers to letters.

He [a third program officer] made an effort to attend our workshops and visited us to show an interest in our problems. He helped with our reports and showed us how to retain the money that we underspent. He made good suggestions about specific implementation problems we were having, but did not dictate.

Director F: Program officers have given little actual direction to the project, and have had little influence, largely because of minimal contact between the program officers and the school district. There has been a great deal of variation in the helpfulness of program officers assigned over the years. My main complaint is that things agreed to in discussions were never confirmed in writing from Washington.

Director G: The program officers who have worked with this program have been very helpful. In twenty years' experience, no federal program officers have been as far in the background. But when they were needed, [the program officers] were ready to help. The major problem has been the rapid turnover of both program officers and directors.

Director H: There has been considerable variation in my experience with program officers. One created a great deal of animosity and strife in the first part of the project because she is a rigid person. She did not understand the problems of administering a school district; and consequently, she had no idea how unrealistic her demands were.

But [another program officer] has been helpful and supportive, and has helped resolve problems that have come up. He has provided technical assistance upon request. And he would sometimes offer it when not requested; however, the final decision as to whether to accept technical assistance was in the hands of the school district.

In general, the program officers did not influence the direction of the project, but they did help to keep it going by encouraging the school district not to withdraw from the program.

IMPACT ON LOCAL PROJECTS: SOME ILLUSTRATIONS OF EACH STYLE

Several examples will be given to illustrate the effects of each of the work styles identified in the preceding chapter (see also Appendix B).

The Uninvolved and Directive Style

When using this style, program officers often fell back on their *managerial* authority to enforce explicit or implicit rules, although even this was subject to negotiation. One describes some of the tension that accompanies this role:

I had said to [the superintendent] that I thought the project consultant should not be the project director for this year on the grounds that this man's greatest effect is in the classroom. . . . But I find out now that he has, in fact, appointed the project consultant as project director. Now I have a dilemma, since this is an appointment over which I have rights of approval or denial.... I was reluctant to get into a power play, because I feel that would be a definite intrusion ... in the research design. I think I've decided that the building principals will function as the administrative personnel on a quarterly basis, and the administrative chairman of their meetings will be the project director, which is some sort of compromise between the superintendent and myself.

In some instances, program officers were directly responsible for the removal of local project directors during the planning period. The superintendent of schools in one of these districts reportedly was very resentful of the fact that refunding was made contingent upon replacing the director, whom the program officer felt did not have the skills necessary to manage the project. In still another project ES/Washington insisted that a project director who had tried to use project funds to finance his personal schooling should be replaced.

Program officers also intervened in program design:

We said, "Look, if you're going to be doing that at the elementary level, then you can't initiate it unless you're going to plan to do something with it all the way through."... They didn't often want to do that.

Many of the criticisms of local projects in the early phases of the program concerned the absence of a central project theme, poor integration among project components, vague plans, unrealistic timetables, and the need to involve more people in the planning. There is less evidence that program officers were pushing particular programs.

But this style was not confined to contract management. Program officers also sometimes adopted this style when serving as project advisors:

I've been particularly cool about their approach to the bilingual education program, and have told them, in fact, that I thought they were not being faithful to what they had agreed to do.... [I] pointed out to them that if they couldn't come up with some kind of program that there was some question if they could be eligible for refunding. That's real pressure. I mean that's really slugging them pretty hard.

Another program officer said that she:

... might really object to a [component]. For instance, "field trips are no big deal," we would say, "unless you can show me programmatically how a few field trips were ever going to do anything for any kid."

Messerschmidt (1979) describes an incident in which ES refused to allow the school district to appoint a separate project director, insisting that only the superintendent of schools could act in that capacity. He notes that:

Such changes in the organization of the school district, however, was equally unacceptable to the school officials. Administrators and trustees alike resented this outside advice, which appeared to totally disregard district administrative policy and established lines of authority. The ES stand on the directorship issue was interpreted by some local individuals as a gross violation of the school district's autonomy (p. 25).

In still another instance, a program officer insisted that a community being funded should establish a relationship with a neighboring community, when in fact there was a long history of rivalry and antagonism between the two communities involved.

The Involved and Directive Style

Often, the program officer became cognizant of some problem in the course of providing technical assistance or when serving in an advisory capacity. In one instance, a program officer had become concerned about the fact that the project had not yet implemented its evaluation plan. He tried to nudge the local project director gently to see implementation as a priority of the project, and to look for that skill when interviewing people to be hired. He also recommended the type of people who should be considered and was present during some of the interviews to explain the problem to the candidates.

Another program officer reported that:

... [T]hey hired a woman to head the [local evaluation], and I went out there and realized that she was very insecure in her role. So, I had a meeting with the superintendent and this person, in which I was attempting to explore with her what her job was all about. And the superintendent exploded. "No, she is working for me, not you." He wanted her to report directly to him and not to us.... She later said that she was glad that I had intervened when I did.

Criticisms from program officers sometimes proved to be irritating to local officials: Donnelly (1979) commented:

> [School district] personnel ... concluded that ES/Washington was criticizing the plan as being overambitious. Such criticism, through written and telephone communications, seemed to be an indication of prejudice against the capabilities of the rural school system; local pride was challenged (p. 19).

At another site, the program officer made harsh and uncomplimentary comments about the local plan charging that it was platitudinous and filled with contradictions. As a result of her criticisms, the superintendent complained to ES that:

> 40 percent of the work that went into preparing the document was spent simply to make it acceptable to NIE and not for the district's benefit. The problem with this type of "help" is that with the departure of the individuals who wrote the project plan, few local personnel are willing to assume responsibility for the ownership of the program; it becomes "just another federal [as opposed to local] program."

The Involved and Nondirective Style

This style was sometimes used in the course of technical assistance as in the instance when the program officer sat down with the project director and worked out the idea of an administrative council to make the overall decisions for the project as a way of maintaining continuity in the face of high turnover. This style was also associated with the advisory role:

> Their ... internal evaluation component was handled by a single individual. I encouraged them to go to a sort of team approach to evaluation, training and using teachers within the system on that team.... Evaluation became less threatening to the teachers, [and] they built up skills within several people in the district.

Even criticism, it seems, could be given in a nondirective way by someone who was accepted as "a friend in court," as he described himself:

> Frankly, I thought they were pulling the wool over their own eyes. I didn't think they had a community action plan at all.... They had a highly selective group of people.... But they hadn't invited the people at all who

would have said anything different.... And I pointed that out.... Well, they were very angry—not angry—they were vociferous in their protestations. I said, "fine, and I've been wrong before, but just bear in mind that that's what it looks like to me." So, after I left and they cooled down a little bit and looked it over, they reported what I had said to the cabinet (which is made up of the school board and some other people) and the cabinet said, "Well, we think he's right." ... So they went to work on it, and they've made some rather interesting changes.

He went on to explain that:

Hell, it's their project. They're the ones who are essentially the contractors. They're the ones who have to deliver the goods. The best I can do is offer my help. And, if in the last resort, they still think I'm wrong, I may submit to them some letter of understanding of our discussion at that particular time, so I go on record as having at least pointed out that this is an area that's very unclear. And then they go ahead. I can't usurp that authority. I wouldn't if I could. I don't think the federal government has any right to tell the contractor he's wrong.

The consequences that can accrue from even a very nondirective style once a program officer has become intimately familiar with a project are illustrated in the case of a program officer who pointed out to members of the school board that their system, with 100 classroom teachers, had approximately 30 to 38 coaches—in other words, one-third of the system or one-third of the personnel; and that they spent over one-third of their budget on athletic programs, including equipment. Many of the board members were not aware of that, and eventually, the local superintendent got into trouble when it was learned that he was spending so much money on one activity. The budgeting procedure required by ES also revealed that he was spending funds given for one component on another.

The Uninvolved and Nondirective Style

Even a program officer who was not intimately familiar with the details of a project or community, and had no definite criticism or alternative in mind, could affect the course of a project by raising basic questions or pushing for a rationale and justification:

They said that one of their goals was to improve the art and cultural offerings. It was having a poet come and attend school twice a year. A: What is its cost? And B: What is its impact? Raising the question itself [was important]; "Why did you do that, over and above six other things?" "Who decided that was what the children of [this discrict] needed?"

In another instance:

Well, in _____, for instance they wanted to do something they called "personalized education." The things they wrote were full of lingo. And I did a lot of questioning about what they meant and whether, in fact, it was different from regular educational procedures, and in what way. And, if they were going to personalize for every kid, had they actually thought about the details of keeping records on every kid? And how would teachers be trained to do that? And where would it be coordinated? It was their idea, and I just tried to work it through.

In another instance, ES/Washington worked out a plan for a local project to hire a resident consultant. The program officer explained how the agency was, indirectly, able to maintain some control over the situation:

Well, the superintendent originally wanted him under his control, to be paid directly out of project funds. But we felt that might be a mistake in a couple of ways, in that, that kind of thing could really hamper the guy's ability to move if he did anything that anybody there was in disagreement with. So instead of that (and I actually did all the setting up and working out details), we set it up so the project would pay [a university]. He would be an employee of [the university], and he would be hired on a contract basis to work in the district full time. This accomplished a couple of things. One, he had the prestige of coming from the university, which means something. It really does mean something in [that community]. And [two], if there was a flare-up, if there was a disagreement, the guy was protected because he was actually employed by the university.

Speaking of this instance, one source concluded:

That's federal imposition. That's federal intervention. And yet there isn't any question in my mind that there would be nothing going on ... if I hadn't gotten this nonthreatening, highly competent man to be an adjunct professor in the sense of assuming the kind of leadership that nobody else would offer.

The uninvolved, nondirective style took several different forms. In one instance, a program officer simply "came in with some packaged evaluation plans that he suggested the community adopt, but the community made the decision independently." In another case:

[ES] required an outside audit done by a private firm. That's impact, on how things are done locally.... Some people got fired. Some people got their jobs shifted. School board members got voted off. Teachers quit, etc. Components were dropped. Some were going to have to go without equipment, or be replaced.

Mixed Styles

The above example also reveals the way styles were sometimes mixed. In this case, the agency insisted upon the audit, but was otherwise nondirective about the outcomes: "Let the chips fall where they may."

Perhaps a more typical example of how program officers used directive methods to achieve indefinite results occurred when they pressured local projects to hire outside consultants chosen or approved by NIE. One program officer, for example, reportedly selected and briefed a consultant paid by the local school district who helped write the formal project plan for the district.

Many of the problems arose because different styles were being used at different times. Thus, several of the on-site observers in different communities independently reported that tension developed between local officials and NIE personnel as the communities realized that they were not to be given the freedom and autonomy that they had been led to expect. Each project was to be developed and designed by persons in the local site based on local conditions and local desires for schooling. However, although the Washington office had intended to remain as nondirective as possible with regard to the planning and implementation of activities of the local school systems, this strategy also presented the problem Donnelly (1979) reported:

[The program officer...] always refrained from offering direct suggestions as to what changes would be necessary for the proposal to be acceptable for funding... the subtle suggestions offered [but never clarified] were enough to produce a condition of anxiety... [Then] following the submission of the "final" version of the proposal to NIE in mid-February, [the program officer] visited [the community] to inform the local project staff that a "complete rewrite" would be necessary due to lack of specificity and organization of that document. By this time, the superintendent and the project coordinator had become convinced that [ES] was trying to force the proposal into a framework which was not compatible with the original objectives of the Letter of Interest (pp. 19–20).

Firestone (1979) independently reported from another school district that:

> The superintendent remembers dealing with ES/Washington as... a very frustrating thing; to say that we have no guidelines and yet to be evaluated on a sub rosa set of guidelines that we didn't know but we found out later they were evaluating on.... If they'd just told us that to begin with, it would have been a lot easier than to try to outguess them all the time and wondering if we were getting the right things in. So what was supposed to be a proposal based on our ideas was instead a proposal based upon what they wanted.... The thing that really bothered me was that we were playing games with each other, rather than just having them say we've got to have this because Congress has said this.... Why not just tell us that (pp. 16–17)?

To understand these vacillations it is necessary to realize that:

- ES/Washington initially was probably more concerned about assessing a community's suitability for the program than in conveying details about monitoring procedures to be followed at each project stage; such details might have only discouraged local officials;
- ES/Washington was in charge of the selection process; local officials were not in a secure position to demand details about the guidelines ES would follow;
- The ES/Washington staff themselves probably did not yet have sufficient experience to stipulate detailed monitoring guidelines; these would evolve over time;
- With the shift from OE to NIE, the ES staff was put under sudden pressure to tighten up the monitoring process.

FAILURES OF INFLUENCE ATTEMPTS

However, it would be a mistake to assume that program officers were uniformly successful whenever they tried to exert influence on a project. A number of instances were reported when local officials either (1) rejected the government's recommendations, or (2) implemented only part of them.

Rejections of Recommendations

In one case, a program officer backed off when he learned the community would resist a plan involving a cultural exchange with a minority group:

> I felt that... I would work on positive things rather than create a confrontation... that's the only case that I felt that I was really totally unsuccessful, and I just didn't pursue it because I knew it wouldn't work.

In another instance, a program officer's suggestion to release a teacher part time to direct the local evaluation effort was not accepted because the superintendent preferred a full-time person from outside the district and did not want to disrupt this teacher's career with a temporary assignment.

In at least one instance, in fact, local officials apparently succeeded in getting a program officer dismissed because of their objections to the condescending way the program officer had treated local people.

One interviewee described an incident that took place when ES/Washington refused to allow a project to hire a new local evaluator after dismissing the first one:

> He and the superintendent didn't get along, and for reasons that are not clear to me, they didn't rehire him the second year. Because they made that mistake, the front office [ES managers] refused to let them use the money the next year to hire another evaluator.... [The superintendent] had some pretty big guns, because he wrote his congressman, and senators, and the governor and everybody else. And so, letters came down from the top and filtered down to our office, and all hell broke loose. It was when [the NIE director] was under tremendous fire from Congress,... and it was just the wrong time for us to get that kind of publicity. And so, they removed the program officer which, of course, as far as I'm concerned, was the wrong thing to do.

Partial Implementation

However, it was probably more typical for communities to choose to implement only part of the government's recommendations. As one program officer saw it, all instances of "successful influence" that he could think of also could be looked upon as partial failures:

By having an aide come into the classroom an hour a day and work with some kids in Spanish, the district has now made a fairly ... honest attempt to create one fully bilingual classroom at each grade level, in the elementary grades, up to grade five. Now, that's a success as far as I am concerned. But my idea was that they had really sort of told us that they were going to do that in *every* classroom ... and they're three years into this project and they're finally, for the first time, designating one bilingual classroom. Now, have I succeeded or have I failed?

IMPACT ON PROGRAM OFFICERS

In addition to the impact that program officers had on communities, the diverse roles and performance styles they tried to employ also had consequences for themselves. Confusion sometimes resulted because they were trying to exercise so many diverse responsibilities. The program officers were typically not clear about their responsibilities during the planning stage, but this problem diminished once a project was under way (Appendix C, Item 20). After the first few months, they also were confident that local school administrators had developed closer agreement with their role definitions (Appendix C, Item 22), although there were still a substantial number of instances (5 out of 16 observations) in which program officers were still not sure how they were perceived by local officials. More important, after a period of optimism early in the program, the majority were unconvinced that administrators at NIE supported their role definitions (Appendix C, Item 21).

In particular, it proved difficult to divorce the advice they offered in the form of suggestions from the fact that they controlled the funds. Several of them commented that they could sense the community often felt intimidated by their advice and listened only because of the program officer's control over the money. As one program officer commented:

> I think I view the relationship a little differently than the superintendents would. I think that they're much more aware of the power I have than I am, and I think they're concerned about it. They think about it.

The inconsistent switching from role to role was sometimes perceived by local officials as insincere "game playing," an attitude of which the program officers were aware. Thus, some program officers looked upon it as a challenge to develop mutual trust and respect under the shadow of their own power. Toward this end, one mused:

> My advice is always a form of suggestion. Usually I couch it that way in the beginning, but I realize it's not always taken that way.... They propose something and they check it out with me to see what my facial expression is like; or they ask me, you know, "What do you think of this?" because they say, "If there's no point in doing it, I mean, we may as well not spend our time discussing the damn thing." Well, that is the power part of the relationship obviously operating right there, and in lots of respects it is hard to break down.

One program officer expressed personal frustration as follows:

> I want not to interfere, I want it to be their project. But at the same time, I have a hard time keeping my mouth shut if I see something that I could directly help with. I don't think we've ever decided whether the responsibility of the program officer is to see to it that they don't fail. My inclination is that, "no, it is not our responsibility"—viewing this as a research project, as an experiment. But as an educator, it's hard not to get in there. I wish that had been more clearly spelled out for us in the beginning.

Another program officer stressed the problems that this combination of roles created for both her and the local community:

> It may have been easier on the project to deal with it directively, "this is what we expect; this is what we want; do it; comply," rather than the ... "well, if you want to do it that way, and if you can explain it, why sure." Because there was nothing clear-cut about that kind of continual negotiations, and that could have actually been a source of greater frustration. In fact, a lot of projects were always saying, "Well, if you'd just tell us what it is, we'll do it." And of course, we didn't believe that we could; there weren't answers; we didn't have one set thing.... We'd say, "Well, if we knew what was acceptable we wouldn't be spending x million dollars having this project. We'd just go out and write the model and then everybody would do it."

The program officers' ambivalence in the situation is also reflected in this comment:

> It's not been possible for me to be of really much help to [that project]. I feel that they would not be too much worse off if they never heard from me, and if I just signed papers as they came in. Sometimes I feel that way.

Other times I say to myself, if they didn't know that I was here thinking about them, there is just quite a strong force in that district to... not do anything. It's quite a strong feeling; that's the way they ought to behave. So that, just my presence is pretty important there.

There were also some unanticipated hazards from working too closely with the communities. One program officer recalled:

I've had to mediate disputes between well-intentioned people who have come to blows over a particular proposal... and if they come to me and say, "You know, this guy sleeps through staff meetings and just doesn't pick up the ball," I think that then I have to be very careful. I could say to them, "Yeah, I know, this guy is a fool" or whatever.... But if I do that, not only do I kill the guy, but it interjects a major variable, or influence, on the porject that I shouldn't be.

Another program officer complained of his vulnerability to being co-opted:

There is a danger, too, that you can be looked upon as "Johnny Nice Guy" or as "Our Man in Washington" as opposed to "Washington's Man in _____." So, the program officer has to avoid being sucked into being somebody else's man. The program officer has to very quickly establish his role and also put across the fact that he is, after all, a government employee who is attempting to make sure that the taxpayers' money is spent properly.

FACTORS RELATED TO IMPACT

It seems clear that the impact of program officers varied from time to time and from community to community. Some communities complained vociferously about federal intervention, while others were less resentful, or at least less vocal about it. Impact seemed to be contingent upon a number of different factors, including: (1) stage of the project; (2) continuity and persistence on the part of the federal agency; (3) instability of the program; (4) the ability of communities to defend themselves; (5) the vulnerability of particular communities.

Project Stage

The needs of the projects for different types of assistance shifted as they matured from selection to planning to implementation.

In the early stages, as communities were designing their projects, they seemed to depend more upon the program officer for advice about the philosophical issues, or about the rationale underlying the design. In describing a colleague, one program officer identified several skills that seemed to be called for during this early stage:

> First of all, she was very good at conceptual work, and that's what was required in planning.... She could go in and say, "No. This isn't what you really want to do." Or, "This isn't going to get you where you are going." She might not be able to tell them how to get there, but she was a critiquer. And she was a good one from what I could see. She also served some functions in helping them translate proposals into plans.... They had wonderful proposals, but we kept saying, "We want a plan." And they would say, "We can't plan for more than one year at a time."

But a different kind of assistance was required once the rationale was worked out:

> It wasn't philosophy they needed; it was "how to." Once I decide that I want to change my system in this way, how do I do it?

According to their questionnaire responses (see Appendix C), the program officers seldom worried about contract management matters (i.e., keeping close surveillance or disapproving requests) during the selection period. But from the planning period on, they typically reported having taken steps toward contract compliance.

There was a similar change in emphasis on the advisory role. Program officers began to offer advice during the planning stage (Appendix C, Item 6). In three-fourths of the instances, they reported having often or very frequently offered suggestions to local administrators regarding ways to implement their plans or resolve their problems.

But their advice was limited to implementation matters, not policy. They seldom claimed to have been responsible for introducing a new project component (Appendix C, Item 11) and they doubted that they had much influence on the conceptual design or project goals (Appendix C, Items 8, 9). They were uncertain, and somewhat divided among themselves, about whether they should have had even more influence on some aspects of local projects (Appendix C, Item 28).

Paralleling these developments, they reported a dramatic increase in the frequency with which they were asked by administrators for technical assistance or advice. During the early stages few of them were solicited for assistance, but during the implementation period most of them were asked to provide technical assistance (Appendix C, Item 13) and nearly all of them said their help was solicited (Appendix C, Item 14). But significantly enough, starting in the planning stage, the majority also frequently offered advice whether or not it was requested (see Appendix C, Item 30).

The program officers could recall a total of 197 specific instances when they felt they had exercised some kind of influence (positive or negative) on a local project.[2] These incidents were divided approximately equally among major, minor, and subtle influences. They affected operating procedures about twice as often as conceptual design. Two-thirds of the incidents occurred during the implementation period, and more occurred during planning than during selection. However, when only major incidents are considered, approximately two out of three occurred before the implementation period, an impact that undoubtedly affected implementation.

As the program evolved, too, the program officers became somewhat more convinced that local officials were committed to the program. Still, in the majority of instances, they remained very unimpressed with the level of local commitment, and more important perhaps, they were even less impressed with the qualifications of local officials to direct projects of this magnitude.

Throughout the program, but especially during the planning period, the program officers did not feel that they had enough backing from the Experimental Schools administration, and they were uncertain about whether ES officials had provided clear interpretations of federal procedures and expectations. The policy changes and inconsistencies that were prevalent during the planning period apparently became more stable during implementation. In most instances, program officers came to believe that they understood their role, and that ES officials agreed with them, but during the selection and planning periods there was apparently much ambiguity. The program officers remained divided on whether local school district administrators shared their own role definitions.

With a couple of exceptions, the program officers seemed convinced that they had helped the local school administrators during the implementation period, although they did not feel that they were of much help during the earlier stages.

Federal Continuity and Persistence

One must also consider how much effort the agency was able and willing to expend to influence a project. The amount of effort that the Experimental Schools' staff devoted to intervention was in turn influenced by the staffing pattern. For some sites there was a high rate of turnover among program officers. Three sites were assigned four different program officers; four others had to deal with three different program officers and three other sites were assigned two program officers. Also, in some cases, there was no active program officer assigned for months at a time. During these periods, the projects tended to slide behind schedule, primarily because the usual delays in payments from Washington became prolonged without someone in Washington to oversee the paper work. It should be noted that many of these small communities did not have enough slack money to tide them over these delays and as a result the teachers and other personnel were kept waiting for their salaries. This intensified local resistance and reduced ES' ability to influence a project.

It has been noted that each program officer tended to stress his or her personal skills and interests. When this idiosyncratic pattern of monitoring is viewed against the swift and often abrupt turnover of monitors, interspersed with periods of neglect, it is evident that projects could be torn in several directions within a few months. The discontinuities were compounded by the fact that the original ES/Washington program director was replaced in midcourse by a sequence of acting directors, and at the same time the ES/Washington office was reviewed and reorganized. Under these conditions it would be natural for local officials simply to give up and withdraw expecting that "This too shall pass."

All of this probably would not have made much difference if the agency had not been so determined to work closely with local projects. Why was the agency so resolute in its commitment to these projects? Part of the answer is that its own reputation and sense of accomplishment depended upon the success of each local project. Once the agency had selected the specific communities, there were few options available to it due to the competition for discretionary funds going on within NIE at this time. If a project were dropped, in all likelihood ES would have lost those funds to other NIE programs.

Program Instability

Another important consideration is the fact that the ES program was never well defined or planned in any detail at the federal level, and its operational capability was never fully appraised before it was funded. It was, of course, reviewed by the administration's budgetary office, but OMB is primarily interested in the ideological and budgetary merits of such programs, not their operational plans (see Summerfield, 1974). Since the program was not enacted as part of a law, it even escaped review by HEW's Office of Legislation. It was authorized directly by congressional budgetary committees, which seldom have the time, interest, or capability to undertake a detailed review of the operational readiness of such a program (see Lowi, 1969). The several task forces that proposed it, debated the program's philosophy but arrived at neither a consensus nor a detailed plan.

Consequently, for example, criteria were never specified for even the key idea, "comprehensive" change. Since the program had been turned down once by Congress, as soon as it was funded, its managers felt compelled to rush into operation to show results. Subsequent circumstances forced ES/Washington to adapt its policies as unforeseen circumstances arose. The policies just evolved.

Of course, there might have been some merit in not being too specific, given the program managers' ideological commitment to local initiative. The general nature of the guidelines certainly left room for the local school districts to negotiate their own preconceptions—had procedures been established to permit such negotiations to take place. The problem is that such procedures did not exist. The districts were thus torn between whatever arbitrary and fluctuating interpretations various federal officials might decide to impose at any time.

These changes in policy undermined the program officer's effectiveness with the local projects. Most program officers agreed that policy changes made by the agency early in this program were a major problem. Moreover, while perhaps the situation improved, apparently ES officials never provided local school administrators with a clear understanding of government procedures and expectations (Appendix C, Item 26). One source observed that:

> The administration, if anything, has been a debilitating influence on Experimental Schools. The sites have been keenly aware of what has happened in this past year. The largest cut that we planned to have to take was two million dollars, and we wound up having to take [almost that amount] 1.8 million dollars.... And I think these districts are relatively conscious of the attitude of the central management of [ES].... They know that the bureaucracy... certainly isn't supporting sending the program officers out to the field. They know that [the ES director] was removed from the program.... I think they feel somewhat hurt at the lack of awareness that NIE has of what they're doing in their district.

He observed that the small districts are probably more adversely affected by erratic policy swings than were the larger ones:

> The people at the bigger projects are much more sophisticated. The leadership [has] been around for years. They've been dealing with the feds for a long, long time. They don't get as rattled as the little fellows do. So it's more crucial with the little projects, because for many of them this was their first experience with a big federal agency, and it hasn't been pleasant, and that's too bad.... The instability of the thing—politically, I think,—has been tremendously devastating to the effort to provide stability in programs.

This kind of program instability is apparently commonplace in Washington. Pressman (1975) reports that local officials associated with various federal programs frequently change their priorities, renege on financial commitments, and yet hold locals responsible for properly administering their projects.

Community Defenses

The amount of impact was of course also a function of the other side of the equation: a community's ability and inclination to resist federal influence. Many instances of overt resistance from local officials were reported. A few informants were convinced that, at least in certain communities, there was little more than "surface [ritualistic] conformity" to the contract and to the government's expectations (Merton, 1957). That is, officials ritualistically fulfilled only the minimum requirements and thus only pretended to implement ES directives. For example, one program officer remarked that, insofar as evaluation was concerned, the school administrators were merely "play acting" to satisfy federal requirements.

In one case, a superintendent was able to minimize the influence of community residents despite an ES requirement for community involvement in planning. The local project staff simply visited a few civic and fraternal organizations to solicit opinions which they used at their own discretion.

Local officials employed several techniques to protect their autonomy. Most of these techniques enhanced their ability to control information available to program officers. For example, an on-site researcher at one site tells how a superintendent limited program officers' access to information during a site visit by managing their schedules. They spent all morning listening to the superintendent and his consultant describe the project and illustrate its success with selected examples. In the afternoon they were taken to one exemplary school where they were introduced to a few teachers who were involved with the most creative aspect of the project.

Most program officers believed they were adequately informed about the local projects (Appendix C, Item 29). Nevertheless, local management techniques were so effective that, reputedly, at one site a program officer was kept from learning, during his site visit, that the superintendent was being fired and had instituted legal proceedings against the school board. In still another instance, a program officer thought that a particular program was operating in the first five elementary grades when in fact it was available in only the kindergarten and first grades.

A few on-site researchers also sensed that limited access to information sometimes caused program officers to overestimate their influence on projects. One researcher, for example, questioned whether a highly touted plan to hire local teachers as evaluators was supported by the teachers involved, who seemed rather uninterested in their new jobs.

In truth, no matter how much a program officer might have tried, he had little chance of influencing what was going on in classrooms if the teachers were not behind it. No one person, it seems—not even outside federal officers with enticing money—

can combat the "slippage" that is characteristic of hierarchical systems. Relatively speaking, it is easy to achieve compliance on paper. New materials can be introduced from the top of an organization. However, because resistance often increases at each lower level of the hierarchy, by the time programs get into classrooms, they have become transformed back into what had already existed. As Gouldner (1952) has observed, conforming to the *letter* of the rules can sabotage an organization because the social system can work only if members are sufficiently committed to exercise their own initiative to make it work. Directives can serve as guidelines to behavior, but they cannot establish the essential attitudes.

Community Vulnerability

Some communities had more power and inclination to resist than others. Several factors help to account for this variation. One program officer identified two reasons:

> Of all the districts, I've probably had more influence in _____ than any of them. And I think that's a result of two things. One, they needed the most help. Two, they react the quickest to the federal government. They need the federal money badly for a number of reasons. The superintendent needs it for political survival, and the district needs it to do anything above the minimum program.... The state has a minimum program outlined that all districts must give, and anything above that is up to the local school district. This is the kind of place that if they had to depend only on their local funds, they would only have a minimum program. Now they aspire to bigger and better things. They've been able to do it primarily because the superintendent's always been able to bring in federal dollars one way or another, and the biggest batch has been the Experimental Schools dollars. But the need for that makes them respond differently than _____. If [the latter] didn't like what we were doing, they'd tell us to "buzz off" and "we'll run our own show." But _____ isn't about to do that.

In addition to the need for help and money, another factor which explains variation in the inclination of communities to resist is the local political situation. Local officials are inclined to think carefully about how participation in federal programs might threaten their own position vis-à-vis the power structure of the local district (Pressman, 1975). One ES program officer commented that the superintendent ignored his recommendation to appoint a principal (rather than an outside consultant) as the project director because:

I think it's easier for the superintendent to be away for a year and know that the project is in the hands of somebody who's going to be a good caretaker (as well as being a creative leader), as opposed to entrusting it to people who have really had sort of untried administrative responsibilities. And, politically, I think, the fact that the project consultant is not from _____ [means that] he doesn't pose a political threat. I think it's possible that there are a couple, or three, building principals who might aspire to the superintendency.

It appears that there was still another factor, although information is vague on this point. Local officials in most of these communities were operating on two fundamental misconceptions:

- While aware of some confusion among the ES staff, they overestimated the extent of consensus and clarity in Washington about what was wanted and expected of the sites, which reinforced their impression that they were being manipulated;
- They were unaware that the ES director felt virtually compelled to retain the projects selected for planning grants (for reasons explained elsewhere). Hence, they underestimated ES/Washington's commitment to them and thus were probably needlessly responsive to ES pressure.

Consequently, at least some communities were very responsive to any suggestions made by federal officials. For example, one source concluded that "[This community] has been highly responsive to program officer 'suggestions,' and often not because they thought it through and wanted it; but because they perceived the program officer desiring it." Another adds:

Now if you suggested a project component, you have two problems going for you. You are already a federal officer, and they are a naive rural school district who hasn't dealt very much with the feds. The school administrator quickly tends to buy it, to say "yes," because it means funding. But the school boards tend to say "No, you are not going to tell us what to do." They were for the most part conservative rural communities.

As a result, as one program officer noted:

[In] some of the rural districts, it may appear that there is more technical assistance given than there really is because of the way they accept and listen to suggestions that are made.

CONDITIONS AFFECTING RELATIONSHIPS WITH LOCAL PROJECTS: SOME PATTERNS

The program officers' responses to selected questionnaire items were combed for clues that might help explain differences in the way they related to the ten communities. Of course, it must be remembered that we are dealing with correlations among statements of the program officers themselves and with some independent measures. But with cautious interpretation, the data can nevertheless point to some conditions that influenced their behavior. Four types of conditions will be explored: those under which program officers said they (1) were able to help local projects; (2) provided technical assistance; (3) stressed the managerial role; and (4) provided advice.

Ability to Be of Help

Judging from the patterns of correlations among program officer responses about the ten projects (see Appendix A), it appears that as program officers' estimates of their ability to help *increases*, so did their estimates of:

- the number of requests for assistance they received ($r = .63$);
- the technical assistance ($r = .76$) and unsolicited advice they provided ($r = .58$);
- the competence of the local project administrators ($r = .71$);
- their influence on implementation ($r = .86$);
- the number of incidents in which they had a major impact on the local project ($r = .65$).

Their estimates of their ability to help were *lower* where they thought that local project personnel agreed on:

- project goals ($r = -.50$)
- project design ($r ; -.43$)

In addition, there is a positive relationship between the amount of help the program officers said they provided and the extent to which ES/Washington had influenced the local project's plans; this last measure was developed independently by Abt Associates (see Herriott and Rosenblum, 1976).[3]

One way to see the basic patterns in these relationships more clearly is to use the "extreme differences" method. Since the cases in the middle of the distribution are likely to demonstrate a mixed effect, any relationship should be most evident in extreme cases. Using this method, the projects have been divided in Table XI.1 into those which the program officers said they helped the most and those they believed they helped least. (See Appendix C, Item 27.) Terms used in Table XI.1 (and Table XI.2) are explained in Figure XI.1.

What do these sites have in common? As the program officers assessed it, their helpfulness does not appear to be related to their management role. In fact, one of the two sites in which management was stressed fell into the most helped category while the other was in the least helped category.

But their helpfulness does appear to be related to the amount of technical assistance they believed they provided. Two of the three sites that were helped most also received the most technical assistance. The site that received the least technical assistance was among those helped least.

In addition, the sites to which program officers said they gave the most help also, according to their estimates, tended to receive the most advice about implementation. However, they did not necessarily give these sites more advice about project goals. In fact, program officers seldom claimed that their advice influenced the conceptual design or goals of any project, although they apparently exerted more influence on the design of projects 4 and 7 than of projects 2 and 5, again using their own estimates as criteria. By contrast, program officers did think they they had a high degree of influence on procedures at two of the sites that they helped most. They also thought they helped least two of the sites in which they had the least influence on procedures.

Program officers could recall a greater number of incidents in which they attempted to exert influence at those sites that they believed they helped most. Although the overall pattern is not very consistent ($r = .42$), the two sites that were most subject to major incidents of influence were among those that were helped the most.

In addition to the way the program officers related to the local school districts, other conditions were present which were associated with their perceived ability to help. Thus, projects that received the most assistance tended to ask for it. The three that were helped most also ranked first, second and fourth in requesting advice and technical assistance. Of course, the program officers tended to offer assistance even when it was not solicited (r = .59), but the *pattern* for this practice is not clear-cut for the extreme cases; for example, the most assisted sites included both extremes—the site where unsolicited help was most frequently offered and the one where it was least frequently offered.

More important is the fact that program officers believed that administrators at the sites they helped most agreed with their role definitions (r = .67). The two sites ranking highest on role consensus are among the three most helped; and the site with lowest consensus is among the three helped least.

Also, there is a slight tendency for program officers to report being of more help to projects where they judged the local administrators to be relatively unqualified, but again the pattern is not well defined for the extreme cases (see Table XI.1).

There is a modest relationship between the program officers' estimates of their helpfulness and a related but independent measure developed by Abt Associates (see Herriott and Rosenblum, 1976): the proportion of local professional staff estimating that Washington Experimental Schools officials had a "great deal of influence" on their school district's formal project plan (r = .42). Two of the most helped projects also were the most subject to Washington influence, and one of the least helped sites ranked low on ES influence as measured by Herriott and Rosenblum (1976). Still, the fact that one of the most helped sites ranked low on this measure and another that was moderately influenced by Washington was not helped much, indicates that Washington influence on the formal plan was not always necessary or productive for the local project.

Receiving help does not appear to be related to the ability of a local program to implement its plan during the early stages (another measure developed by Herriott and Rosenblum, 1976). It is probably significant that all three of the most helped sites ranked high on their initial readiness for change, as estimated by Herriott and Rosenblum (1976), but the most helped sites ranked lower (though still above the median) on measurements of their ability to actually initiate change.

The extent of help provided to the local projects also is vaguely connected to the commitment expressed by the local staffs to this project (r = .50). Using an estimate of commitment developed by Herriott and Rosenblum (1976), the staff was *highly* committed in two of the three most helped sites and demonstrated only *low* commitment in two of the three sites that were helped least. But the amount of commitment of the local leaders seems to be a less important factor than the commitment of the staff. In fact, leadership commitment is high in two of the three least helped sites and mixed in the sites that were helped most.

Technical Assistance

Judging from the patterns of the correlations (see Appendix A), it appears that the more technical assistance that program officers said they provided, the more:

- helpful they thought they had been (r = .76);
- requests for assistance they have received (r = .76);
- favorably they evaluated the competence of the local school administrators (r = .75);
- influence they believe they have had on implementation (r = .79);
- incidents they recalled in which they had a major impact (r = .70).

The goal consensus of local project personnel was lower where program officers said they provided more technical assistance (r = −.53).

According to the program officers' estimates, the most technical assistance was provided to three sites; three other sites received the least technical assistance (see Table XI.2). Two of the former sites also received the most advice about implementation, and two of the latter were among the three sites which received the least advice. In general, the amount of technical assistance program officers said they provided is not associated with the management role. It is true, though, that the two sites at which there was the *least* stress on management were among those that received the *most* technical assistance, which suggests that there may be a tradeoff between these two roles, at least in extreme cases.

Also, it is worth noting that although the correlation between

Text continued on page 192

Table XI.1. Characteristics of the Three Local Projects Helped Most and the Three Helped Least by Program Officers

PROJECT RANK	RANKS ON INDEPENDENT VARIABLES																	
			Advisory Role		Assistance		Local Programs		Role	Impact Incidents			ES Inf.	Commitment of:*		Readiness for	Initiation	Effectiveness of Early
Most helped Sites	Mgt. Role	TA Role	Imp.	Goals	Req.	Off.	Cons.	Comp.	Cons.	Total	Major	Minor	On Plan*	Leaders	Staff	Change*	of Change*	Implementation*
1 Saint Martin	9	1	1	1	1	1	10	10	1	3	3	2	1	L	M	2	5	8
2 Uppsala Valley	4	2	2	9	4	10	3	5	2	4	2	4	3	M	H	4	3	2
3 Northampton	1	6	5	10	2	4	1	2	4	7	8	8	8	H	H	1	3	3
Least helped sites																		
8 Glasgow	6	10	9	7	8	5	4	7	6	2	4	3	7	M	L	7	5	7
9 Mount Olivia	2	5	6	7	4	3	2	1	3	6	3	5	5	H	L	4	7	1
10 Dover	8	7	10	6	7	9	6	3	10	8	4	8	9	H	M	4	7	4
Pearson Correlations (All Ten Projects)	.12	.76	.86	.24	.63	.58	-.32	-.53	.67	.42	.65	.25	.42	.32	.50	.37	.25	.05

Note:
*Independent measures developed by Abt Associates, Inc. Signs have been changed to reflect actual directions of correlations.

Table XI.2. Characteristics of the Three Local Projects Receiving the Most Technical Assistance (TA) and the Three Receiving the Least TA

PROJECT RANK	RANKS ON INDEPENDENT VARIABLES																
	Mgt. Role	Advisory Role Assist				Local Proj.		Role Cons.	Impact Incidents			ES Infl. on Plan*	Commitment of:*		Readiness for Change*	Initiation of Change*	Effectiveness of Early Implementation*
		Impl.	Goals	Req.	Off.	Cons.	Comp.		Total	Major	Minor		Leaders	Staff			
Received most TA																	
1 Saint Martin	9	1	1	1	1	10	10	1	3	1	2	1	L	M	2	5	8
2 Uppsala Valley	10	7	3	6	8	6	4	9	1	6	1	6	M	L	7	9	6
3 New Brunswick	4	2	9	2	4	3	5	2	4	2	4	3	M	H	4	3	2
Received least TA																	
8 New Rheinland	7	8	5	8	10	5	8	8	10	10	10	4	L	M	9	3	9
9 Yorktown	3	10	2	10	4	8	6	6	9	9	8	2	L	L	10	10	10
10 Glasgow	6	7	3	5	8	4	7	6	2	4	3	7	M	L	7	5	7
Pearson Correlations (All Ten Projects)	−.33	.79	.37	.76	.51	−.39	−.75	.61	.53	.70	.43	.35	.14	−.26	.37	.09	−.21

Note:
*Independent measures developed by Abt Associates

189

Figure XI.1. An Explanation of Terms Used in Tables XI.1 and XI.2

Most Helped Sites—The three projects which program officers estimate they have helped the most. (See Appendix C, Item 27. This variable used in Table 1 only.)

Least Helped Sites—The three projects which program officers estimate they have helped the least. (See Appendix C, Item 27. This variable used in Table 1 only.)

Projects Which Received Most TA—The three projects which program officers estimate were provided the most technical assistance. (See Appendix C, Items 5–9. This variable used in Table 1 only.)

Projects Which Received Least TA—The three projects which program officers estimate were provided the least technical assistance. (See Appendix C, Items 5–9. This variable used in Table 2 only.)

Linear Correlations—Pearsonian correlations among all ten sites for each independent variable and the variables listed in the left-hand column.

Rank on Independent Variables—The ranking of the ten projects on each independent variable.

Management Role—Stress that program officers said they placed on the managerial role (See Appendix C, Items 1–4.)

Technical Assistance—Amount of technical assistance the program officers said they provided. (See Appendix C, Items 5–9.)

Advisory Role: Implementation—Amount of advice program officers said they provided. (See Appendix C, Items 10–12.)

Advisory Role: Goals—Amount of advice program officers said that they had given concerning project goals. (See Appendix C, Items 8, 9.)

Assistance Requested—Frequency with which program officers said a local project had requested assistance. (See Appendix C, Items 13, 14.)

Assistance Offered—Frequency with which program officers said they had offered assistance to a local project. (See Appendix C, Item 30.)

Local Project Consensus—Extent to which program officers believed local administrators agreed among themselves about the project. (See Appendix C, Items 15, 16.)

Local Project Competence—Level of competence of local administrators as estimated by program officers. (See Appendix C, Items 17, 18.)

Impact Incidents: Total—Total number of incidents program officers recalled concerning a particular project. (See Appendix C, "Impact Index.")

Impact Incidents: Major—Total number of incidents program officers recalled concerning a particular project which they considered "major" incidents. (See Appendix C, "Impact Index.")

Impact Incidents: Minor—Total number of incidents program officers recalled concerning a particular project which they considered "minor" incidents. (See Appendix C, "Impact Index.")

ES Influence on Plan—An independent measure developed by Abt Associates based on the percentage of professional staff in each local project reporting that ES/Washington had a "great deal" of influence on the local project plan. (See Herriott and Rosenblum, 1976, p. 64.)

Commitment of Leaders—An independent measure developed by Abt Associates based on the degree to which the local superintendent was involved in preparing a letter to express interest in participating in the ES program. (See Herriott and Rosenblum, 1976, pp. 38–39.)

Commitment of Staff—An independent measure developed by Abt Associates based on the percentage of teachers in the district who said they consider the ES program a "good idea." (See Herriott and Rosenblum, 1976, p. 66.)

Readiness for Change—An independent measure developed by Abt Associates based on estimates of the following combination of factors: (a) the range of groups within the school system which participated in identifying local needs and project goals; (b) the variety of sources of influence on the formal project plan; (c) independence of the project plan from the influence of ES/Washington; (d) the degree of congruence between locally identified problems and formal project goals; and (e) the extent to which the local professional staff accepted the project plan. (See Herriott and Rosenblum, pp. 57–66.)

Effectiveness of Early Implementation—An independent measure developed by Abt Associates estimating the amount of change that had taken place during the first years of implementation. The measure is based on estimates of the following combination of factors: (a) the number of "facets" of a school district that exhibit change (i.e., change in the curriculum, instruction, community participation, governance, and evaluation); (b) the proportion of the school district affected by these changes; and (c) a qualitative estimate of the "difference" that each innovation has made in the district. (Details can be obtained by writing directly to Robert Herriott, in care of Abt Associates, 55 Wheeler Street, Cambridge, Massachusetts 02138.)

Text continued from page 187
the two advisory roles (i.e., advice about implementation and about goals) is low ($r = .28$); and although program officers seem to have exerted less influence over goals than over implementation, the program officers had a high degree of influence over goals at two of the sites that received the most technical assistance. It is possible that in some cases technical assistance can, advertently or inadvertently, shape goals.

In general, the sites which were estimated to have received the most technical assistance seem to have requested at least some of it. The two which received the most technical assistance ranked first and second on this measure. There is also a tendency on the part of program officers to say they offered technical assistance whether it was requested or not ($r = .51$) to sites which had previously requested it ($r = .48$). Apparently they tended to expand the technical assistance role at those sites.

Role consensus between the program officer and local administrators may contribute to the amount of technical assistance provided ($r = .61$); two of the most assisted sites ranked first and second on role consensus. However, the fact that one of the most

assisted sites was ranked low on role consensus indicates that consensus is not always necessary.

The program officers' answers suggest that the lack of commitment of the local administrators may be an incentive for help (r =
−.39) provided that they otherwise seem to be competent
(r = .75).

Program officers tended to recall more influence incidents at
the sites that received the most technical assistance. All three that
received the most assistance rank high on this measure. The two
that rank lowest on influence also are among those that rank
lowest on technical assistance. However, the fact that one of the
latter sites ranks second on influence indicates that influence can
also be exerted apart from technical assistance. For the ten sites as
a whole, the relationship with technical assistance is clearer with
major influences (r = .70) than with minor influences (r = .43).
The two sites with the most major incidents were both among the
most assisted sites.

The amount of technical assistance they believed they were able
to provide is not clearly related to independent measures of the
amount of influence the Washington Experimental Schools office
exerted on the formal plan (r = .35), nor to the local district's
ability to initiate change (r = .13). But there is a loose relationship
with another independent measure—the district's readiness for
change (r = .42); two of the least helped sites rank low on readiness and one (possibly two) of the most helped ranks high. The
leaders and staff of the most helped projects were not necessarily
highly committed (r = .13, r = .26), but it may be significant that
staff commitment was low in two of the three sites that had the
least help.

Although it is not reflected in the correlation (r = −.21) there is
some tendency for the local projects receiving the most technical
assistance to have changed the most in the early stages of the
project. At least, the three sites that received the least technical
assistance all ranked very low on effectiveness of implementation,
and one of the three which received the most technical assistance
ranked very high (second) on the measure of early implementation. However, it is true that the one site that received the most
technical assistance is also relatively low (eighth) on early
implementation.

Similar analyses were undertaken with a focus on the managerial role and on advisory roles. The patterns in the data can be summarized as follows:

The Managerial Role

As managerial responsibilities increased, it appears that:

- program officers' estimates of local consensus on goals and design increased (r = .80; r = .67);
- their estimated influence on goals diminished (r = −.62);
- they offered more unsolicited advice (r = .48);
- they could recall fewer incidents in which they have had an impact (r = −.52).

Advisory Roles

As the amount of advice they provided about *implementation* problems increased, so did:

- ES/Washington influence on project plans (r = .56);
- program officers' estimates of their ability to help (r = .86);
- the amount of unsolicited advice they gave (r = .82);
- the technical assistance they gave (r = .82);
- requests for assistance (r = .66);
- program officers' estimates of the competence of local school administrators (r = .86); and
- their ability to recall major incidents in which they had an impact (r = .54).

Where program officers' influence on project *goals* was higher:

- the project was less ready for change (r = −.48);
- the amount of change was greater (i.e., magnitude: r = .75; pervasiveness: r = .60) and early implementation (r = .72);
- the commitment of the leaders (and to a lesser extent the staff) was greater (r = .73; r = .41);
- local consensus on goals and design has been lower (r = −.81; r = −.88);
- they employed their managerial responsibilities less (r = −.62).

SUMMARY

I have selected comments from the interviews, supplemented by reports from on-site observers, to highlight some of the consequences of different performance styles. It was noted that the influence attempts were not always or completely successful and that the effects were not limited to local projects; the program officers themselves also seemed to be affected in various ways by the styles they used.

Impact seemed to be contingent upon a number of interrelated factors, including the stage of the project, the persistence of the federal agency and the continuity of its policies, changing expectations at the federal level, instability of the program, the ability of communities to defend themselves, and the vulnerability of particular communities.

An exploratory analysis of the program officers' own beliefs and observations provided some additional clues about conditions that might affect their ability to provide help, to render technical assistance and advice, and to fulfill their contract management responsibilities.

They thought they were of most help when it was requested, especially by local administrators whose competence they respected. But they also believed that their advice was helpful even when not solicited. They seemed to think their assistance had been helpful, and where they believed they had been helpful, they also estimated they had a significant impact on the project, especially on implementation procedures. Also, their own estimates of their helpfulness seemed to be related to local perceptions of the amount of influence that ES/Washington had on project plans.

Program officers stressed their managerial responsibilities in situations where local officials seemed in agreement on project goals and did not solicit their advice. When they did stress this role, they felt they had less impact on a project, especially on its goals.

Where program officers provided a lot of advice about implementation problems, they thought they had more impact, and (through an independent measure) the Washington office apparently had more influence on project plans at these sites. The more advice they said they gave, the more helpful they thought they had been. They were especially inclined to offer advice when they respected the competence of local administrators and when their assistance was requested, although they also gave unsolicited advice. Where they gave advice, they also provided more technical assistance.

Program officers reported having more influence on the goals of those projects that, by an independent measure, were most ready for change. The leaders of such projects were committed to comprehensive change, but according to the program officers, disagreed among themselves about the particulars of the project. The more influence they had on goals, the less emphasis they said they placed on managerial responsibilities, and (through an independent measure) the more change that occurred in the project.

NOTES

1. The word impact was chosen because it seems more neutral than either the term "influence," which several respondents thought implied unwarranted intervention, or the term "help," which is the way some program officers preferred to think of their activities. The reader is again reminded that much of the information about federal impact was provided by program officers themselves. Reasonable precautions were taken to corroborate these reports with other program officers, local project directors, written reports and informal conversations with on-site researchers employed by Abt Associates, and ES files in Washington. Nevertheless, it is important to remember that program officers themselves are one of the primary sources.

2. This measure is based on the number of incidents in which the program officer could recall having exercised major, minor, or subtle influence on the design, procedures or other aspects of the project (see Appendix C). The number reported was weighted 3 for major influences, 2 for minor influences and 1 for subtle influences. The final score is the sum of the total number multiplied by these weights.

3. This measure and some subsequent measures in this section were developed by Abt Associates Inc. from a survey administered to the teachers and administrators who participated in this program in each of the ten school districts. (See Herriott and Rosenblum [1976] for details.)

Chapter XII

Federal Assistance: An Appraisal

The tensions apparent in the ES program are part of a larger conflict in American society: while local organizations are pressing for autonomy, reintegration is being sought at higher levels. Federal control over education does not seem to be a real threat, because there is a system of checks and balances that assures a measure of compromise and negotiation between local and federal control. While the federal level often exercises great influence, dominance changes from time to time and from issue to issue.

Issues raised by the ES program have been observed in other programs as well (see Van Horn and Van Meter, 1976). Speaking of the ESEA Title I, Bailey and Mosher (1968) ask:

> How could the [agency] be specific, even coercive, with regard to fiscal accounting, and at the same time be flexible in establishing criteria for local project *design* (emphasis added)? ... What degree of uniformity in applying national standards should be expected or required (p. 99)?

Such questions ultimately lead to what is a fundamental dilemma. To what extent should a federal agency defer to local autonomy, and to what extent should it enter into an active partnership with local agencies in order to influence and/or control the planning and implementation of local projects? The technical assistance and advisory roles of the ES program were clearly designed to do the latter. Are these two "assistance roles" appropriate? Are they feasible?

197

APPROPRIATENESS OF THE ASSISTANCE ROLES: THE POSITIVE SIDE

An argument can be made in favor of the assistance roles. Many local communities simply do not have the required expertise or the degree of commitment necessary to implement categorical programs by themselves. In this regard a study by the General Accounting Office concluded that ES projects did not prepare operational plans that could be used to carry out and evaluate changes, and did not provide adequate financial information (Comptroller General of the United States, 1976). Furthermore, local projects were able to delay potentially threatening evaluations. Given the inclination of local communities to use outside funds to underwrite existing programs, it appears that some outside stimulus for change is often necessary (Griffiths, 1965; Kirst, 1973).

Even if the *need* for federal influence could not be justified, the *fact* of some kind of federal influence is undeniable. Influence is not control, however, and there is little evidence in this or in other programs to indicate that federal control is an imminent or inevitable threat. ES program officers appeared to be more aggressive and less inclined to defer to local officials than some authors suggest is typical of federal employees (Kirst, 1973; Murphy, 1971), and yet they were never in full control. These and other studies demonstrate the ability of local officials to protect themselves (Corwin, 1973; Kirst, 1973). For example, Ripley and his colleagues (1976) concluded that the federal representatives in CETA programs had less influence on decisions than any other group involved, including the staff of the state agency. Thomas (1976) concludes from a study of the Environmental Protection Agency's implementation strategies that far from providing central direction, the grant-in-aid device resulted in expanded control for the states, because of (1) the uncertainty of federal appropriations, which nullified the agency's ability to define clearly the nature of environmental problems, and (2) the inadequacy of data, which forced the agency to bargain with the clientele. Finally, regional federal administrators followed contrasting leadership styles, which ranged from strong federal control to almost no direction at all.

Similarly, Murphy (1971) concluded that local school districts have primary control over how Title I funds are spent. Among the contributing causes identified were: differences between those who developed and those who implemented the policies, inadequate number of federal staff, disinclination to monitor, the tradition of local control, the absence of pressure from the clientele (the poor), and most important, the dispersion of control and power within the federal system.

At most, federal agencies act as a countervailing force, play a mediating role in a larger system of checks and balances, and exert a real but modest overall influence. Not only are government agencies only one of many sources of national influence, but also their power is restricted on all sides by controversy, congressional constraints, internal bureaucratic controls, and the small proportion of the total operational costs of any program that are typically provided by the federal government (Derthick, 1970). Local governments continue to exercise veto power over those policies that are most repugnant to them (Thomas, 1976).

The fact is that if federal agencies are forced to rely only upon their legal and economic sanctions, they have very little leverage (Berke and Kirst, 1972; Nagi, 1976; Thomas, 1976). Despite concerted efforts for over nearly two decades, the federal government has been unable to completely enforce legal decisions or to fully implement federal guidelines concerning desegregation and the ways in which schools have used federal monies intended to improve education for the poor. Federal agencies can try to *coerce* local agencies to comply through legal proceedings, but since this is a lengthy and expensive route, the courts can be used only in selected cases. Once a project has been funded, the *economic* sanctions available to agencies are limited to their authority to withhold funds and their ability to audit projects. For practical reasons, the former sanction can be used only rarely and in extreme situations. Federal guidelines are usually so vague that it is difficult to prove violations (Derthick, 1970). Moreover, congress is more responsive to the wishes of local officials than to federal bureaucrats. Thus, it is often virtually impossible to cut off local funds (Murphy, 1971). And the effectiveness of audits is limited by the inaccessibility of information, especially information about program operations in addition to fiscal expenditures (see Nagi, 1976; Van Horn and Van Meter, 1976).

In principle at least, the technical assistance and advisory roles provide another and perhaps more effective *normative* leverage (Etzioni, 1961). They help distribute another type of resource—expertise. At the same time they create relationships in which socialization, occupation, persuasion and other normative controls can be brought to bear.

APPROPRIATENESS OF THE ASSISTANCE ROLES: THE NEGATIVE SIDE

However, good reasons exist to question whether government agencies should try to provide either advice or technical assistance since both roles constitute a potentially powerful and disruptive force. They have had clearly discernible negative as well as positive impacts on local projects. Even if Program Officers cannot *control* the local projects, the federal position is consolidated when the authority of expertise is added to the program officer's powerful managerial role. There are logical contradictions in attempting to cultivate collegial relationships against a backdrop of power. The close working relationships involved in providing technical assistance and advice permit federal employees to influence, and on occasion even to co-opt certain aspects of local projects. For, the local agency must not only comply with *explicit regulations* (a restriction that accompanies appropriations at any level of government), but also may find itself being led in directions that would not have been followed on the basis of local priorities alone. Low income communities, which depend on outside funds, are particularly vulnerable to federal intimidation and infringement on individual and local autonomy.

There are other, perhaps even more important considerations. One is that it is difficult for a government agency to provide assistance without compromising its contract management responsibilities. Because it is always possible that public funds will be misused, the federal program officer in this role must be regarded by local officials as a potential adversary. But to provide assistance the program officer must become an ally and in the process will tend to become personally identified with a project's fate. If the advice is accepted by locals, the program officer has a personal investment in the project; if it is not followed, he or she may become unduly critical of the project. To the extent that a project seems to reflect personally upon him, the program officer will be inclined to act as its advocate, perhaps minimizing its faults or exaggerating its strengths. This conflict of loyalty can become especially acute when a program officer also assumes responsibility for reviewing and making recommendations about the very same project components he or she has helped to design and implement.

In the course of providing technical assistance, program officers inevitably become much more familiar with some projects than others. This familiarity can distort their perceptions and perhaps ultimately undermine their objectivity. This places on the director of the overall program the entire burden of making comparative evaluations across all projects, but to do so, he or she must rely heavily upon the recommendations of several program officers each of whom may be acting as an advocate for a different project.

The problem can become aggravated when the program officers are also professional educators, perhaps only temporarily employed by the government. Their sympathy with professional colleagues accustomed to local autonomy and peer control can conflict with organizational responsibilities (i.e., federal regulations and contract compliance). This situation, of course, is not without solution. For example, a centralized decision structure staffed by career bureaucrats could serve as a check on such situations. However, if their agency supervisors are also professional educators, the agency will be vulnerable to cooptation by "the field" (see Corwin and Nagi, 1972; Van Horn, 1976).

In short, such conflicts of loyalty need not always compromise contract management responsibilities, but given the cross-pressures from the assistance roles, the *potential* for role conflict is real.

Even in the rare case, which existed in ES, where all projects are assured continuation, a federal agency still can be criticized for giving some projects more help than others, because (1) the projects receiving aid thereby have an edge in the competition for larger budgets at times of refunding, and (2) it seems improbable that such active federal assistance can be made widely available. This last point is important. Under such conditions it will be virtually impossible to replicate on a wider scale even the most promising projects.

CONDITIONS NECESSARY FOR FEDERAL ASSISTANCE

This mixed evaluation of federal assistance (as embodied in the project advisor and technical assistance specialist roles) is not merely an instance of investigative indecisiveness. It is impossible to make conclusive evaluations without considering the *conditions* that determine a federal agency's capacity to render advice and technical assistance. This study has suggested that such federal assistance requires some rather exceptional circumstances to be effective. I now turn to the task of reviewing some of the conditions uncovered in the course of this investigation.

Because a given condition might affect the various components of each role in different ways, in discussing each condition consideration will be given (as appropriate) to each of the four role components described in Chapter IX: intensive role involvement, collegial relationships, specialized competence, and focused influence.

Project Stage

The amount and type of advice and technical assistance that seems appropriate changes during the course of a project. Advice is especially useful during the preliminary stages, whereas technical assistance can be most effective at very specific times, especially as problems arose during implementation. Also, it takes a certain amount of time (1) for the mutual trust essential to a collegial relationship to evolve, and (2) to allow local officials to establish their priorities and identify areas of greatest need. The stage of the project, then, helps dictate the amount and type of involvement that a program officer can hope to accomplish.

A problem arises, however, from the fact that program officers must alter their relationships with local officials as a project reaches transition points. A person whose skills are needed at one stage of the project might be less useful or effective at another stage, and it is not clear how to prepare for those changes. *Clearer job descriptions* and thorough *in-service training* would help, but there is no assurance that job applicants can be found who possess the range of skills, experience, and personality traits necessary to undertake such a complex set of responsibilities. Even if ways could be found to prepare program officers for these adjustments, the local project directors involved in the relationship would also need background to prepare them for these transitions. *Periodic orientation programs* might be one solution.

Another option is to *organize program officers into teams.* A division of labor might permit individuals to bring their various skills to a project at different times as needed. The obstacles involved in fixing the locus of final authority for contract management and working out coordination would be difficult though not insurmountable.

Administrative Continuity

The amount of planning that has gone into a federal program obviously has an important bearing on its quality and the agency's ability to offer advice and technical assistance. Of course, planning is not the entire answer. Indeed, it is probably *impossible* to fully implement a controversial program as planned, because invariably general policies must be negotiated with the local communities and shaped to particular circumstances. (See Comptroller General of the U.S., 1976; Bailey and Mosher, 1968; Murphy, 1971; Van Horn, 1976:12–13.) The Congress, the public, and program evaluators should not hold program managers responsible for circumstances beyond their control.

However, at a minimum, there must be a certain amount of continuity in the federal-local relationship if advice and technical assistance are to be effective. On this score, the fact that the local ES projects were given a *long-term* (five-year), *irrevocable "moral commitment"* was probably an important incentive behind Washington's efforts to provide assistance. For, having forfeited its right to terminate struggling projects, ES/Washington felt compelled to help them succeed. Nevertheless, in this instance, the local project directors were never fully persuaded that their projects would survive, if only because their contracts had to be renegotiated periodically. Some of them felt that they had no choice but to ritualistically accept whatever assistance was offered.

Nor is assurance of survival enough. *Program continuity* at the federal level is also necessary if program officers are to establish their authority and build the mutual trust necessary to maintain a collegial relationship with local officials. In this case, frequent policy fluctuations and reversals early in this program and rapid turnover of program officers and directors proved to be very disruptive.

Prior Experience of Federal Program Director

The source of leadership for such federal programs is another factor to consider. The first ES program director came from outside the federal civil service. Diverse backgrounds can often help to infuse an agency with new ideas and energy. If the person is a professional educator, he or she can also bring an important grasp of the practitioners' problems to the agency. Nevertheless, outside leaders face a handicap when they have not had practical experience with the federal bureaucracy and when they do not have enough internal support to protect a new, controversial program from attack. And, as mentioned, their identification with the professional education community can also interfere with their ability to enforce organizational procedures and goals.

If program directors are recruited from outside the federal government, perhaps they should be required to serve an apprenticeship in another capacity within the agency prior to being assigned major leadership responsibilities.

Another alternative is to *recruit the best candidates from the super grades of the civil service roster,* and then *monitor their actions through a panel of outside consultants* from relevant professional fields. In addition, such a director's main assistants might be drawn from creative talent outside the agency.

Administrative Support

Providing advice and technical assistance also requires extra funds to pay for lower project loads and the higher travel costs necessary to enable program officers to obtain detailed knowledge about a project. Because the Congress usually maintains strict control over salaries and expense monies, agencies often find it difficult even to obtain sufficient staff to routinely monitor programs (see Murphy, 1971). Technical assistance, being labor intensive, is particularly expensive. At best, such assistance probably can be justified and *supported only in selected large-scale efforts* where monitoring costs can be kept to a small percentage of total program cost.

Type of Legal Relationship

In a sense, the wrong instrument may have been used in the ES program. Given the existence of contracts between NIE and the school districts, the program officer's formal power was always in the background overshadowing any overtures he or she made toward collegiality. Moreover, under such contractual arrangements, federal officers are not *expected* to become personally involved in projects (Baker, 1975). Indeed, local officials can use explicit written agreements to parry federal influence. Even when the contract is not fully explicit, attempts on the part of a program officer to interpret it broadly can be seen as capricious and unwarranted distortions of the formal relationship. Even when a program officer is able to exert influence under such circumstances, his or her *authority* will still be in doubt, and is subject to appeal to the federal contracting officer.

Grants differ from contracts in an important respect. Whereas federal agencies use contracts to secure outside services for their own objectives, grants are awarded to support the recipient's objectives (Baker, 1975). The terms of grants are more flexible and hence more compatible with collegial relationships. There are also disadvantages, of course. Local officials will be vulnerable in some ways when they do not have explicit agreements to protect them. However, only very *explicit contracts* can protect them from federal caprice, and the novel social experiments undertaken in recent years do not seem to lend themselves to the required degree of explicitness. *Still another option is the "Cooperative Agreement."* This instrument is used less frequently than grants or contracts, but in some cases it is useful. NIE has entered into cooperative agreements with its Regional Educational laboratories. The basis of the instrument is an equal partner relationship between the funding agency and the contractor, which gives the later a great deal of autonomy from federal controls. Funding is contingent upon evidence of performance. However, cooperative agreements require long-term relationships in which trust and mutual expectations can be established.

The Program Officers' Expertise

How anxious local officials will be to receive federal advice and technical assistance depends in part on whether the program officers can demonstrate expertise in fields of relevance to the local project. Three conditions must be met to satisfy this requirement: (1) the agency must be able to employ people with particular specialties who *also* have the necessary administrative and managerial skills; (2) the program officers' areas of expertise must be relevant to the needs of the particular project to which they are assigned; (3) the program officers must be able to convince local officials that their advice and assistance will be useful.

Two critical problems can arise. First, local officials sometimes follow a program officer's advice irrespective of their own priorities. In extreme cases, a program officer's interests could virtually dictate the direction a local project takes. Secondly, contract management responsibilities might tend to be neglected by specialists. The program officer's *primary* obligation is to manage the contract. But were these managerial duties to be stressed when program officers were recruited and evaluated, their specialized skills would become a secondary consideration. And, were the needed specialties given priority, the program officers might tend to depreciate or neglect their routine and often mechanical managerial responsibilities.

One option already has been suggested, namely *for several program officers with different skills to work in teams.* As mentioned, this would complicate the maze of relationships that local projects already have to deal with in most federal programs.

Sophistication and Expertise of the Local Community

Local officials seem to be more receptive to federal advice and technical assistance when: (1) they are committed to the objectives of the program (not merely participating to obtain the money); (2) they have not had prior unfavorable experience with federal agencies that would cause them to distrust program officers; (3) they are relatively competent individuals; and (4) they are not in full agreement among themselves concerning project goals or design.

These conditions cannot be met unless the projects are carefully selected for participation in a program. The selection process is usually handicapped by political considerations, deadlines, budgetary constraints, and lack of information. Consequently, it seems that agencies often have little choice but to select poor risk projects and either terminate them in midcourse or attempt to salvage them. However, when technical assistance is provided under these adverse circumstances federal officials have an overwhelming advantage. They can use money as leverage to force their own personal ideas on a local district. This is especially true when: (1) local personnel lack the necessary competencies, but (2) nevertheless want the money, and (3) are easily intimidated and thus vulnerable to advice offered. The submissive, compliant districts that lack local expertise are the best candidates for federal assistance, but they are precisely the ones that are least able to defend themselves against the misuse of federal power and possible infringements upon local initiatives.

While it was not especially evident in this study, a potential irony should be mentioned. There is always a possibility that once an agency makes a commitment to render advice and technical assistance, it will be inclined to select those projects most likely to look to the federal government for such counsel. *Closer monitoring of the process through which local projects are selected to participate in programs would provide some safeguard. An appeals system* to enable communities to take grievances against federal agencies to a neutral body is another possibility. Finally, perhaps federal agencies should exercise restraint and *render counsel only within explicit guidelines and upon explicit request from local officials.*

The Parties in the Relationship

The managerial role can be established vis-à-vis a few high level officials in a local school district who in turn can be held responsible for fulfilling the contract. However, the advice and technical assistance roles require a more complicated set of relationships. If a program officer is to become intensively involved in a project and work with local project members on a collegial basis, he or she must be prepared to establish relationships with a variety of individuals directly responsible for implementing the project; particularly, classroom teachers and principals. But these individuals are often peripheral to the local authority structure. The dilemma is that while program officers need the support of school district administrators, their support is not a sufficient basis for establishing rapport with lower echelon employees; and in fact in some school districts official endorsement simply puts employees on guard. Again, it seems that *the situation requires either very sensitive and skillful individuals as program officers or a team of specialists* to work in different ways with various people at the local level.

Implications

It seems apparent from the experience of the ES program that federal agencies sometimes can provide effective advice and technical assistance, but only under rather complex conditions. In practice, most agencies are severely limited in their ability to meet these conditions. Whether or not such federal assistance can be made more feasible in the future depends upon the answers to at least three practical questions.

- Can a federal agency *provide* comparable assistance to all school districts wishing to implement a given program? And if not, how can the uneven treatment of different local projects be justified; indeed, how can the experiments that have received extensive assistance be replicated elsewhere?
- Can a federal agency employ enough specialists with the range of skills necessary to help local projects operating under diverse circumstances as they evolve through different stages? And if so, what safeguards can prevent federal employees from misusing their authority with local officials dependent on outside funds?
- Can program officers assume responsibility for providing assistance *without* compromising their managerial responsibilities?

While these issues cropped up repeatedly in the course of this study and some options were mentioned, they have not been satisfactorily resolved here. They should be addressed more thoroughly in future research on this neglected topic. In the meantime, I personally doubt that federal assistance has been shown to be superior to the option of requiring local projects to secure their own advice and technical assistance from qualified external sources.

SUMMARY

A case can be made for federal advice and technical assistance. Many communities need it, and under some circumstances, may even require it. Fears about impending federal takeover of local projects are not persuasive. While such assistance does imply a degree of federal influence, communities are by no means defenseless. Federal *control* does not seem to be an imminent threat.

The problems associated with growing federal dominance should not be minimized. Sustained federal assistance could interfere with local autonomy. However, this political issue should not be allowed to drown out equally serious questions about the *feasibility* of such moves, when they are thought desirable.

Feasibility is not an "either-or" issue. It depends upon whether the necessary conditions are present, that is, the conditions which permit an agency to provide effective assistance. A number of these conditions became evident in the course of this study. At a minimum, it seems that a federal agency cannot provide effective advice and technical assistance unless at least the following factors have been taken into account: the stage of the project, the amount of administrative continuity, the program director's experience with the federal bureaucracy, the amount of support and funds to pay for the costs of assistance, whether or not assistance is encouraged or inhibited by the contract/grant mechanism, the combined expertise of the program officers, the sophistication and experience of the local community, and the parties in the relationship.

It is not now clear how federal agencies can meet most of these contingencies. Assistance can compromise an agency's contract management responsibilities, impair the ability of program officers to remain objective toward all projects, and jeopardize any chance of replicating promising projects. Moreover, it is questionable that any federal agency can afford to employ enough specialists with the range of skills demanded of complex research and development projects. And even if that were possible, it would be necessary to devise novel methods of organizing and deploying these specialists, and to establish safeguards to protect communities from the arbitrary actions of aggressive federal employees.

In any event, we have seen that the major question is not merely whether it is *appropriate* for the federal government to provide advice and technical assistance to local projects. An equally important question is whether it is *feasible*. This study has provided some clues, but my answers are by no means conclusive. It is hoped that this volume will stimulate further research on this important topic.

Part IV

Reflections

Chapter XIII

The Entrepreneurial Bureaucracy

In Chapter I, I called NIE an entrepreneurial bureaucracy, and mentioned some major features of this intriguing organizational form. With the events surrounding ES and RDU now before us, it is now time to return to this topic and consider it in greater detail.

THE RATIONAL AND NATURAL SYSTEMS MODELS

First, the reader may have recognized the entrepreneurial bureaucracy as a species of the so-called open, natural systems model of organization. I will begin then by outlining the generic characteristics of natural systems, especially as they contrast with rational models of organization.

Gouldner (1959) posited two fundamentally distinct models used by social scientists to study organizations, which he called the "rational" and the "natural systems" models. Each is derived from a different source of authority—expertise in the first case, and sheer incumbency of office in the second. Dahrendorf (1958) referred to comparable models of society as the "integration" and "coercion" models.

The Rational Model

The following assumptions underlie the rational model:

1. Organizations have clear-cut goals that are understood and subscribed to by the members.
2. Activities are planned.

3. Activities are closely coordinated.
4. The necessary information is available for making the informed decisions necessary to achieve the goals.
5. Officials have sufficient control over the organization to ensure compliance with long-range plans.
6. Rank in the hierarchy is closely coupled with task expertise; expertise in turn is presumed to increase with longevity in the organization.

In short, organizations serve as instruments for realizing group goals. "Rationality" results from integration between means and ends, which is produced by interdependency and firm control by enlightened administrators. As Gouldner (1959) observed, in this model the structure appears to be entirely manipulatable and designed solely for purposes of efficiency (pp. 404, 405). Significant changes are due to planned efforts to increase efficiency, and any departures from rationality can be attributed to mistakes, ignorance, or miscalculation. The keys to this model then, are administrative control coupled with expertise and integration among the various components of the organization.

The Bureaucratic Ideal Type. Bureaucracy as an ideal type is a version of the rational model. Although Weber's (1946) work characteristically was based on a "social-action" framework, his discussion of bureaucracy is more closely allied to "formal theory," in which the essence of organization is found in the various structures or forms of social action abstracted from the specific contents, objectives, or personalities involved. Domination-subordination, the division of labor, clique structure, and group size are all concepts central to this model, although they are not unique to it. The bureaucratic ideal type presumes goal consensus; power is centralized; authority is based on expertise which is in turn reflected in rank; there is close-knit coordination and extensive planning; and the components of organization are highly interdependent. Bureaucracies can be relatively autonomous and impervious to outside attempts to influence them, although in a larger sense they are products of society. Although Weber (1946) considered the nonrational elements in organizations, such as charisma, he was preoccupied with the distinctive rationality that bureaucratic organization provides and that he believed would make it the dominant form in the Western world.

Many traditional, "old line" bureaucracies are undergoing significant transformations. Through systems of "participatory democracy," for example, even low-ranking employees can have some voice in decisions that affect them. Similarly, simple authority hierarchies do not reflect the influence that labor unions and professional associations have on management decisions. The growing influence of specialists is another complication. Purchasing officers, budget analysts, architects, engineers, lawyers, researchers, management and personnel consultants, logistics experts, and other specialists typically do not have "line" authority over other employees, but through their advice to top management, they shape policy more than their formal position suggests. Military rank, for example, has been literally transformed because of the influence specialists have on the decisions of command officers. And then, too, the formerly simple act of delegation has become quite complicated by the growing reliance on subcontracts through which one organization pays another to perform some of its tasks. For example, some government agencies rely heavily on consulting firms to assist with their work, and school districts may contract for food service, police protection, or even the teaching of certain subjects. Of course, these changes apply to some organizations more than to others, but there are enough complications to suggest that one should be cautious about applying the label"bureaucracy" to modern organizations.

The Natural Systems Model

In view of accumulating evidence that organizations frequently do not conform to the rational model (and given sociologists' preference for models that can deal with "unintended" consequences of deliberate action), many social scientists hold an image of organizations as organic, adaptive systems. In Dahrendorf's (1958) coercion model, for example, every organization is subject to ubiquitous change, filled with dissention and conflict, and on the verge of disintegration. His answer to how such organizations are controlled is simply that coercion is imposed on most members by others. The problem of maintaining control is of course far more complicated. The "natural systems" model proposed by Gouldner (1959) seems more sophisticated. It has these features:

1. Consensus on goals is problematic. Members in different parts of an organization are subject to different constraints and often place the interests and objectives of their own unit above those prescribed for the overall organization.

2. Official goals are readily displaced, distorted or neglected as the organization strives to survive and expand. The "direction" of an organization simply evolves from the accumulation of unforeseen commitments made by subordinates as well as by management, and from adjustment to external constraints.

3. Functional autonomy is endemic. One's status and activity in an organization take on value as ends in themselves; salary schedules often are based on conformity and seniority, independently of demonstrated competence or contributions to explicit goals.

4. Power is diffuse. No one group has sufficient information or power to compel a high degree of coordination among the subgroups.

5. Coordination is achieved through a process of exchange, within the organization and with the environment. Decisions are the outcomes of compromise and adaptation among competing groups.

6. Formal authority, as reflected in rank or title, is not necessarily indicative of specialized expertise in carrying out tasks; task expertise is less important than specialized knowledge; neither type of expertise is necessarily reflected in either formal rank or in longevity; control (obedience) is derived from position irrespective of expertise.

Distinctive Features. Knowledge, functional autonomy, and the distribution of power represent three distinct aspects of the natural systems model. First, expertise in the natural system is based primarily on systematic knowledge about a specialized field and only secondarily on a task specialization (training for a specific job) or experience in the organization. These different sources of competence tend to be partially independent. Rank assumes priority over expertise as a basis of authority.

Secondly, given the importance of functional autonomy in the natural systems model, organization "policy" accumulates crescively, that is, in an unplanned manner. Members independently commit the organization to lines of action as they cope with constraints imposed by outside conditions (Selznick, 1943). Gouldner (1959) speaks of "functional autonomy" in recognition of the fact that there is systematic variation in the extent to which different parts of an organization can be independent of one another (pp. 419–27). That is, (1) some roles bestow (or require) more autonomy than others, and (2) some subgroups have more independent support outside of the organization.

Third, the model implies that power is dispersed, partly because authority is decentralized and also because of "slippage" that can occur between the levels at which policies are formulated and those at which they are implemented. Selznick (1948) attributes many of the nonrational properties of organizations to the act of delegating responsibility to individuals who might be in a position to resist demands made of them. Mechanic (1962) identifies several sources of subordinates' power, including their control over other persons and over information, the unavailability of people to replace them, the extraordinary effort that they are sometimes willing to expend, and their capacity to form coalitions. Also, the hierarchy accentuates communication problems; the longer the hierarchy, the more distortion that can take place at each successive lower level due to misinterpretations as well as to conflicts of interest between subordinate and superordinate groups.

To underscore the primacy of power, some writers have portrayed organizations as "political systems" responding to the cross-pressures of their diverse clientele within and outside the organization (Baldridge, 1971). Decisions are products of compromise or coercion. Some attempts have been made to adapt social conflict theories to the study of organizations by portraying an organization as a balance of power. The investigator uses the conflict model to discover whether conflict is based on certain structural arrangements and hence arises when these arrangements are present (Collins, 1975; Corwin, 1970:22–28; Dahrendorf, 1958). Zald (1970) extended the political model by linking it with economic variables. By the "political economy of organizations," he means how the goals are related to power and to the incentive system.

Hierarchy.　The concept of natural system lies at the core of the sociology of organizations, especially the so-called institutional school of sociology. Consider, for example, their view of the *hierarchy*. Conceding that organizations are supposed to be rationally ordered instruments, Selznick (1948) concluded that "as we inspect these formal structures, we begin to see that they never succeed in conquering the non-rational dimensions of organizational behavior," because (1) people act in their own self-interests and (2) the institutional environment exerts its own independent pressures on the organization to adapt.

For Selznick, delegation is the primordial organization act. It is a precarious venture which can never be fully controlled because of overriding institutionalized patterns of deviation. Delegation fosters the inconsistencies that arise between the intent of the policymakers and the way subordinates execute policies for two reasons: because policies must be interpreted, and subordinates often resist and subvert them. As noted, a variety of ways that subordinates can circumvent the intent of a policy have been identified (Mechanic, 1962). Indeed, the difficulty of securing compliance in hierarchical organizations is one theme underlying Etzioni's (1961) typology of organizations.

Parsons (1956) has even questioned whether it is accurate to speak of "delegation." The functions of each level are so essentially different, and they operate under such different pressures, different sources of support, and different bases of reputations that he concludes that "breaks" or discontinuities are part of any line of authority.

Autonomy. Parallel arguments have been advanced about how zones of authority within organizations are often used as bases of *autonomy* interfering with programmed coordination. "All complex organizations," said Barnard (1938:113) "are built up of 'working' or 'basic' organizations overlaid with units of executive organizations." As mentioned, Gouldner (1959:419–27) uses the term "functional autonomy" in recognition of the fact that there is systematic variation in the amount of independence (or looseness) among various parts of an organization. Some roles bestow (or require) more autonomy than others; superiors must rely on the judgments of specialists; some groups have more outside support than others; and "zones of indifference" permit discretionary behavior.

Employing what he calls a "strategic model" of organization, Crozier (1964:156) assigns competition for autonomy among various groups and echelons in an organization a central role:

Each group fights to preserve and enlarge the area upon which it has some discretion, attempts to limit its dependence upon other groups and to accept such dependence only insofar as it is a safeguard against another and more feared one, and finally prefers retreatism if there is no choice but submission. The group's freedom of action and the power structure appear clearly to be at the core of all these strategies.

Crozier's (p. 163) view is that hierarchical order evolves out of the necessity to arbitrate among competing groups and individuals. Accordingly, the power of the hierarchy is incomplete, vulnerable, and negotiable, not absolute. But Simmel (1950) observed the converse, namely that the division of labor can weaken the unity of subordinates and make them more dependent upon their superiors than their peers.

Autonomy is of central importance in Argyris's (1959) definition of organization. He maintains that the essence of organization is not found in either its goals or its structures, but in the patterning among semi-autonomous but interdependent parts. He and others have proposed that organizational stability (and horizontal conflict) increases with the density of "linkages" among these parts. (See also Corwin, 1969; Dubin, 1959; Loomis, 1959; Thompson, 1960; Wilson, 1966.) Young (1970) notes one way that autonomy ("group differentiation") can promote hierarchical conflict: groups become more cohesive when their distinctness is not sufficiently acknowledged by the larger system.

In an uncommonly illuminating discussion of schools as organizations Lortie (1969) also stresses the importance of autonomy. Indeed, the central problem that schools must resolve, he says, is how to achieve a necessarily delicate balance between control and autonomy. He notes several conditions in schools which act as restraints on the ability of administrators to exercise control over teachers, notably that each school is a self-contained organizational unit and that teachers are further isolated within self-contained classrooms. Zones of autonomy are carved out because administrators tend to use controls only at points of possible trouble and in restricted spheres. As a result, executives dominate administrative matters, but their control is muted in instructional areas.

Rules. Still other writers have described the lax enforcement of *rules* in natural systems. The growth of bureaucracy is, in part, an expression of faith in the infallibility of rules. And yet, ironically, rule evasion is widespread because after all, rules are often vague and in any event require interpretation, they encounter resistance for personal reasons, and they often violate community and organizational mores (see Anderson, 1966). Clearly, subordinates are not merely the conformists whom Merton (1957) portrayed conscientiously interpreting rules in only the most literal sense. Indeed, Kohn's (1971) analysis leads to the opposite conclusion: bureaucratic structure provides security and a challenge that requires employees to use their initiative. With reference to teachers, I (1965) found that the large majority of them were compliant rule followers, but there was an important leadership group who were predisposed to exercise their own initiative.

Rules are sometimes employed to strategically support decisions made on nonrational grounds. The Federal Employment Security Investigators in the Francis and Stone (1956) study selected rules that would confirm their intuitive judgments about dubious clients. In another context, Turner (1947) observed that naval officers were often forced to evade rules when they were given direct orders that contradicted the rules. Gouldner (1954) spoke of the "leeway" function of rules, that is, the rhythmic relaxation and tightening of rule enforcement in accordance with worker motivation. Supervisors, he said, use "strategic leniency" to increase their control. However, it is possible that the implicit rules governing rule enforcement (i.e., rules about rules) may be more rigidly followed than the rules themselves.

Goals. The very foundation of rational organizational control has been attacked by writers questioning the utility and significance of organizational *goals* because of the typically loose connection between ends and means. Although Selznick (1943) did not give up the idea of goals, he stressed the process of goal displacement and transformation and the "institutional drift" that can result when organizational policy accumulates in an unplanned manner. Long-range plans must be interpreted, executives lose sight of the goals in the press of day-to-day problems, outside pressures deflect the organization, and members often unintentionally commit the organization to unplanned lines of action as they cope with constraints imposed by outside groups (see also Clark, 1956).

Yuckman and Seashore (1967) maintain that organizations announce goals only in order to justify their efforts to obtain more resources. Accordingly, goals are formulated and changed on the basis of expediency as opportunities arise (see also Corwin, 1973). Thompson and McEwen (1958) suggest that goals are products of negotiation among organizations and with their environment. In addition, goals are shaped in the process of accomodating potentially disruptive, alien subcultures. The end-means schema implicit in the goal-structure dichotomy obscures the fact that action has no ultimate end. For every act, there are innumerable consequences, each in turn creating new actions.

Definitions of Organization. Natural Systems concepts are even the core of some *definitions.* Barnard's (1938) definition of formal organization as a system of consciously coordinated activities of two or more persons is one of the few that avoids imputing to workers common motives and the acceptance of common goals. The essential bond between organization and the individual is contractual. This is Etzioni's (1961) "utilitarian" organization, in which the worker bargains to exchange his services for economic, emotional, and other rewards. Argyris's (1959) definition even more explicitly emphasizes the central role of autonomy and mutual adjustment mechanisms. The definition includes several dimensions: (1) plurality of parts; (2) each part achieving limited objectives; (3) each maintaining itself even while interrelated with others; (4) simultaneously adapting to the external environment, thereby (5) maintaining coordination among the parts. I have defined complex organization as a coalition of subgroups having an indeterminate connection between structure, program, activities and outcomes. More specifically, an organization is a relatively permanent and complex social system that (1) consists of subgroups (or coalitions) and that has (2) a name and a location (that is, an unequivocal collective identity), (3) an exact roster of members, (4) an authority structure, (5) a division of labor, (6) a program of activity, and (7) procedures for replacing members (Caplow, 1964; Corwin, 1970).

Reconciliation of the Models

The rational and natural systems models can be reconciled. They each refer to different points on at least seven variables pertaining to mechanisms used to integrate social organizations. Four of the variables can be regarded as primary integrating mechanisms: (1) consensus among the membership on values, norms, and objectives; (2) functional interdependence among the parts of an organization (such that each part must cooperate in order to achieve its own objectives); (3) reciprocity, or a balanced exchange of goods and services among the parts of an organization; and (4) centralized power, which enables the central office to impose its will on members of the organization. Three additional variables act as supplemental integrating mechanisms; (5) expertise, or the authority bestowed to persons in recognition of their knowledge; (6) task competence based on experience; and (7) coordinated planning, as reflected in the number of alternatives considered in making policy decisions and the time taken into consideration.

The rational model is a limiting case, since it describes one extreme on this set of variables. The natural systems model, on the other hand, refers to organizations that occupy the other extreme on each variable, namely: (1) absence of consensus, (2) functional autonomy, (3) bargaining and compromise, (4) decentralization, (5) incomplete information, (6) separation of rank, experience and expertise, and (7) lack of coordination (Corwin, 1970). In the absence of consensus, planning and coordination will be inversely related to the amount of functional autonomy and decentralization of power in the organization. In many cases, effective planned control in a decentralized organization is likely to be imposed from outside rather than from within the organization itself. In any event, decisions will be based on bargains between different subgroups.[1]

OPEN VERSUS CLOSED MODELS

There is also another set of primary models which helps account for the different approaches researchers have taken to organizations. Parallel to the patterns of functional autonomy within organizations are patterns of autonomy between the organization and its outside environment. The open and closed models of organization are based upon different assumptions about the extent to which organizations can be autonomous from the environment and how important the environment is for understanding processes internal to the organization.

Closed Models

Most studies have concentrated on internal organizational characteristics as though they function independently from external influences. Research on the "span of control" of organizations, which extends from the work of Gulick and Urwick (1937) to that of Blau and Schoenherr (1970) illustrates this approach. However, sociologists have become increasingly uneasy about the narrowness of this focus.

Open Models

Social scientists have employed a variety of concepts dealing with very limited, albeit important, aspects of the environment: local versus cosmopolitan (Gouldner, 1959; Waller, 1932), employee versus professional norms (Blau and Scott, 1962; Corwin, 1961, 1970; Hall, 1968) status versus office (Davis, 1949:88–89), institution versus organization (Selznick, 1943). However, these concepts were only stopgap measures.

Some writers now regard openness as the key to organizational analysis (Katz and Kahn, 1966; Lawrence and Lorsch, 1967; Levine and White, 1961; Selznick, 1943; Stinchcombe, 1965; Terreberry, 1968; Thompson and McEwen, 1958). Several distinct approaches have been taken to organization-environment relations, including (1) studies of interorganizational relationships, (2) boundary maintenance studies, and (3) studies of the organization's relationships with the sociocultural environment.

Although the open model provides a broader perspective on organizations than any other available approach, several types of problems remain unresolved. First, mechanisms have not been identified to account for how the sociocultural characteristics exert their influence and why organizations located within the same context often differ from one another. Secondly, the interpretations tend to be rather speculative since it is difficult to demonstrate that it is the environment operating independently of other associated factors, such as characteristics of the membership. Third, the direction of influence usually has been viewed only from society to a passive organization. Little attention has been given to influences that organizations can have on their environments.

One way around some of these problems is to examine the way people define, and play, boundary-spanning roles. Thus, for example, in ES it was shown that NIE exerted influence on local projects by offering advice and technical assistance, and in the process it played an active aggressive role in some local projects. The way program officers used their discretion in shaping different roles was only partially determined by their backgrounds. Other conditions within the society and the agency were also critically important in determining which roles received priority and how effectively they could be performed.

PROPERTIES OF THE ENTREPRENEURIAL BUREAUCRACY

Given that the EB is a special case of the open natural system, we can next identify the distinguishing features that separate it from other natural systems. The EB is a "hybrid" form of organization in that it represents a synthesis, or mutation, of selected extremes associated with natural systems. It is probably an "emergent" form of organization as well, in that it seems to be produced by, and confined to, a unique configuration of social conditions. An attempt will be made to identify some of these conditions at the end of this chapter.

The EB is based on a unique constellation of the three properties mentioned in the first chapter. First, in EBs subordinates are given more encouragement to take initiative than is characteristic of most natural systems. While all natural systems are decentralized, decentralization itself does not ensure that subordinates will use the discretion available to them. The EB not only permits discretion but aggressively capitalizes on it by explicitly rewarding initiative and competition.

Moreover, the initiative demanded of subordinates in EBs can be consequential. Both Bendix (1942) and Gouldner (1954) stressed the fact that executives always must rely on their subordinates to take a great deal of initiative. Accordingly, "representative" organizations, where subordinates participate in decisions, are tolerated and even cultivated. And, there is some support for this proposition in some of Blau's (1970) work. His data indicate that after a threshold point, decision making becomes decentralized in large and hierarchical organizations, thus giving subordinates more discretion in large hierarchical organizations than in small, flat ones. However, when these writers speak of "initiative," they are thinking of the occasions when executives consult their subordinates and the minor ways that anyone can exercise influence in the course of his or her daily work routine. In contrast to these minor actions, in EBs subordinates are formally rewarded for assuming the managerial responsibilities and the risks associated with establishing new programs, activities, and relationships.

Secondly, in comparison to other natural systems, personnel in EBs frequently rotate between government agencies and other institutions such as universities, state and local governments, research firms, and businesses. That is, experts from outside the EB, who have not had experience in it and who do not plan to confine their careers to such organizations, are routinely given temporary appointments. EBs are used as stepping-stones to still other types of organizations and opportunities. To hold a temporary appointment in an EB at most means that the expert must divide his or her loyalties between the agency and colleagues and practitioners in client organizations in the "field" outside the agency, to which one day he or she might return. Thus, split loyalties and allegiances to external constituencies are prevailing features of EBs.

Third, specialized knowledge (expertise) assumes even greater priority in EBs than in other natural systems. At times, expertise constitutes a competing basis of authority. At other times, it becomes a basis for promotion and recruiting new leadership. Consequently rank and knowledge are more closely associated in EBs than in other natural systems, that is, high-ranking officials are often recognized subject matter specialists. However, the role and type of expertise in EBs differs in two respects from other natural systems: (1) in EBs most subordinates also possess expertise and (2) in EBs expertise takes priority over other bases of competence such as job training and on-the-job experience.

ENTREPRENEURIAL BUREAUCRACIES AND OLD LINE AGENCIES

The significance of the entrepreneurial bureaucracy (EB) can be best appreciated when contrasted with an old-line agency (OLA).

Of course, these are constructed or "ideal types" and they do not exist in pure form. All organizations are hybrids containing various mixtures of both types at different times, for different functions, and at different levels of the hierarchy. But it is reasonable to assume that the entrepreneurial form will be more prominent in some agencies than in others, and I believe that this form has dominated NIE since it was created in 1972. It is important to note, too, that NIE was in turn (until 1980) encysted within old-line agencies in the HEW complex.

Entrepreneurial and old-line agencies share some features of natural systems, but they differ in several respects, including the career incentives used, the basis and structure of authority, and the type of expertise required, the division of labor, and the allegiances of employees (see Figure 8).

The Entrepreneurial Bureaucracy

In this type of agency, as noted, the incentive system is the key. In the EB, the managerial strategy is to recruit bright, aggressive functionaries and give them the freedom they need to initiate and manage their own programs. They are rewarded with visibility, influence, and autonomy with respect to the field as well as to the agency. However, they are never given *carte blanche*. They must compete with others for resources, and therefore they must cultivate internal and external support for their plans. It follows that they must remain sensitive to the market and they must aggressively merchandise their ideas. They must possess the interpersonal skills necessary to maneuver their projects through the bureaucracy, and they must have the political savvy needed to form and work with fluid external constituencies. Because of this dependency upon personal constituencies, their loyalties are split between aggrandizing their position in the hierarchy and satisfying the clientele whom they are serving.[2] But the staff person who can satisfy these demanding political constraints will be relatively free from many of the bureaucratic controls characteristic of OLAs. In lieu of close supervision, the management relies upon subordinates to use their discretion to produce "results."

This heavy reliance on creativity and personal initiative also calls for a diffuse decision-making structure with corresponding autonomy for individuals and groups. Power is personalized, and some activities are relatively unstructured just as they are in so-called personal bureaucracies; the difference is that in the latter authority is centralized exclusively in the top leader. However, the fact that power is diffuse does not mean that EBs are "anarchies" (Sproul et al., 1978).[3] We have already identified certain patterns (see Figure XIII.1). Moreover, in this intensely competitive environment, employees often find it advantageous to trade off their individual autonomy in order to form temporary coalitions and power blocks. The result is a fluid and fickle division of labor, which produces numerous but often short-lived and poorly coordinated new initiatives. But the whole process is nonetheless governed by norms and results in a kind of understandable social order.

Such an agency recruits experts who are specialized in substantive areas of research and practice, and who can provide advice and technical assistance to contractors. As specialists they can call upon their expertise to inspire and direct centralized programs of research, and they can relate to their counterparts in the field as colleagues. They freely offer solicited and unsolicited advice and technical assistance to local projects, which can immerse them in every phase of project operations from writing the proposal to revising the final report. In competitive and rapidly changing fields of research and development, youth is valued over experience. Temporary term appointments are commonly used to attract outside experts for short stays. Personnel turnover tends to be high and programs short in duration.

The Old-Line Agency

Old-line agencies can exhibit features of natural systems, but they use fundamentally different mangement strategies. They reward functionaries for their commitment to long-standing policies, for implementing centrally planned, long-term programs, and for their administrative skills, especially their ability to coordinate and conscientiously monitor operating programs. These skills accrue from experience in bureaucratic agencies and on-the-job training rather than from formal training in a subject matter field. The subordinate staff of OLAs do not have much opportunity to initiate programs on their own, although they may be consulted. Instead, they are closely supervised through staff

Figure XIII.1. Management Strategies Used in Entrepreneurial Bureaucracies and Old-Line Agencies

	Entrepreneurial Bureaucracies	Old-Line Agencies
1. Incentives	visibility and influence within the agency and in the field	predictable promotions and salary increases; increased responsibility
2. Behavior Rewarded	initiative, responsiveness to clientele, giving technical assistance and advice to contractors	compliance; loyalty to established policies and practices; monitoring contracts
3. Abilities Required	merchandising skills; interpersonal and political skills	administrative skills: coordinating and monitoring
4. Basis of Authority	professional expertise in a substantive field of research or practice	administrative experience in bureaucratic agencies
5. Authority System	decentralization: autonomy, discretion	centralization: compliance, close supervision
6. Division of Labor	fluid; temporary coalitions based on shifting loyalties and markets; intense competition	stable; clearly defined responsibilities and interdepencies
7. Allegiance or reference orientation	loyalty split between a specific agency and external constituencies; personal mobility and turnover	loyalty to the bureaucratic system rather than to a specific agency or its constituencies

| 8. Outcomes/ products | new programs based upon current theory; often discretionary; often short term | long term service programs with established clientele and constituencies |

meetings, routine reports, and budgetary controls and are guided by central policy. They find other rewards in predictable promotions, increased responsibilities, and salary increments.

Whereas employees of EBs are expected to take bold initiatives with the support of external constituencies, career bureaucrats in OLAs are characteristically predisposed toward gradualism, avoidance of direct assaults on problems, and political cautiousness (Heclo, 1977). Since functionaries are not closely identified with a particular substantive area, they rely heavily on the advice of outside expert consultants to make judgments about technical matters. Constituency building is handled at central management levels of the agency, subordinates cultivate ties with their supervisors, and political pressures filter down through the hierarchy.[4] With no binding commitment to either a specialty or a constituency, the loyalties of the staff extend to the bureaucratic system as a whole. They are not bound to a particular position or government agency, but they do not readily transfer outside the system in which they have tenure. Instead they are free to rise through the government bureaucratic system in pursuit of new opportunities anywhere their administrative skills and government experience can be applied.

SOME CONSEQUENCES

Using this thumbnail sketch, we can inquire into the consequences likely to result from these differences. Some clues can be inferred from the way RDU and ES were designed and managed.

Advantages

First, EBs offer numerous advantages over OLAs. These include:

- Extensive influence exercised by experts employed within the agency;
- Assistance and advice from experts readily available to clients;
- Responsiveness to social change via continual review and readjustment of priorities;
- Sensitivity to external, diffusely organized constituencies;
- Creativity, high energy, and organizational renewal facilitated by stress on initiative and by continual rotation of professionals from the field through the agency; and
- Flexibility in approaches to management and problem solving.

However, EBs also pose some unresolved problems that merit further consideration.

Problems

Fragmentation. Probably the most serious problem is the high degree of fragmentation among programs associated with EBs. Fragmentation is particularly pronounced because of competitiveness and tension created by the incentive system. It seems a gross contradiction to hold an agency, that is itself so loosely organized, responsible for coordinating a maze of programs generated by competition among bureaucrats. The ultimate irony is that, rightly or wrongly, federally initiated programs have been deemed necessary because the research community was presumed to be too disorganized to plan coherent programs of research. And yet, EBs duplicate at another level the chaotic approach to R & D that federal planning was supposed to correct. I do not mean to say that funding overlap and alternative approaches to a problem are necessarily ineffective strategies. But it is not clear that a federal agency is needed to promote laissez-faire approaches.

Inability to Plan and Monitor. Beyond this incapacity to coordinate, EBs have special difficulty when relating to contractors in the field. This difficulty is due to the delicate conflict between egalitarianism and competition for prestige characteristic of professional relationships. When expertise and the collegial role are introduced into a bureaucratic funding agency, so too are the vicious competition and the status hierarchies that are often associated with the academic disciplines. In attempting to juggle collegial and bureaucratic forms of authority, the official has a special problem with colleagues in the field concerning how much control to exercise. The dilemma can be resolved in two different ways.

1. *Vague Plans*—In one scenario, the official defers to the judgments of colleagues in the field. For example, the official may write program plans that are deliberately vague and contain enough gaps so that contractors are able to exercise their own discretion over extensive areas of implementation. While it can sometimes be useful to treat government program plans as little more than general guidelines, thus allowing contractors to fill in the details, the vagueness also can compromise the government's ability to monitor. In some cases, responsiveness to the field seems to border on *collusion* between federal employees and their clients.

2. *Improper Exercise of Power*—Another scenario is equally plausible and has comparably serious implications. As acknowledged specialists, professionals in EBs can call upon not one, but two bases of authority: their official position as custodians of research money, and their professional role as experts. This dual authority structure contributes to an ambiguous commingling of professional ambition with scaler status in the organization hierarchy, which can give them the leverage they need to satisfy their entrepreneurial ambitions in relation to their colleagues. The fact that they are rewarded for their ability to influence the direction of R & D in a particular field puts them in an opportune position to persuade, coerce, or intimidate colleagues to adopt their ideas as a condition of receiving or maintaining money—the epitome of federal control. There is, at best, a fragile line between an expert who initiates and directs a program of research and one who, in the capacity of a colleague offering advice or technical assistance, negotiates with particular individuals to change their procedures or theories as a condition for being funded. Employees of OLAs can also act coercively, of course, but since they are less likely to think of themselves as experts, their requests do not carry the sanction of professional authority; and, moreover, they will prob-

ably be less tempted to assume the advisory or technical assistance roles or to adopt either egalitarian or superior postures in technical matters.

The standard government procurement instruments are not well suited to EBs. RFP contracts can protect contractors from being co-opted against their will, but for the reasons already noted, EBs have difficulty enforcing them, and the contracts do not prevent subtle bargaining and collusion. Grants are in some ways more compatible with the client orientation of EBs, but they preclude the kind of federal direction that officials must exercise if they are to take full advantage of opportunities to influence a particular field.

Poor Articulation of Temporary Systems. There is still another problem which, though shared with OLAs, is particularly acute in EBs. Whereas the bulk of career executives in the federal government have worked in the same agency at least since reaching middle management ranks (with only about 3 percent of positions filled from outside the government) (Helco, 1977), EBs rely heavily on temporary personnel for term appointments to import fresh ideas into the agency from the field. They in turn cultivate short-term projects (like RDU) whose fates become closely tied to the career exigencies of their program directors. It is no easy task to integrate the rotating personnel. They walk a fragile line between being so abrasive that they will lose the support of the insiders upon whom they depend to carry out their ideas, and becoming so thoroughly co-opted that they lose the peculiar perspectives they brought to the agency in the first place.

Similarly, it is not always easy to terminate a temporary program when it is so closely tied to the personal careers and fortunes of individuals. More generally, special mechanisms are needed if good ideas are to be salvaged from limited, term projects. Each of these problems can be handled with some simple policies but, in EBs especially, such policies must be made explicit from the outset of a new program.

Tensions with the Contracts Office. Finally, generic tensions between program officers and contract officers tend to be exacerbated in EBs. Even though situated in EBs, contract offices are modeled after OLAs. Contract officers have difficulty tolerating the liberties taken by aggressive program officers in their direct negotiations with contractors. At best, these internal conflicts can create inconveniences for contractors, or grantees, and at worst they can tear the contractor between conflicting expectations.

SUMMARY

Warwick (1975:183) asserts that organizational theories based on factories, schools, prisons, hospitals, insurance companies, and other organizations are inapplicable to government agencies where, he is convinced, there are irrepressible pressures toward bureaucratization. Government agencies face many problems—such as communication overload, accountability to oversight committees, the struggles of appointed officials to control powerful career employees, and subordinates' demands for clarity and protection. Warwick believes they can respond only by adding levels of hierarchy and proliferating rules. While this might be an accurate portrayal of old-line agencies where bureaucracy has already taken hold, such an immutable monolithic stereotype of government agencies is inaccurate. The case of NIE clearly shows that business, professional, and political norms compete as viable options to more bureaucracy. Whereas Barton *distinguishes* between public bureaucracies and business and professional organizations on the basis of some of the features noted here, what makes EBs unique is precisely that they are *emergent hybrids* based on *constellations* of norms associated with all those organizational types. In particular, the competition and redundancy that Barton attributes to free market business organizations are the prevailing means of coordinating bureaus and programs in EBs. What *can* be said is that the way government agencies respond to crises is determined by their basic administrative style. Entrepreneurial bureaucracies are predisposed to handle problems by decentralizing and placing more reliance on the initiative and influence of temporary, middle- and lower-echelon experts.

A question that naturally arises is, why do EBs evolve alongside OLAs? Of course, this question cannot be fully answered from a single case, but the situation at NIE does provide some plausible clues. One possibility is that the functions of an organization are responsible for this type of structure. NIE was responsible for fostering and disseminating research on education, and it would not be difficult to develop a convincing argument that research flourishes better in an organization where experts are encouraged to use their creativity and initiative. Following this reasoning would lead one to expect that EBs are characteristic of a variety of scientific, research and development based organizations.

Another possibility is that different types of organizational structures evolve during each historical era, and that EBs are currently in "vogue" for all types of recently created organizations. Or, still another related possibility is that new organizations often begin as EBs and tend to become transformed into OLAs as they "mature."

But I think there is another critical factor in this case. As stressed at the beginning of the volume, NIE was thrust into a precarious environment. It seems to me that OLAs tend to be associated with secure "domesticated" environments (Carlson, 1964), where there is some assurance that the organization will have a continuing demand for its services, stable resources, and above all, powerful constituents, benefactors, and sponsors. NIE was not able to cultivate a powerful loyal constituency. Many of the constituents it tried to serve were at best indifferent to its fate, and others were often skeptical or hostile to some of its policies and practices. NIE has always existed in a "wild" enviornment with few assurances for survival. EBs seem best suited to organizations struggling to survive.

In any event it seems reasonable to think of the EB as an *emergent hybrid* form or organization, or administration pattern. It is an "emergent hybrid" in the sense that it represents a unique combination of organizational properties that, I believe, still occurs with relative infrequency. And, it is also "emergent" in the sense that it is a unique product of modern conditions, including the requirements of complexly organized research systems, modern management philosophies, and the uncertain fate of newly established public organizations. It is indeed significant that currently even government agencies are not immune to the threats to survival that characteristically have been associated with organizations competing in the private sector. In fact, it is conceivable that the survival of many private sector organizations is far less problematic than that of some public institutions. If so, do they have characteristics comparable to old-line government agencies? The question is beyond the scope of this book, but the possibilities for applying the framework developed here to other settings are intriguing.

Whatever the explanation of its origins, the EB can inject creative energy, expertise, and responsiveness into the federal government, but at a possible cost of fragmentation, lax monitoring, intimidation of colleagues in the field, conflict between short-term and long-term employees, and fragile programs that become closely linked to the personal fortunes of their sponsors and that are not supported by highly bureaucratized components of the government. It is not merely a question of whether EBs are worth these costs. There is no doubt that they perform some important functions. They sustain technical competence, social concern, imagination and flexibility in what otherwise might be highly static, remote areas of government. The policy question is how to maintain a productive *balance* between these two managerial systems. The first step is to become more fully aware of the differences between these forms of bureaucracy.

NOTES

1. For a more extensive treatment of the implications of rational and natural systems models for coordination and conflict in organizations see Corwin, 1981.

2. Rourke (1979) distinguishes between "constituency" agencies which have been co-opted by specialized segments of the population and "self-directing" agencies. The latter normally deal with deferential publics, and the outside groups with which such an agency interacts have very often been created by its activities. EBs do not fit neatly into either category. They devote much of their energy to identifying and creating constituencies to which they can be responsible. That is, while they build their own constituencies in the manner of self directing agencies, they are often subservient to these same specialized interests in the way that constituency agencies operate.

3. According to Sproull et al. (1978:5) an "organized anarchy" is an organization characterized by "ambiguous goals, unclear Technology, and fluid participation." Beliefs and actions, problems and solutions are only loosely connected in such organizations. Elsewhere (Corwin, 1981) I have tried to demonstrate that these ideas were anticiapted in the literature on Natural Systems reviewed in this chapter. The open natural system model provides more precise criteria for differentiating the non national elements of an organization. The ambiguities which surround goals, technologies, and participation can be accounted for as by products of the way EB's as open, natural systems were structured.

4. The point here is that staff specialists at *lower* rungs of the hierarchy are discouraged from cultivating their own constituencies. High-level administrators

do often have political connections to protect their budgets. However, control over political contacts is jealously guarded even at the highest levels of bureaucracy. Many OLAs have a special office to handle all contacts with Congress. When the Teacher Corps lost its status as an independent program and became incorporated into the OE hierarchy, its director was fired. Part of the problem was that the contacts he had cultivated with members of Congress and in the administration challenged the position of his adminmistrative superiors.

Appendices

APPENDIX A. PEARSON CORRELATION MATRIX FOR SELECTED VARIABLES*
(N = 10 PROJECTS)

Variable	1	2	3	4	5	6	7	8	9	10	11	12	13	14	15	16	17	18	19	20	21	22
1. ES Influence	—	-.20	-.35	.36	.46	.20	.37	.65	.12	-.29	.15	.42	.38	-.15	.35	.08	.56	.36	.47	.44	.13	.12
2. Readiness for Change	-.20	—	.41	-.59	-.69	-.48	-.65	-.57	-.56	.21	.42	.37	.25	-.65	.46	.00	.18	-.48	.50	.64	.24	.48
3. Initiation of Change	-.35	.41	—	-.20	.00	-.11	-.26	-.08	-.70	.25	.00	.24	.13	-.20	.09	-.38	.22	-.33	.26	.29	-.19	.20
4. Magnitude of Change	.36	-.59	-.20	—	.70	.93	.98	.86	.29	-.58	-.81	.15	-.11	.24	-.13	.37	.08	.75	-.20	-.22	.05	-.14
5. Extensiveness of Change	.46	-.69	.00	.70	—	.59	.72	.84	.04	-.41	-.53	.12	-.12	.20	-.17	-.11	.17	.40	-.13	-.19	-.11	-.06
6. Pervasiveness of Change	.20	-.48	-.11	.93	.59	—	.84	.68	.20	-.51	-.71	.14	.04	.03	.20	-.25	.07	.60	-.11	-.23	-.15	-.07
7. Early Implementation	.37	-.65	-.26	.98	.72	.84	—	.86	.35	-.51	-.75	.05	-.21	.36	-.21	-.38	.04	.72	-.33	-.31	-.05	-.25
8. Commitment of Leaders	.65	-.57	-.08	.86	.84	.68	.86	—	.15	-.60	-.76	.32	.01	.20	.14	-.30	.36	.74	.06	.05	.02	.00
9. Commitment of Staff	.12	-.56	-.70	.29	.04	.20	.35	.15	—	-.16	-.15	-.50	.36	.35	-.26	-.19	-.38	.41	-.34	-.28	.25	-.18
10. Local Consensus on Goals	-.29	.21	.25	-.58	-.41	-.51	-.51	-.60	-.16	—	.79	-.43	.00	.13	-.53	.80	.34	-.81	-.17	-.20	-.46	-.49
11. Local Consensus on Design	.15	.42	.00	-.81	-.53	-.71	-.75	-.76	-.15	.79	—	-.16	.13	-.15	-.20	.67	.15	-.88	.09	.07	.00	-.04
12. P.O. Helpfulness	.42	.37	.24	.15	.12	.14	.05	.32	-.50	-.43	-.16	—	.58	-.31	.76	-.12	.86	.24	.71	.63	.42	.65
13. Offering Unsolicited Advice and Criticism	.38	.25	.13	-.11	-.12	.04	-.21	.01	.36	.00	.13	.58	—	-.38	.51	.49	.82	.00	.80	.48	.53	.28
14. Clarity of NIE Policy and Procedures	-.15	-.65	-.20	.24	.20	.03	.36	.20	.35	.13	-.15	-.31	-.38	—	-.31	.02	-.27	.28	-.66	-.69	-.15	-.64
15. Technical Assistance	.35	.46	.09	-.13	-.17	.20	-.21	.14	-.26	-.53	-.20	.76	.51	-.31	—	-.33	.79	.37	.75	.76	.53	.70
16. Managerial Role	.08	.00	-.38	.37	-.11	-.25	-.38	-.30	-.19	.80	.67	-.12	.49	.02	-.33	—	.13	-.62	.19	-.06	-.52	-.34
17. Influence on Implementation	.56	.18	.22	.08	.17	.07	.04	.36	-.38	.34	.15	.86	.82	-.27	.79	.13	—	.28	.86	.66	.20	.54
18. Influence on Goals	.36	-.48	-.33	.75	.40	.60	.72	.74	.41	-.81	-.88	.24	.00	.28	.37	-.62	.28	—	.00	.01	.22	.07
19. Project Competence	.47	.50	.26	-.20	-.13	-.11	-.33	.06	-.34	-.17	.09	.71	.80	-.66	.75	.19	.86	.00	—	.90	.27	.70
20. Assistance Requested	.44	.64	.29	-.22	-.19	-.23	-.31	.05	-.28	-.20	.07	.63	.48	-.69	.76	-.06	.66	.01	.90	—	.47	.76
21. Total Impact	.13	.24	-.19	.05	-.11	-.15	-.05	.02	.25	-.46	.00	.42	.53	-.15	.53	-.52	.20	.22	.27	.47	—	.75
22. Major Influence	.12	.48	.20	-.14	-.06	-.07	-.25	.00	-.18	-.49	-.04	.65	.28	-.64	.70	-.34	.54	.07	.70	.75	.75	—

*Legend: The correlations for variables 1 through 9 are based on *ranks*. These scores were developed by Abt Associates. The correlations for variables 10–22 are based on measures developed from questionnaires completed by program officers. Between 2 and 4 program officers answered for each site. Their responses were summed and averaged by site. Also, all project stages have been combined. (See Figure XI.1, pp. 190–192, for details.)

Incidents Related to Contract Manager Role* (N = 36)

- Refusing to continue financing a physical education program until board agreed to continue program after termination of contract. (1)
- Withholding funds until the promised project objectives/plans were formulated, or reformulated. (3)
- Threatening to cancel contract unless district proceeded to implement project plans. (1)
- Requiring prior approval from ES before spending project money for hiring consultants, staff training activity, travel plans, teaching supplies and materials, or renovation of buildings, or making program changes. (5)
- Disapproving a superintendent's request to appropriate project funds for his own personal use. (2)
- Denying requests by local projects to create a separate position for the project director. (3)
- Requesting local districts to replace project directors. (3)
- Interviewing a new superintendent of schools to evaluate him as a project director. (2)
- Disapproving a proposed project director. (1)
- Ordering a school district to reduce the size of its request (but without stipulating how much). (1)
- Requiring schools to increase administrative costs at the expense of staff development. (1)
- Pressuring a district to staff a promised bilingual program under threat of a budget reduction.
- Requiring a community to broaden the base of citizen participation in planning. (3)
- Disapproving a request to paint walls in connection with renovation of a school room for early childhood education. (1)
- Criticizing local officials for not following SOP. (3)
- Refusing to issue guidelines after repeated requests from local districts. (1)

*The number of times this type of incident was reported is in parentheses ( ).

- Slow processing of local project's requests for reimbursement. (1)
- Providing simplified forms and procedures to expedite payments to local districts. (3)

Incidents Related to Project Advisor Role (N = 72)

- Disapproving plans for summer workshops for teachers in career education and cultural education. (1)
- Blocking a proposed math component. (3)
- Informing autonomous school districts they must collaborate as a condition for receiving funds. (3)
- Criticizing the project or plan for:
    Lack of coordination (6);
    Too much authority granted to consultants to set priorities and policy (1);
    Lack of meaningful local evaluation (5);
    Lack of meaningful "comprehensiveness" (1);
    Lack of detail about how plan would be implemented (1);
    Excessive personnel and/or costs (1);
    Vague project goals (and characterizing the plan as a "loose collection of ideas") (7);
    Lack of relationship between goals and the purpose of the project (5);
    Inconsistencies among proposed changes (2);
    Lack of detail about proposed staff training (2);
    Inadequacies in the plans for administration and governance of the project (6);
    Lack of detail about procedures for developing the career and the vocational components of the plan (5);
    Lack of detail in plans regarding curriculum changes (3).
- Insisting that a summer staff development plan be prepared and submitted for approval. (1)
- Requiring detailed plan for integrating Head Start children into early childhood education program. (1)
- Challenging and criticizing school officials during meetings. (3)
- Criticizing a school principal, which directly led to his resignation. (1)

- Informing local officials of the availability of equipment, which was then budgeted into their plan. (1)
- Encouraging a project to establish a training program for the local evaluation staff. (4)
- Encouraging a district to use a team approach to the local evaluation. (5)
- Urging districts to abandon formal evaluation designs for activities that would be more immediately useful to the district. (1)
- Providing moral support to a group of teachers who were encountering resistance to a proposed resource center. (1)
- Expressing sympathy and understanding about local problems and providing support to local personnel. (1)
- Encouraging a local district to go beyond the original plan in curriculum reform. (1)

Incidents Related to Technical Assistance Role (N = 21)

- Requesting and helping a project to revise the materials that had been developed because of their poor quality. (4)
- Suggesting that a position be created for a full-time on-site project consultant. (1)
- Proposing definition of, and criteria for, behavioral objectives related to an evaluation/design. (4)
- Recommending a specific teacher to be director of the local evaluation. (1)
- Selecting and/or briefing a consultant to work with the local project. (2)
- Proposing a way to reorganize the project's governance system. (1)
- Instructing a local evaluation staff person about her responsibilities. (3)
- Acquainting districts with packaged evaluation and curriculum plans. (3)
- Helping implement a packaged math program in an elementary school. (2)

Incidents Unrelated to Official Roles (N = 4)

- Entering school building and interviewing teachers without informing principals. (1)

- Prematurely informing a school board member about a superintendent's confidential decision to resign. (1)
- Informing a school board that a disproportionate amount of money was being spent for the athletic program. (1)
- Intervening in a local dispute between teachers and board. (1)

APPENDIX C. RESPONSES OF PROGRAM OFFICERS TO SELECTED QUESTIONNAIRE ITEMS, BY STAGE PROGRAM

		Stage of Program					
Type of Item or Index		*Selection*		*Planning*		*Implementation*	
		Percent	*N*	*Percent*	*N*	*Percent*	*N*
Management Role Index							
1. I have had to take steps	S/AN	46	(5)	20	(4)	20	(4)
to assure compliance to	SM	27	(3)	35	(7)	35	(7)
the proposal or contract	O/VF	27	(3)	45	(9)	45	(9)
because the local project							
seemed to be in violation.							
2. I have advised local ad-	S/AN	43	(3)	30	(6)	30	(6)
ministrators that their	SM	43	(6)	25	(5)	25	(5)
practices were inconsis-	O/VF	14	(1)	45	(9)	45	(9)
tent with the proposal or							
contract.							
3. I have disapproved re-	S/AN	50	(4)	18	(3)	24	(4)
quests formally submitted	SM	25	(2)	35	(6)	29	(5)
to NIE by local project	O/VF	25	(2)	47	(8)	47	(8)
administrators.							
4. I have advised local offi-	S/AN	27	(3)	28	(5)	31	(5)
cials that their plans	SM	36	(4)	33	(6)	31	(5)
probably would not be	O/VF	36	(4)	39	(7)	38	(6)
approved by NIE.							
Technical Assistance Role Index							
5. I have worked along with	S/AN	70	(14)	48	(9)	27	(4)
local administrators in a	SM	5	(1)	26	(5)	13	(2)
technical capacity.	O/VF	25	(5)	26	(5)	60	(9)
6. I have offered sug-	S/AN	47	(10)	30	(6)	6	(1)
gestions to local admin-	SM	24	(5)	35	(7)	19	(3)
istrators about ways to	O/VF	29	(6)	35	(7)	75	(12)
implement their plans, or							
to resolve the problem(s)							
they were faced with.							
7. I have helped local ad-	S/AN	43	(9)	35	(7)	19	(3)
ministrators formulate or	SM	29	(6)	25	(5)	19	(3)
clarify their plans.	O/VF	29	(61)	40	(8)	65	(10)
Advice about Goals Index							
8. I have influenced the	D/SD	62	(13)	60	(12)	56	(9)
conceptual design of this	U	5	(1)	10	(2)	13	(2)
local program.	A/SA	34	(2)	30	(6)	31	(5)
9. I have influenced the	D/SD	66	(14)	75	(15)	75	(12)
goals of this project.	U	24	(5)	20	(4)	13	(2)
	A/SA	10	(2)	5	(1)	13	(2)

		Stage of Program					
		Selection		Planning		Implementation	
Type of Item or Index		Percent	N	Percent	N	Percent	N
Advice about Implementation Index							
10. I have influenced specific decisions about imple- mentation procedures.	S/AN	52	(11)	40	(8)	13	(2)
	SM	19	(4)	5	(1)	25	(4)
	O/VF	29	(6)	55	(11)	62	(9)
11. I have proposed a pro- cedure or component that was eventually imple- mented in this program.	S/AN	81	(17)	70	(14)	44	(7)
	SM	10	(2)	15	(3)	44	(7)
	O/VF	10	(2)	15	(3)	13	(2)
12. Local school district ad- ministrators have sought to implement my advice.	S/AN	34	(7)	31	(6)	13	(2)
	SM	14	(3)	16	(3)	20	(31)
	O/VF	52	(11)	54	(10)	67	(10)
Requests for Assistance Index							
13. Local administrators have asked me to assist them in a technical capacity.	S/AN	71	(15)	55	(11)	13	(2)
	SM	14	(3)	25	(5)	38	(6)
	O/VF	14	(3)	20	(4)	50	(8)
14. Local administrators have solicited my advice.	S/AN	71	(15)	40	(8)	12	(2)
	SM	10	(2)	20	(4)	13	(2)
	O/VF	19	(4)	40	(8)	75	(12)
Local Consensus Index							
15. The people involved in the Experimental Schools (ES) Program in this school district have agreed on what the pro- gram is trying to accomplish.	S/AN	24	(5)	18	(4)	31	(5)
	SM	43	(9)	27	(6)	31	(5)
	O/VF	34	(7)	55	(12)	38	(6)
16. The people primarily re- sponsible for implement- ing the ES Program have agreed about how the project should be de- signed and implemented.	S/AN	33	(7)	18	(4)	13	(2)
	SM	38	(8)	36	(8)	44	(7)
	O/VF	29	(6)	46	(10)	44	(7)
Local Competence Index							
17. Most local people respon- sible for implementing this project have been highly committed to com- prehensive change.	D/SD	43	(9)	20	(4)	25	(4)
	U	38	(8)	60	(12)	31	(5)
	A/SA	19	(4)	20	(4)	44	(7)
18. The local administrators who have been in charge of the project are well qualified to direct a com- prehensive change effort.	D/SD	48	(10)	40	(8)	31	(5)
	U	24	(5)	35	(7)	38	(6)
	A/SA	29	(6)	25	(5)	31	(5)

			Stage of Program				
Type of Item or Index		*Selection*		*Planning*		*Implementation*	
		Percent	*N*	*Percent*	*N*	*Percent*	*N*
Clarity of Role Items							
19. I have had enough back- ing from ES administra- tors in my dealings with the local project.	S/AN SM O/VF	10 38 51	(2) (8) (11)	15 50 35	(3) (10) (7)	7 53 40	(1) (8) (6)
20. I have been clear about what my responsibilities are as an officer in the Rural ES Program.	D/SD U A/SA	14 19 67	(3) (4) (14)	55 15 30	(11) (3) (6)	6 13 81	(1) (2) (13)
21. NIE administrators have agreed with me about my responsibilties as a pro- gram officer.	D/SD U A/SA	19 43 38	(4) (9) (8)	10 30 60	(2) (6) (12)	0 31 69	(0) (5) (11)
22. Local school district ad- ministrators have agreed with me about what my responsibilities are as a program officer.	D/SD U A/SA	10 33 57	(2) (7) (12)	65 10 25	(13) (2) (5)	13 38 50	(2) (6) (8)
23. ES policies and/or re- quirements have changed with respect to this project.	S/AN SM O/VF	14 33 52	(31) (3) (11)	23 50 27	(5) (11) (6)	13 19 69	(2) (3) (11)
24. ES policies and/or re- quirements have changed importantly with respect to this project.	D/SD U A/SA	30 5 65	(6) (1) (13)	40 40 20	(8) (8) (4)	41 24 35	(7) (4) (6)
25. ES procedures have been interpreted and imple- mented in a consistent way with respect to this project.	D/SD U A/SA	35 20 45	(7) (4) (9)	15 60 25	(3) (12) (5)	12 24 65	(2) (4) (11)
26. The statements of ES of- ficials have provided local school district administra- tors with a clear under- standing of procedures and expectations.	D/SD U A/SA	60 30 10	(12) (6) (4)	60 25 15	(12) (5) (3)	35 47 18	(6) (8) (3)
Program Officer Assessment of *Impact*							
27. My relationship with the key school district admin- istrators has been produc- tive for them.	S/AN SM O/VF	35 35 30	(7) (7) (6)	25 50 25	(5) (10) (5)	6 6 88	(11) (1) (14)
28. I should have experi- enced more influence	D/SD U	33 24	(7) (5)	75 5	(15) (1)	38 44	(6) (7)

Type of Item or Index		Stage of Program					
		Selection		*Planning*		*Implementation*	
		Percent	*N*	*Percent*	*N*	*Percent*	*N*
over some aspects of the project than I was able to achieve.	A/SA	43	(9)	20	(4)	19	(3)
Program Officer Information Items							
29. I have a good grasp of	D/SD	29	(61)	21	(4)	20	(3)
the progress being made	U	0	(0)	53	(10)	19	(3)
and the problems that have arisen in all ten Rural ES Projects.	A/SA	71	(15)	26	(5)	63	(10)
30. I have felt free to offer	S/AN	57	(12)	25	(5)	12	(2)
criticism and advice to lo-	SM	14	(3)	15	(3)	13	(2)
cal administrators even when they do not ask for it.	O/VF	28	(6)	60	(12)	75	(12)

Impact Index	*Stage of Program*			
Number of Specific Influence	*Selection*	*Planning*	*Implementation*	*Total*
Incidents Recorded	*N*	*N*	*N*	*N*
I. Extent of influence				
A. Major perceptible influence	14	32	27	73
B. Minor perceptible influence	5	14	54	73
C. Subtle influence	3	1	47	51
D. TOTAL: Major, minor, subtle	22	47	128	197
II. Aspect Influenced				
A. Conceptual design	7	17	17	41
B. Operating procedures	14	27	44	85
C. Others	1	2	65	68
D. Non-Response	—	1	2	3
E. Total	22	47	128	197

*Each program officer made separate observations for each program for which he was responsible. The numbers reflect the *situations* observed (not the number of program officers or number of programs). Since some program officers were responsible for more programs than others, some of them have a disproportionate influence on these programs.

EXPLANATION OF LETTERS:
S/AN — Seldom or almost never
SM — Situation is mixed
O/VF — Often, very frequently
D/SD — Disagree or strongly disagree
U — Undecided
A/SA — Agree or strongly agree

APPENDIX D.   A SUMMARY OF MEASURES USED

Several indices were assembled from a pool of questionnaire items answered by eight program officers (see Appendix C):

Management Role: Items 1–4; Mean Inter-item Correlation r = .66

Technical Assistance: Items 5–7; Mean Inter-item Correlation r = .94

Advice about Goals: Items 8, 9; r = .78

Advice about Implementation: Items 10–12; Mean Inter-item Correlation r = .78

Requests for Assistance: Items 13–14; Correlation r = .85

Local Consensus: Items 15, 16; Correlation r = .79

Local Competence: Items 17–18; Correlation r = .81

References

Aldrich, Howard E.
 1979 Organizations and environments. Englewood Cliffs, NJ: Prentice-Hall.
Anderson, J. G.
 1966 "Bureaucratic rules: bearers of organizational authority." Educational
       Administrative Quarterly 2:7–34.
Argyris, Chris
 1959 "Understanding human behavior in organizations: one viewpoint." P.
       125 in M. Haire (ed.), Modern Organizational Theory. New York:
       Wiley.
Attewell, Paul, and Dean R. Gerstein
 1979 "Government policy and local practice," American Sociological Review
       44:311–327.
Bailey, Stephen K., and Edith K. Mosher
 1968 ESEA: The Office of Education administers a law. Syracuse, NY: Syr-
       acuse University Press.
Baker, Keith
 1975 "A new grantsmanship." The American Sociologist 10(November):
       206–219.
Baldridge, Victor
 1971 Power and conflict in the university. New York: Wiley.
Banfield, Edward C.
 1976 "Making a new federal program: model cities, 1964–68." Pp. 183–218
       in Walter Williams and Richard Elmore (eds.), Social Program Imple-
       mentation. New York: Academic Press.
Bar-Josef, Rivka, and E. O. Schied
 1966 "Pressures and defenses in bureaucratic roles." American Journal of
       Sociology 71:665–673.
Bardach, Eugene
 1977 The implementation game: what happens after a bill becomes a law?
       Cambridge, MA: MIT Press.

Barnard, Chester A.
  1938 The functions of the executive. Cambridge, MA: Harvard University
        Press.
Barton, Allen
  1979 "A prognosis of bureaucratic maladies." Pp. 7–26 in Carol H. Weiss
        and Allen H. Barton (eds.), Making Bureaucracies Work. Beverly Hills,
        CA: Sage Publications.
Bendix, Rinhard
  1942 "Bureaucracy: the problem and its setting." American Sociological Re-
        view 12:502–504.
Berke, Joel S., and Micheal W. Kirst
  1972 Federal aid to education: who benefits? who governs? Lexington, MA:
        Lexington Press.
Berman, Paul, and Milbrey McLaughlin
  1977 Federal programs supporting education change, Vol. II: factors affect-
        ing implementation and continuation. Washington, DC: USOE.
Bernstein, Ilene N., and Howard E. Freeman
  1975 Academic and entrepreneurial research: the consequences of diversity
        in federal education studies. New York: Russell Sage Foundation.
Blau, Peter M.
  1970 "A formal theory of differentiation in organizations." American So-
        ciological Review 35:201–218.
Blau, Peter M., and Richard A. Schoenherr
  1970 The structure of organizations. New York: Basic Books.
Blau, Peter M., and W. Richard Scott
  1962 Formal organizations. San Francisco: Chandler
Budding, David
  1972 Draft discussion paper on experimental schools. Washington, DC: Ex-
        perimental Schools Program. (Original carries no title, author or date.
        Facts of publication established in conversation with the author.)
Caplow, Theodore
  1964 Principles of organization. New York: Harcourt Brace.
Carlson, Richard O.
  1964 "Environmental constraints and organizational consequences: the pub-
        lic school and its clients." Pp. 262–276 in Daniel E. Griffiths (ed.),
        Behavioral Science and Educational Administration Yearbook, Part II.
        National Society for the Study of Education. Chicago: University of
        Chicago Press.
Chabotar, K. J., et al.
  1978 "Linking R&D with schools: an NIE program and its policy context."
        Cambridge, MA: Abt Associates.
Clark, Burton R.
  1956 "Interorganizational patterns in education." Administrative Science
        Quarterly 10:224–237.
Clinton, Charles A.
  1979 "Shiloh county: a matter of agendas." Ch. 8 in Robert E. Herriott and

Neal Gross (eds.), The Dynamics of Planned Educational Change. Berkeley, CA: McCutchan.

Collins, Randall
1975   "A conflict theory of organizations." Ch. 7 in Conflict Sociology: Toward an Explanatory Science. New York: Academic Press.

Comptroller General of the United States
1975   Report to the Congress: experimental schools program—opportunities to improve the management of an educational research program. April 27. Washington, DC: NIE, HEW.

Corwin, Ronald G.
1961   "The professional employee: a study of conflict in nursing roles." The American Journal of Sociology 66:604–615.

Corwin, Ronald G.
1965a   "Militant professionalism, initiative, and compliance in public education." Sociology of Education 38:310–331.

Corwin, Ronald G.
1965b   A sociology of education. New York: Appleton-Century-Crofts.

Corwin, Ronald G.
1969   "Patterns of organizational conflict." Administrative Science Quarterly 14:507–520.

Corwin, Ronald G.
1970   Militant professionalism: a study of organizational conflict in high schools. New York: Appleton-Century-Crofts.

Corwin, Ronald G, and Saad Z. Nagi
1972   "The case of educational research." Pp. 351–396 in Saad Z. Nagi and Ronald G. Corwin (eds.), The Social Context of Research. New York: Wiley.

Corwin, Ronald G.
1973   Reform and organizational survival: the teacher corps as an instrument of educational change. New York: Wiley Interscience.

Corwin, Ronald G.
1974   Education in crisis. New York: Wiley.

Corwin, Ronald G.
1981   "Patterns of organizational control and teacher militancy: theoretical continuities in the idea of 'loose coupling'." In Ronald G. Corwin (ed.), Research in Sociology of Education and Socialization, Vol. 2: Research on Educational Organizations. Greenwich, CT: JAI Press.

Corwin, Ronald G.
1982   "Patterns of federal–local relationships in education." In Ronald G. Corwin (ed.), Research in the Sociology of Education and Socialization, Vol. 3. Greenwich, CT: JAI Press.

CPI Associates, Inc.
1977   "The roles and functions of project officers in DHEW region VI program agencies." Mimeo.

Cronin, Joseph M.
1976   The federal takeover: should the junior partner run the firm?" Phi Delta Kappan (November):499–501.

Crozier, Michael
1964 The bureaucratic phenomenon. Chicago: University of Chicago Press.
Dahrendorf, Ralf
1958 Class and class conflict in industrial society. Stanford, CA: Stanford University Press.
Davis, Kingsly
1949 Human society. New York: Macmillan.
Dershimer, Richard A.
1976 The federal government and educational R&D. Lexington, MA: Lexington Books.
Derthick, Martha
1970 The influence of federal grants. Cambridge, MA: Harvard University Press.
Dissemination and Resources Group
1976 "R&D utilization, request for proposal, scope of work." Washington, DC: National Institute of Education.
Donnelly, William L.
1979 "Arcadia: local initiatives and adaptation." Chapter 7 in Robert E. Herriott and Neal Gross (eds.), The Dynamics of Planned Educational Change. Berkeley, CA: McCutchan.
Downs, Anthony.
1967 Inside bureaucracy. Boston: Little Brown.
Dubin, Robert
1959 "Stability of human organization." Pp. 218–251 in M. Haire (ed.), Modern Organizational Theory. New York: Wiley.
Elmore, Richard
1976 "Follow through planned variation," Pp. 101–123 in Walter Williams and Richard Elmore (eds.), Social Program Implementation. New York: Academic Press.
Etzioni, Amati
1961 A comparative analysis of complex organizations. New York: Free Press.
Etzioni, Amati
1965 "Organizational control and structure." In James March (ed.), Handbook of Organizations. Chicago: Rand McNally.
Eveland, J. D., Everett M. Rogers and Constance Klepper
1977 "The innovation process in public organizations." March. Nostrand Science Foundation Report, Mimeo.
Farrar, Eleanor, J. Desanctis and David Cohen
1979 Views from below: implementation research in education. Cambridge, MA: Huron Institute.
Firestone, William A.
1979 "Butte-Angels camp: conflict and transformation." Chapter 6 in Robert Herriott and Neal Gross (eds.), The Dynamics of Planned Educational Change. Berkeley, CA: McCutchan.

Francis, Roy G. and Robert Stone
  1956   Service and procedure in bureaucracy: a case study. Minneapolis: University of Minnesota Press.
Fullan, Michael
  1981   "Research on the implementation of educational change." In Ronald Corwin (ed.), Research in the Sociology of Education and Socialization. Greenwich, CT: JAI Press, Inc.
Gouldner, Alvin W.
  1952   "Red tape as a social problem." Pp. 410–418 in R. Merton, A. Gray, B. Hockey and H. Selvin (eds.), Reader in Bureaucracy. Glencoe, IL: Free Press.
Gouldner, Alvin W.
  1954   Patterns in industrial bureaucracy. Glencoe, IL: Free Press.
Gouldner, Alvin W.
  1959   "Organizational analysis." In R. K. Merton, L. Bloom and L. S. Cottrell, Jr. (eds.), Sociology Today. New York: Basic Books.
Griffiths, Daniel E.
  1965   "System theory and school districts." Ontario Journal of Educational Research 8.
Grodzins, Morton
  1966   "The American scene: the new view of government in the U.S." In Daniel J. Elazor (ed.). Chicago: Rand McNally.
Gulick, L., and L. Urwick (eds.)
  1937   Papers on the science of administration. New York: Institute of Public Administration.
Hall, Richard H.
  1968   "Professionalization and bureaucratization." American Sociological Review 33:92–104.
Hannan, Michael, and John Freeman
  1977   "The population ecology of organizations." American Journal of Sociology 82:929–964.
Hargrove, Erwin C.
  1979   "The bureaucratic politics of evaluation: a case study of the Department of Labor." July. Mimeo.
Havelock, R. G.
  1973   "R&D utilization strategies and functions: an analytical comparison of four systems." Ann Arbor: University of Michigan.
Helco, Hugh
  1977   A government of strangers: executive politics in Washington. Washington, DC: The Brookings Institution.
Herriott, Robert E.
  1979   "The funding context: the experimental schools program." Chapter 3 in Robert E. Herriott and Neal Gross (ed.), The Dynamics of Planned Educational Change. Berkeley, CA: McCutchan.
Herriott, Robert E., and Sheila Rosenblum
  1976   First steps towards planned change (organizational change study, interim report No. 1). March 3. Cambridge, MA: Abt Associates Inc.

Hutchins, C. L.
n.d.   "Promoting change in schools: a diffusion casebook." Mimeo.
Jones, Charles O., and Robert D. Thomas
1976   Public policy making in a federal system, Vol. 3. Beverly Hills, CA: Sage Publications.
Kane, Michael B.
1976   Educational change in rural America: an interim report to the experimental schools program. July. Cambridge, MA: Abt Associates Inc.
Katz, D., and R. L. Kahn
1966   The social psychology of organizations. New York: Wiley.
Katz, Elihu, and Brenda Danet
1973   Bureaucracy and the public. New York: Basic Books.
Kirst, Michael
1973   "The growth of federal influence in education." Pp. 448–477 in The Uses of the Sociology of Education. National Society of the Study of Education Yearbook. Chicago: University of Chicago Press.
Lawrence, P. R., and J. W. Lorsch
1967   "Differentiation and integration in complex organizations." Administrative Science Quarterly 12:1–47.
Lazin, F. A.
1973   "The failure of federal enforcement of civil rights regulations in public housing from 1963–1971: the co-optation of a federal agency by its local constituency." Policy Sciences 14:263–273.
Levien, R. E.
1971   "National Institute of Education: preliminary plan for the proposed institute." Santa Monica, CA: Rand.
Levine, S., and P. E. White
1961   "Exchange as a conceptual framework for the study of inter-organizational relationships." Administrative Science Quarterly 5:583–601.
Lipsky, Michael
1976   "Toward a street-level bureaucracy." In Willis Hewlen and Michael Lipsky (eds.), Theoretical Perspectives in Urban Politics. Englewood Cliffs, N.J.
Loomis, Charles P.
1969   "Tentative types of directed social change involving systematic linkage." Rural Sociology 24:352–369.
Lortie, Dan D.
1969   "The balance of control and autonomy in elementary school teaching." Pp. 1–53 in A. Etzioni (ed.), The Semi-Professionals and Their Organizations: Teachers, Nurses, Social Workers. New York: Free Press.
Louis, Karen Seashore, and Ronald G. Corwin
1982   "Doing policy research in a policy vacuum." In Ronald Corwin (ed.), Research in the Sociology of Education and Socialization, Vol. 3. Greenwich, CT: JAI Press.
Louis, Karen Seashore, James A. Molitor, Gregory J. Spencer and Robert K. Yin
n.d.   "Linking R&D with schools: an interim report." Cambridge, MA: Abt Associates Inc. Mimeo.

Lowi, Theodore
1969   The end of liberalism. New York: Norton.

McGowan, Eleanor Farrar
1976   "Rational fantasies." Policy Sciences 7:439–454.

McLaughlin, Milbrey
1976   "Implementation as mutual adaptation: change in classroom organization." In Walter Williams and Richard Elmore (eds.), Social Program Implementation. New York: Academic Press.

Mechanic, David.
1962   "Sources of power of participants in complex organizations." Administrative Science Quarterly 7:349–364.

Merton, Robert K.
1957   "Bureaucratic structure and personality." Pp. 131–160 in Social Theory and Social Structure. Glencoe, IL: The Free Press.

Messerschmidt, Donald A.
1979   "River district: a search for unity amidst diversity." Chapter 4 in Robert E. Herriott and Neal Gross (eds.), The Dynamics of Planned Educational Change. Berkeley, CA: McCutchan.

Michelson, Stephen
1979   "The working bureaucracy and the non-working bureaucracy." Pp. 175–200 in Carol H. Weiss and Allen H. Barton (eds.), Making Bureaucracies Work. Beverly Hills, CA: Sage Publications.

Murphy, Jerome T.
1971   "Title I of ESEA: the politics of implementing educational reform." Harvard Educational Review 41:35–63.

Nagi, Saad
1976   "Disability policy and programs: an analysis of organizations, clients, and decision making." Columbus, OH: Mershon Center, mimeo, pp. VII-37.

Nash, Nicholas, and Jack Culbertson
1977   Linking processes in educational improvement. Columbus, OH: University Council of Educational Administrators.

National Institute of Education
1973   Building capacity for renewal and reform. Washington, DC:

Parsons, T.
1956   "Suggestions for a sociological approach to the theory of organizations." Administrative Science Quarterly 1:64–85.

Pressman, Jeffrey L.
1975   Federal programs and city politics. Berkeley, CA: University of California Press.

Pressman, Jeffrey L., and Aaron B. Wildavaky
1973   Implementation. Berkeley, CA: University of California Press.

Raizen, Senta A.
1979   "Dissemination programs at the National Institute of Education: 1974–1979." Knowledge: Creation, Diffusion, Utilization 1:259–292.

Reagan, M.
1972   The new federalism. New York: Oxford University Press.

Riker, William H.
1964   Federalism. Boston: Little Brown.
Ripley, Randal, et al.
1976   "The implications of CETA in Ohio." July 31. Columbus, OH: The Ohio State University, mimeo.
Rivilin, Alice, and Michael Timpane
1975   Planned variation. Washington, DC: The Brookings Institution.
Rourke, Francis E.
1979   "Bureaucratic autonomy and the public interest." Pp. 103–112 in Carol H. Weiss and Allen H. Barton (eds.), Making Bureaucracies Work. Beverly Hills, CA: Sage Publications.
Selznick, Philip
1943   "An approach to a theory of Bureaucracy." American Sociological Review 8:51–52.
Selznick, Philip
1948   "Foundations of the theory of organizations." American Sociological Review 13:25–35.
Selznick, Philip
1953   TVA and the grass roots. Berkeley, CA: University of California Press.
Selznick, Philip
1957   Leadership in administration. Evanston, IL: Row, Peterson.
Sieber, Sam
1982   "Scholarship and contract evaluation research—a problem of integration." In Ronald G. Corwin (ed.), Research in Sociology of Education and Socialization, Volume 3: Policy Research in Education. Greenwich, CN: JAI Press.
Sieber, Sam, Karen Seashore Louis and Loya Metzger
1972   The use of educational knowledge. New York: Columbia University, 2 Volumes.
Simmel, G.
1950   The sociology of Georg Simmel. K. Wolff, trans. Glencoe, IL: Free Press.
Smith, T. B.
1973   "The policy implementation process." Policy Sciences 4:197–209.
Sproull, Lee, Stephen Weiner and David Wolf.
1978   Organizing an anarchy: belief, bureaucracy and politics in the National Institute of Education. Chicago: University of Chicago Press.
Stinchcombe, Arthur
1965   "Social structure and organizations." Pp. 142–193 in J. G. March (ed.), Handbook of Organizations. Chicago: Rand McNally.
Summerfield, Harry
1974   Power and process: the formulation and limits of federal educational policies. Berkeley, CA: McCutchan.
Terreberry, Shirley
1968   "The evolution of administrative environments." Administrative Science Quarterly 12:590–613.

Thomas, Robert D.
1976 "Intergovernmental coordination in the implementation of national air and water pollution policies." Pp. 39–62 in C. G. Jones and R. D. Thomas (ed.), Public Policy Making in a Federal System. Beverly Hills, CA: Sage Publications.

Thompson, James D., and William McEwen
1958 "Organizational goals and environments: goal setting as an interaction process." American Sociological Review 23:23–31.

Turner, Ralph H.
1947 "The navy disbursing officer as a bureaucrat." American Sociological Review 12:342–348.

Van Horn, Carl E.
1976 "Implementing CETA: the federal role." Columbus, OH: The Ohio State University, mimeo.

Van Horn, Carl E., and Donald S. Van Meter
1976 "The implementation of intergovernmental policy." Pp. 39–64 in C. O. Jones and R. D. Thomas (eds.), Public Policy Making in a federal system. Beverly Hills, CA: Sage Publications.

Wacaster, C. Thompson
1979 "Jackson county: local norms, federal initiatives, and administrator performance." Chapter 5 in Robert E. Herriott and Neal Gross (eds.), The Dynamics of Planned Educational Change. Berkeley, CA: McCutchan.

Waller, W.
1932 The sociology of teaching. New York: Wiley.

Warwick, Donald P.
1975 A theory of public bureaucracy: politics, personality and organization in the state department. Cambridge, MA: Howard University Press.

Weatherly, Richard
1979 Reforming special education: policy implementation from state level to street level. Cambridge, MA: MIT Press.

Weber, Max
1946 Essays in sociology. New York: Oxford University Press.

Weiss, Carol A.
1979 "Efforts at bureaucratic reform: what have we learned?" Pp. 26–36 in Carol H. Weiss and Allen H. Barton (eds.), Making Bureaucracies Work. Beverly Hills, CA: Sage Publications.

Weiss, Robert S., and Martin Rein.
1970 "The evolution of broad-aim programs: experimental design, its difficulties and an alternative." Administrative Science Quarterly 15(March):97–109.

Williams, Walter
1976a "Implementation analysis assessment." In Walter Williams and Richard Elmore (eds.), Social Program Implementation. New York: Academic Press.

Williams, Walter
1976b "Implementation problems in federally funded programs." Pp. 15–42

in Walter Williams and Richard Elmore (eds.), Social Program Implementation. New York: Academic Press.

Williams, Walter, and John W. Evans
  1969 "The politics of evaluation: the case of head start." The Annals of the American Academy of Political and Social Science: Evaluating the War on Poverty vol. 385 (September).

Wilson, James Q.
  1966 "Innovation in organization: notes toward a theory." In James D. Thompson (ed.), Approaches to Organizational Design. Pittsburgh: University of Pittsburgh Press.

Young, Frank W.
  1970 "Reactive subsystems." American Sociological Review 35:297–307.

Yuchtman, Ephraim, and Stanley S. Seashore
  1967 "A system resource approach to organizational effectiveness." American Sociological Review 32:891–903.

Zald, M. N.
  1970 Organizational change: the political economy of the YMCA. Chicago: University of Chicago Press.

Author Index

Subject Index